OTHER MINDS

OTHER MINDS

CRITICAL ESSAYS 1969–1994

THOMAS NAGEL

New York   Oxford
OXFORD UNIVERSITY PRESS
1995

Oxford University Press

Oxford   New York
Athens   Auckland   Bangkok   Bombay
Calcutta   Cape Town   Dar es Salaam   Delhi
Florence   Hong Kong   Istanbul   Karachi
Kuala Lumpur   Madras   Madrid   Melbourne
Mexico City   Nairobi   Paris   Singapore
Taipei   Tokyo   Toronto

and associated companies in
Berlin   Ibadan

Copyright © 1995 by Oxford University Press, Inc.

Published by Oxford University Press, Inc.
198 Madison Avenue, New York, New York 10016

Oxford is a registered trademark of Oxford University Press

Library of Congress Cataloging-in-Publication Data
Nagel, Thomas.
Other minds : critical essays, 1969–1994 / Thomas Nagel.
p. cm.   Includes bibliographical references and index.
ISBN 0–19–509008–X
1. Philosophy of mind.   2. Ethics.   3. Ethics, Modern—20th
century.   4. Political science—Philosophy.   I. Title.
B945.N333O74   1995
128'.2—dc20   94–3162

The author gratefully acknowledges the support of the Filomen D'Agostino and
Max E. Greenberg Faculty Research Fund of New York University Law School.

1 3 5 7 9 8 6 4 2

Printed in the United States of America on acid-free paper

To the memory of
Carlos Nino
1943–1993

Contents

OTHER MINDS

Introduction: The Philosophical Culture

These essays were all written on request, so they don't discuss all and only the philosophers I am most interested in, but the topics are those that have always occupied me: subjectivity and consciousness, objectivity and ethics, liberalism and reason. Even though there isn't much about some parts of the philosophical mainstream—language, logic, general metaphysics—it all belongs to the common universe of argument that defines analytic philosophy: these subjects and the methods used in treating them cannot be isolated from one another. I've revised most of the pieces slightly for inclusion in this book and have in some cases added afterthoughts, particularly for the earlier ones. But I've included only things that I still think are mostly right, even after a couple of decades. My basic sympathies and antipathies—antireductionist and more or less realist—haven't changed much.

Let me here add a few personal opinions and reminiscences about the philosophical culture to which these essays and most of their subjects belong, with the firm acknowledgment that the sociology of a subject is no substitute for reflection on its substance. When I entered the field, analytic philosophy was only beginning to approach its ascendancy in the United States. The Continental branch of philosophical analysis had made inroads with the help of émigrés such as Carnap, Tarski, Reichenbach, Hempel, and Feigl. The English branch was just starting to have an influence, but I was exposed to it early because I went to Cornell as an undergraduate in 1954, when it was probably the best place in the country to learn about Wittgenstein and ordinary language philosophy. I intended to major in physics—the great romantic field of that date—but took an introductory philosophy course and soon concluded that my real motive for studying physics (which was to discover whether there was such a thing as objective reality), not to mention my aptitudes, would make the philosophy department a more suitable choice.

At Cornell I encountered Norman Malcolm, John Rawls, and Rogers Albritton, teachers whose influence on me was strong and permanent. Malcolm was a large, charming, ferocious man whose capacity for pleasure and displeasure at what one said in philosophical discussion was a cause of great anxiety in his students. Though his tendency to moralize the subject was not altogether healthy, I acquired from him and Albritton a sense of the distinctive and unnerving character of philosophical problems and of the importance of Wittgenstein, and from Rawls a conviction of the priority of substantive moral theory over metaethics. A Fulbright scholarship then took me to Oxford, which in 1958 was pretty near its peak of confidence and activity as the vanguard of a movement. J. L. Austin was my thesis supervisor for the B.Phil., a brilliant and riveting lecturer, a sarcastic and withering critic, and a wonderfully attentive adviser, but not really interested in the sorts of questions that interested me: he distrusted "depth" and the agonized Wittgensteinian style, and depth was what I thirsted for. Austin died toward the end of my second year there, at what now seems to me the unbelievable age of forty-eight. Apart from the theory of speech acts, his form of detailed empirical study of ordinary language, though delightful to witness, has not left much trace—nor has the conviction, then common, that many of the traditional problems of philosophy could be made to disappear by clearing up confusions about how ordinary language works.

I had a term's tutorial from Paul Grice, which was the single most transforming educational experience of my life. Every week I would come in with a paper to read aloud, with Grice heaped in his chair opposite looking bored and unreceptive, and when I was a few sentences into it, he would ask a short question I couldn't answer. Eventually I would try something, but it was met by another such question, and I was soon reduced to silence. At the end of an hour spent mostly in silence, I went away with my entire view of the issue, whatever it had been, transformed. While saying hardly anything, he managed to show that this or that fashionable approach to some traditional problem would not work. I have never encountered anything like it.

Because of its size, with rafts of graduate students from all over the world, and many more seminars than you could possibly take in, and because of its traditional dedication to teaching through discussion, Oxford was a great feast. There was an enormous amount going on: Strawson's lectures that became *Individuals*, Hart's that became *The Concept of*

Law, Anscombe's on Wittgenstein and the theory of action, Philippa Foot's on moral beliefs and motivation. I had valuable tutorials with David Pears, James Thomson, and G. E. L. Owen. Blackwells was the world's best philosophy bookstore, and books were as cheap as pocket calculators are now. It was a wonderful place to be in that excitable condition when you are just finding your legs and trying to make up your mind about everything.

At the end of two years I returned to the United States and much less enlivening Harvard. Quine, descending from the tradition of reconstructive logical empiricism (the other great branch of Frege's dynasty), was engaged in a philosophical project, baffling to me, of redescribing the world. I wrote my dissertation with Rawls (who had moved to Harvard) and was able to read and discuss with him successive drafts of *A Theory of Justice.* And I encountered both Noam Chomsky and Saul Kripke, then an undergraduate, but already distinguished for his work in logic. Gilbert Harman, Robert Swartz (fellow graduate students), and I met regularly with Kripke to discuss Wittgenstein's *Philosophical Investigations,* and the new interpretation Kripke was beginning to work out transformed my understanding of the book.

Harman and I would slog down Massachusetts Avenue to M.I.T. several times a week to hear Chomsky's lectures. (He and Austin both had the remarkable gift of making you hang on every word, without the slightest hint of the dramatic.) Those were the lectures that eventually became *Cartesian Linguistics* and *Aspects of the Theory of Syntax.* While I was occasionally exasperated by his polemics against other writers, Chomsky's work had a large impact on me. I never learned much linguistics; it was his extraordinary imagination and his attitude toward the mind as a field wide open for combined empirical and theoretical investigation that attracted me, together with his strong sense that we were only at the beginning of our understanding and that we might be constitutionally incapable of making the kind of progress here that humans had been able to make in physics. I was also interested by the lack of "purity" in his approach. He didn't care about the boundaries between empirical, theoretical, and philosophical questions and methods. While these distinctions are often important, he seemed interested in everything at once.

In 1963 I left for Berkeley, my first job. There I was particularly influenced by Thompson Clarke's technique of making the naturalness of philosophical problems themselves an object of investigation and a resource for the understanding of basic human concepts and forms of thought. The 1960s began with a bang in Berkeley shortly after I got there, and after three years I went back east, to Princeton, which was in the process of becoming a large and powerful department. It supported active research in several areas, including ethics and the history of philosophy, but the center of gravity was a mixture of metaphysics, epistemology, philosophy of language, philosophy of logic and mathematics, and philosophy of science. In recent years these topics have come more and more to be approached in a spirit of theory construction that sees philosophy as continuous with science, only more abstract and more general. This outlook, which has never appealed to me, is now very common among analytic philosophers, including many of the best minds in the subject; somehow the Carnap-Quine tradition has come to dominate the profession, though the other, problem-centered style is still in existence, and I think it is important to keep it alive. Without a strong grasp of the uniquely philosophical character of certain problems, it is too easy to fall prey to scientism, the idea that any genuine question can be handled as part of the development of a scientific worldview, and that what can't be, isn't a real question. This outlook can lead to work of astounding superficiality, like eliminative materialism in the philosophy of mind.

In other regions of the subject, developments were affected by Rawls's revival of substantive political theory and by a rise in the political temperature associated with the Vietnam War, the civil rights movement, and the fight over abortion. In the late 1960s Marshall Cohen, T. M. Scanlon, and I started *Philosophy & Public Affairs* (though the first number didn't appear till 1971); and Robert Nozick and I, with Rawls's encouragement, started a small monthly discussion group called SELF (The Society for Ethical and Legal Philosophy). Most of the members were already friends, but there were some, such as Ronald Dworkin, Michael Walzer, Charles Fried, Judith Thomson, and Frank Michelman, whom I came to know well only through its meetings. The speed and level of discussion were exceptional, and some significant work in progress passed before that group, which was unified by confidence that moral intuition and systematic reasoning could be combined to yield substantive progresss on real normative questions.

Altogether, I was very lucky in the philosophical chums I found early on. In my twenties and early thirties I had some of the best times of my life discussing philosophy with friends: Tom Clarke, John Searle, and Barry Stroud at Berkeley; Gil Harman and Tim Scanlon at Princeton; Saul Kripke and Bob Nozick in New York (when they were at the Rockefeller University and I lived nearby in Manhattan); and Ronald Dworkin, Derek Parfit, David Wiggins, and Bernard Williams on both sides of the Atlantic. At that age you have energy to burn, you haven't yet begun to husband your resources, and everything seems undecided. There is a kind of highly exhilarating discussion, often very rapid, that takes place only between people on the same wavelength who already know a subject inside out. It becomes rarer as you get older—the synapses get tired, the categories harden, and the capacity for excitement fades—but it plays for most of us an important role in the development and spread of philosophical ideas.

That is why philosophy of this kind is usually a local phenomenon, in spite of its universality of concern. Like painters who look at one another's work, analytic philosophers talk to each other, and the original developments have involved small groups in one city or with easy geographical access. Subsequently, through travelling fellowships plus emigration, the tradition has spread from Vienna, Cambridge, and Oxford first to all the Anglophone countries and Scandinavia and now to the whole world. It has been a pleasure to participate in this flow of ideas and to make friends in so many places as a result. I dedicate this book to the memory of one of them who was very dear to me—a man of incomparable largeness of heart, sweetness of temper, bravery, gaiety, and intelligence—Carlos Nino of Buenos Aires, who died in 1993 at the age of forty-nine, after having played a vital role in the intellectual and public life of his country and in guiding it toward the rule of law.

I was once interviewed by two French philosophers who were traveling around the United States doing a survey of the field. When I told them, in answer to a question about my early interests, that I had switched to philosophy from physics, they smiled knowingly at each other, and when I asked why, they told me that every American philosopher they interviewed had given a similar answer: science or mathematics had been what first attracted them all. In my case, this was partly because those were the only subjects that offered any intellectual stimulation whatever in the high school I went to: they could not be spoiled by ignorance, incompetence, or political propaganda. But I also found the rigor and universality of the physical sciences and mathematics enchanting, and this attitude has never left me. While an early love of science does not characterize all American analytic philosophers, it is true of a great many, and it has consequences for the field. Adolescent science buffs are a different intellectual type from those with historical or literary interests, the more usual background in Europe. In the United States, philosophers don't have to know much about history or anything about literature, but they are expected to know some science, to have at least an amateur's grasp of the contributions of Newton, Maxwell, Darwin, Einstein, Heisenberg, Cantor, Gödel, and Turing, as well as of some representatives of the human sciences like Chomsky, Sperry, and Arrow—all of which provide data for philosophical reflection. Also important is the concept of philosophy not as a critical or historical subject but as an enterprise of primary research in which most of us are actively engaged, even if only in a small way. A more or less scientific ethos means that everything must be explicitly set out and, if possible, argued for, and that the persuasiveness of the arguments is what counts;

rhetoric and textual reference cannot take up the slack. That at least is the ideal, even if it is often violated.

The philosophical community by which I was formed, in all its varieties of interest and outlook, also valued philosophical argument as an activity, in some cases more highly than philosophy as a product. This went along with an unusual appreciation for the active quality of people's minds, whatever their views or their record of publication. Analytic philosophy has been wonderfully hospitable—more, I think, than any other academic field—to individuals of obvious talent who have published a few distinguished papers, or even less, and also to philosophers who pick up creative speed only gradually, publish little at the beginning of their careers, and then, in middle age, come out with major bodies of work (Rawls, Grice, and Donald Davidson, for example).

It is also a field in which sheer brains—I.Q., logical speed, raw mental muscle—play a powerful role, even though they are not the same thing as philosophical ability. Philosophy is like basketball: being preternaturally tall doesn't ensure that you'll be a good basketball player, but it helps an awful lot, and in philosophy it helps to be supersmart. Such people can simply travel farther and faster than the rest of us, and I wish philosophy attracted more of them. But the effects of this sort of intelligence are complex: sometimes, if all that power is put to the service of harebrained intuitions, it yields logically dazzling but implausible results. Even when it goes off the rails, though, brilliance generates structures of thought that command attention and have a life of their own, and their impact on the field doesn't depend on whether anyone thinks they're right. This can be a nuisance, but I suppose the devaluation of plausibility is unavoidable in a field so dominated by argument.

A crucial determinant of the character of analytic philosophy—and a piece of luck as far as I am concerned—is the unimportance, in the English-speaking world, of the intellectual as a public figure. Fame doesn't matter, and offering an opinion about practically everything is not part of the job. It is unnecessary for writers of philosophy to be more "of their time" than they want to be; they don't have to write for the world but can pursue questions inside the subject, at whatever level of difficulty the questions demand. If the work is of high quality, they will receive the support of a large and dedicated academy that is generally independent of popular opinion. This is an enviably luxurious position to be in, by comparison to writers who depend for their status and income on the reaction of a broader public. Of course, there are plenty of silly fashions and blind spots inside the academic community, but in philosophy, at least, their effect has not been as bad as the need to compete for wider literary fame would be. I think arid technicalities are preferable to the blend of oversimplification and fake profundity that is too often the form taken by popular philosophy. A strong academy provides priceless shelter for the difficult and often very specialized work that must be done to advance the subject.

Lately some purveyors of philosophy-made-easy have become world famous, and there has been a rise in amateur philosophizing outside the field, but this hasn't made much difference on the inside. Analytic philosophy has escaped almost completely the facile relativism that seems to be so influential elsewhere in the humanities, originally stirred up by Derrida and now defended by references to Richard Rorty, Paul Feyerabend, and Thomas Kuhn. Philosophy seems to export its worst products, as happened earlier in the century with behaviorism and logical positivism and their influence on the social sciences and psychology.

Developments like this pose a difficult choice. When debased philosophy is very influential elsewhere, the only way to combat it actively is to enter the arena and compete for popular conviction, in other words, to take up the traditional role of a public intellectual. While I admire those, like Dworkin and Searle, who have the stomach and the talent for this sort of polemic, I have lost what appetite I ever had for it, and hope instead that the current wave of confusion will subside if we just ignore it. I think it is a great burden for a field of theoretical inquiry if its practitioners have to compete for the approval of those who don't understand the issues. Sometimes it can't be helped, as when governmental funding is needed to support scientific research, but philosophy luckily doesn't cost much.

There have certainly been useful connections recently between philosophy and other fields: law, economics, politics, medicine, linguistics, psychology, and information technology. But they have been due to common interests in specific issues, rather than to the exportation of all-purpose epistemological or metaphysical doctrines. And while these connections are important and can be expected to continue, the real life of the field depends on the work being done on its central problems.

Substantively, there has been plenty of good work, but how good is hard to say. Which philosophical writings of this century will be of more than historical interest in another hundred years? Near the end of the twentieth century, very few philosophers of the nineteenth are much read: Peirce and Frege, Mill, Bentham, and Sidgwick, Hegel, Nietzsche, and perhaps Schopenhauer. What will a comparable list look like next time around? But then, who would have bet on Peirce, Frege, or Nietzsche in 1894? Greatness is rare and the fourth century B.C. and the seventeenth and eighteenth centuries A.D. remain, in my view, unrivaled. The strongest recent candidate for immortality is Wittgenstein; he certainly identified a new set of problems, though his response to them is still poorly understood and very difficult to evaluate. Russell, Husserl, Sartre, and

Carnap will continue to be familiar names for a while, and so, unfortunately, will Heidegger. Of those who have flourished in the second half of this century, however, it is difficult to guess who will actually be *read* more than a hundred years from now. I would bet on Rawls and perhaps Nozick, partly because of the linear character of the history of Western political thought and its need for exemplary figures, but I have no confidence that the most influential recent work in metaphysics, epistemology, and philosophy of language will survive. But perhaps it is the wrong question; perhaps it is possible to contribute greatly to the development of philosophy without writing a classic.

Bernard Williams once posed the awkward question, What is the point of doing philosophy if you're not extraordinarily good at it? The problem is that you can't, by sheer hard work, like a historian of modest gifts, make solid discoveries that others can then rely on in building up larger results. If you're not extraordinary, what you do in philosophy will be either unoriginal (and therefore unnecessary) or inadequately supported (and therefore useless). More likely, it will be both unoriginal and wrong. That is why most of the philosophy of the past is not worth studying. So isn't there something absurd about paying thousands of people to think about these fundamental questions?

If there is an answer to this question, it would have to depend on the idea that we are engaged in a collective enterprise whose results can't always be easily traced. Some kind of marketplace of arguments and ideas may generate developments of value that wouldn't have been produced just by the greatest thinkers working individually and responding to each other. Original contributions are thus disseminated and interpreted, and an environment is produced in which others can occasionally and unpredictably develop. I am not sure whether this is true, but it does seem to me possible that the widely extended cooperative activities of philosophical research and teaching, in which this subject has its life, contribute something to the development of intellectual tools that over the long run advance our common capacity to think about language, science, knowledge, politics, morality, and what human beings are.

Anyway, something will happen next. It always does.

I

PHILOSOPHY OF MIND

1

Freud's Anthropomorphism

It is difficult to decide whether a mentalistic psychology, dealing with either conscious or unconscious processes, can be regarded as a higher-level theory of the operation of the brain. Psychology deals with persons and with the causes and influences that explain what they do, think, feel, and so on. These causes and influences must have some physiological basis, but it remains obscure what the relation must be between the different levels of explanation in order for them both to be true. A psychological theory need not, I suspect, be a rough sketch of the underlying physiological or physical structure. So long as there is no inconsistency at the level of particular causal connections, it may be that both levels of description and explanation can be true, without anything like a reductive relation between the theories. This applies both to ordinary, commonsense psychology and to its psychoanalytic extension. Whether this was also Freud's belief, I do not know.

Freud was a materialist, and at an early stage of his psychological inquiries attempted to construct an explicitly physiological psychology based on the interaction of neurons. This attempt, by now well known under the title "Project for a Scientific Psychology," was abandoned shortly after Freud sent the draft to Fliess in October 1895. And when he learned in 1937 that Marie Bonaparte had unearthed the manuscript, he sought to have it destroyed.

His subsequent theories were of an entirely different character, for they

---

First published in *Freud: A Collection of Critical Essays,* Richard Wollheim, editor (Doubleday, 1974).

contained only psychological terminology and did not refer explicitly to neuron interaction. Nevertheless, there is a good deal of structural continuity between the earlier and later views, and Freud continued to be convinced that the psychic apparatus he was investigating and describing in mentalistic terms was in its true nature a physical system—though too little was known about neurophysiology to permit anyone to think about psychology in physical terms. That is why Freud felt it necessary to abandon the line of investigation represented by the *Project*.

The question therefore arises in what sense it is possible to think about a physical system in mentalistic terms, taken from the vocabulary of experience, perception, desire, and the like, without having any idea of the physical significance of those descriptions. This question bears not only on psychoanalytic theory but also on current disputes about the status of mentalistic hypotheses in linguistics and in other areas where it is maintained that a mentalistically or anthropomorphically described process or function can be assumed to have a physical realization. What is the meaning of such claims?

Freud was not silent on the subject, and his explanations of how it is possible to think anthropomorphically about a physical system when one lacks an explicitly physical understanding of that system are among the most philosophical passages in his writings.[1] They also contain a contribution to discussion of the mind-body problem, which deserves examination.

The remarks that will occupy us form part of Freud's general defense of the existence of unconscious mental states. There are four main locations: *The Interpretation of Dreams*,[2] "The Unconscious,"[3] *An Outline of Psychoanalysis*,[4] and "Some Elementary Lessons in Psychoanalysis."[5] It will be useful to quote one typical passage at length.

> The hypothesis we have adopted of a psychical apparatus extended in space, expediently put together, developed by the exigencies of life, which gives rise to the phenomena of consciousness only at one particular point and under certain conditions—this hypothesis has put us in a position to establish psychology on foundations similar to those of any other science, such, for in-

[1] Freud often gives the impression of being hostile to philosophy, but in a letter to Fliess of January 1, 1896, he says, "I see that you are using the circuitous route of medicine to attain your first ideal, the physiological understanding of man, while I secretly nurse the hope of arriving by the same route at my own original objective, philosophy. For that was my original ambition, before I knew what I was intended to do in the world." (Letter 39 in *The Origins of Psychoanalysis* [Basic Books, 1954], p. 141).

[2] *Standard Edition of the Complete Psychological Works of Sigmund Freud*, ed. James Strachey (Hogarth Press, 1961) [hereafter *S.E.*], vol. 5, esp. 612–13, 615–16.

[3] *S.E.*, vol. 14, esp. 166–71.

[4] *S.E.*, vol. 23, Chapters 4 to 8, esp. 157–60 and 196–97.

[5] *S.E.*, vol. 23, esp. 282–83 and 285–86.

stance, as physics. In our science as in the others the problem is the same: behind the attributes (qualities) of the object under examination which are presented directly to our perception, we have to discover something else which is more independent of the particular receptive capacity of our sense organs and which approximates more closely to what may be supposed to be the real state of affairs. We have no hope of being able to reach the latter itself, since it is evident that everything new that we have inferred must nevertheless be translated back into the language of our perceptions, from which it is simply impossible for us to free ourselves. But herein lies the very nature and limitation of our science. It is as though we were to say in physics: "If we could see clearly enough we should find that what appears to be a solid body is made up of particles of such and such a shape and size and occupying such and such relative positions." In the meantime we try to increase the efficiency of our sense organs to the furthest possible extent by artificial aids; but it may be expected that all such efforts will fail to affect the ultimate outcome. Reality will always remain "unknowable." The yield brought to light by scientific work from our primary sense perceptions will consist in an insight into connections and dependent relations which are present in the external world, which can somehow be reliably reproduced or reflected in the internal world of our thought and a knowledge of which enables us to "understand" something in the external world, to foresee it and possibly to alter it. Our procedure in psycho-analysis is quite similar. We have discovered technical methods of filling up the gaps in the phenomena of our consciousness, and we make use of those methods just as a physicist makes use of experiment. In this manner we infer a number of processes which are in themselves "unknowable" and interpolate them in those that are conscious to us. And if, for instance, we say: "At this point an unconscious memory intervened," what that means is: "At this point something occurred of which we are totally unable to form a conception, but which, if it had entered our consciousness, could only have been described in such and such a way."[6]

Freud appears to have arrived at this position by the following process of reasoning. If one tries to construct a science of psychology dealing only with conscious processes, the task seems hopeless, for there are too many evident causal gaps. The conscious material is fragmentary and unsystematic, and therefore unlikely to be theoretically understandable in terms that do not go beyond it. It is natural to suppose these gaps filled in by neurophysiological processes, which give rise from time to time to conscious states. And the purposes of theoretical unity are served by supposing that, instead of an alternation and interaction between unconscious physical processes and conscious mental ones, there is a causally complete physical system, some of whose processes, however, have the property of consciousness in addition, or have conscious concomi-

[6] S.E., vol. 23, 196–97.

tants. The mental then appears as the effect of a certain kind of physical process.[7]

Further reflection, however, suggests that it may be wrong to identify with the physical processes themselves. These can appear to consciousness but are in themselves unconscious, as all physiological processes are. And since the true nature of the mental processes that appear to consciousness is physical, with consciousness being just one added quality of them, there can be no objection to also describing as mental those intermediate processes, occurring in the same physical system, which do not appear to consciousness even though they may be in many respects physically and functionally similar to those that do. Moreover, as we do not have the requisite physical understanding of the nervous system to be able to think about these processes in physical terms (perhaps we will never be able to reduce them to *cellular* terms), our best hope of progress in understanding the physical system is to think about it in terms of the conscious aspects under which some mental processes appear to us. This is analogous to our use of visualization in thinking about physics—even about physical phenomena that are not actually visible. By thinking about mental processes in terms of the appearances of consciousness, we do not imply that their intrinsic nature is conscious. In fact, the intrinsic nature of both conscious and unconscious mental processes is unknown to us, and both types are merely represented, and not exhausted, by conscious imagery. Thus all of the psychical, and not only the unconscious, is *in itself* unconscious.

> Just as Kant warned us not to overlook the fact that our perceptions are subjectively conditioned and must not be regarded as identical with what is perceived though unknowable, so psycho-analysis warns us not to equate perceptions by means of consciousness with the unconscious mental processes which are their object. Like the physical, the psychical is not necessarily in reality what it appears to us to be.[8]

I want to consider three questions about this view. First, is the analogy with the use of visual imagery in physics accurate? Second, does the view imply a particular position on the mind-body problem (e.g., materialism), or is it compatible with several alternatives? Third, does the view supply a rationale for the employment of mentalistic concepts, taken from the

---

[7] This is the view expressed in Freud's monograph *On Aphasia:* "It is probable that the chain of physiological events in the nervous system does not stand in a causal connection with the psychical events. The physiological events do not cease as soon as the psychical ones begin; on the contrary, the physiological chain continues. What happens is simply that, after a certain point of time, each (or some) of its links has a psychical phenomenon corresponding to it. Accordingly, the psychical is a process parallel to the physiological—'a dependent concomitant'" (*S.E.*, vol. 14, 207).

[8] *S.E.*, vol. 14, 171.

psychology of consciousness, in theorizing about processes of whose physi-ological or chemical nature we are unable to form a conception?

It is certainly true that we find visual imagery helpful in thinking about structures that are invisible, invisible either because they are too small or because they do not reflect light. Thus we can imagine the DNA molecule as a double helix. Does this mean that we believe that if our vision were acute enough, that is how it would look to us? Perhaps so; but for some objects, such as atomic nuclei, the supposition that our vision should be-come acute enough to enable us to *see* their structure makes doubtful sense. It is more plausible to suppose that *if* we believe the hypothetical proposition, it is because we believe something else: namely, that there is a similarity in structure between the invisible thing we are talking about and other, visible things that look a certain way; and that this structural feature is responsible for their looking that way. If the structural feature is what we see in the case of the visible objects, then we can use this kind of visual image to represent the same structural feature in invisible objects. Hence our image of the DNA molecule.

An important aspect of such cases is that the structure being imagined can be independently characterized. A double helix can be described in purely geometrical terms, without reference to its visual appearance, and it is the former, not the latter, that the DNA molecule and a visible model have in common.[9] But if the significance of the hypothetical, "If we could see it, it would look like this," depends on the availability of an indepen-dent characterization in nonvisual terms, then the usefulness of this exam-ple as an analogy for the relation between conscious and unconscious mental processes is problematic. For in the latter case we have no indepen-dent way to characterize the unconscious mental process, "which, if it had entered our consciousness, could only have been described in such and such a way."

However, we can still make sense of the supposition in terms of the *possibility* of an independent characterization of the unconscious process. We may be supposing that, although we are at present totally unable to form a conception of it, nevertheless it shares features with a correspond-ing conscious mental process, and that these features are partly responsi-ble for the latter process appearing to consciousness in the form it does. This supposition seems to legitimate the peculiar counterfactual condi-tional, even if we do not now possess the vocabulary or concepts for describing the common features. They need not, for example, be features describable in the terms of current neurophysiology. They may be de-

---

[9] Similarly, it is possible to speak of sounds so faint or so high that they cannot be heard by any organism, because we have a physical theory of sound.

scribable only in the terms of a future psychology whose form will be in part determined by the development of psychoanalytic theory. And there may be no reduction of the general terms of that theory to the terms of current neurophysiology (though it is possible that Freud himself thought there would be). I believe that this interpretation makes Freud's mentalistic discourse about what he regards as a physical system comprehensible, and makes the analogy with visualization in physics acceptable, though not so close as might initially appear. Instead of inferring specific similar causes from similar effects, he infers *similarity* of causes in unknown respects from observed similarity of effects.

Our knowledge of the unconscious, he says, is very like our knowledge of another person's mind, for it rests on circumstantial and behavioral grounds.[10] Since we have standard reasons of this kind for believing that certain features of our own and others' behavior have a psychical explanation, and further reasons to deny that these psychic phenomena are conscious,[11] the natural conclusion is that they are unconscious but otherwise similar to the potentially or actually conscious mental processes to which our ordinary explanations refer. Since they do not appear similarly to consciousness, the resemblance must be found in other, presumably physical, characteristics.

Since consciousness does not exhaust the nature of, for example, conscious hostility, it is possible to employ the imagery of consciousness to think about that which is common to both the conscious and the unconscious forms, as we use visual imagery in thinking about the structure of both visible and invisible double helices.

The main difficulty with this view is that it may assume too much, even though what it assumes is less specific than in the case of visual images of

[10] In neither case does he believe these grounds have to operate as the premises of a conscious *inference*, however: "(It would no doubt be psychologically more correct to put it in this way: that without any special reflection we attribute to everyone else our own constitution and therefore our consciousness as well, and that this identification is a sine qua non of our understanding)" (*S.E.,* vol. 14, 169).

[11] He may be overhasty in this assumption. His main reason for refusing to extend the analogy with other minds to the attribution of consciousness to the Unconscious is that "a consciousness of which its own possessor knows nothing is something very different from a consciousness belonging to another person, and it is questionable whether such a consciousness, lacking, as it does, its most important characteristic, deserves any discussion at all" (*S.E.,* vol. 14, 170). But, of course, if the Unconscious were conscious of *itself,* then it would have a "possessor" distinct from the subject of ordinary consciousness in the same person, and it would be only the latter who was unconscious of these conscious states of the Unconscious. However, Freud also offers other reasons against their consciousness, namely, problems of inconsistency, peculiarity, and incoherence, as well as indeterminateness in the number of subjects required to accommodate all other states consciously in more or less unified fashion.

submicroscopic or invisible entities. It assumes that there *is* some definite objective character or disjunctive set of characters common to the states that are ordinarily grouped together by their similarity of appearance to consciousness (and their contextual and behavioral connections and significance.) Only if that is true can we pick out a type of state of the nervous system by a mentalistic concept without implying anthing about its conscious manifestations. But it is by no means obviously true, at least for many of the examples important to Freud, like beliefs, wishes, identifications.

It is most implausible, of course, that there is a general *neurological* character or set of characters common to all instances of the desire to kill one's father, but that is not the problem. A defender of the Freudian view need not claim that the objective character of these states can be accounted for in terms of any existing physical concepts. Perhaps it is only a developed psychology, not reducible to current neurophysiology, that can accommodate them.[12] But even to assume this—that is, to assume that an objective psychology, whose concepts refer to physical phenomena, will roughly preserve the distinctions and categories embodied in common-sense mental concepts—is to assume a great deal. (It is perhaps less implausible in the case of sensations than in the case of thought-related mental states.) If this criticism should be correct, and the assumptions of Freud's account too strong, there may be other accounts of the significance of the attribution of unconscious mental states that would involve weaker theoretical assumptions: dispositional accounts referring only to the behavioral and circumstantial similarities, perhaps with an added condition that the unconscious state can reach consciousness under certain conditions. Certainly such accounts have been offered by philosophers. But they are different from Freud's, and in this case his remarks about what he means are not so easily dismissed as the philosophical *obiter dicta* of a scientist commenting on the nature of his primary professional activity.

[12] See, however, *Beyond the Pleasure Principle:* "We need not feel greatly disturbed in judging our speculation upon the life and death instincts by the fact that so many bewildering and obscure processes occur in it—such as one instinct being driven out by another or an instinct turning from the ego to an object, and so on. This is merely due to our being obliged to operate with the scientific terms, that is to say with the figurative language, peculiar to psychology (or, more precisely, to depth psychology). We could not otherwise describe the processes in question at all, and indeed we could not have become aware of them. The deficiencies in our description would probably vanish if we were already in a position to replace the psychological terms by physiological or chemical ones. It is true that they too are only part of a figurative language; but it is one with which we have long been familiar and which is perhaps a simpler one as well" (*S.E.*, vol. 18, 60).

Let us now turn to the second of the three questions we have posed: since Freud's view is that both conscious and unconscious mental processes are *in themselves* physical—though we can think of them at present only in mentalistic terms—it might appear that he is committed to a materialistic position on the mind-body problem. However, I believe that this is not the case. Freud apparently *accepted* a materialist position, but it is not *entailed* by the views we are now considering. Everything depends on what is said about consciousness itself. Only if it, too, is a physical phenomenon or a physical feature of those brain processes that are conscious mental processes would Freud's account be materialistic.

In the *Project* this is in fact his position, for he posits a special class of neurons, the ω-neurons, whose activation is in some sense identified with conscious experience. His most careful statement of the view is as follows:

> A word on the relation of this theory of consciousness to others. According to an advanced mechanistic theory, consciousness is a mere appendage to physiologico-psychical processes and its omission would make no alteration in the psychical passage (of events). According to another theory, consciousness is the subjective side of all psychical events and is thus inseparable from the physiological mental process. The theory developed here lies between these two. Here consciousness is the subjective side of one part of the physical processes in the nervous system, namely of the ω processes; and the omission of consciousness does not leave psychical events unaltered but involves the omission of the contribution from ω.[13]

To say that consciousness is the *subjective side* of a certain kind of neurophysiological process is not compatible with dualism, although it may also be a mistake to call it materialism. The view appears to combine the following points. (1) Every conscious mental process is[14] a physical process, of which consciousness is an aspect. (2) The consciousness is not an *effect* of the physical process; its existence is not compatible with the nonoccurrence of that physical process, nor is its absence compatible with the occurrence of the physical process. This view, though not developed, is subtle and interesting. His later views on the subject are probably contained in the lost metapsychological paper on consciousness, written in the same year as "The Unconscious."[15] Unfortunately it was never published and appears to have been destroyed.

---

[13] *S.E.*, vol. 1, 311.

[14] The identification is made explicitly in the following passage: "Thus we summon up courage to assume that there is a third system of neurones—ω perhaps (we might call it)—which is excited along with perception, but not along with reproduction, and whose states of excitation give rise to the various qualities—are, that is to say, *conscious sensations* (*S.E.*, vol. 1, 309).

[15] See the editor's introduction to the papers on metapsychology, *S.E.*, vol. 14, 105–7.

Freud might have retained the double-aspect view (if that is what it can be called), in which case the other doctrines we are considering could provide a justification for thinking about physical phenomena in mentalistic terms, without implying the existence of any nonphysical processes. It would also be possible, however, to hold that consciousness makes us aware of psychic processes that are in themselves physical and can exist unconsciously, *without* allowing that the events of consciousness are themselves physical. In either case the rationale for thinking about the unconscious psychical in terms of conscious appearances is the same, and the analogy with physics can be appealed to.

But the position that consciousness too is a physical process, or the "subjective side" of certain physical processes, while obscure, is more interesting philosophically. It is worth saying a few words about how such a view may be construed, since it may bear on current discussion of the mind-body problem. Ordinarily, when the phenomenal appearance of something is constrasted with its objective nature, the former is explained as an *effect* of the latter on human observers. Thus ice feels cold in virtue of its effect on our sense of touch, and the physical property we identify with its coldness—low average kinetic energy—is something distinct from this sensory effect. If a corresponding view were taken about the relation between consciousness and the brain processes of which it is an appearance, then the conscious state would have to be described as an *effect* of the brain process on the subject's awareness, the brain process being something distinct.[16]

The view suggested by Freud, however, is that the brain process corresponding to a conscious state is *not* something distinct from the consciousness that is the awareness of it. The conscious qualities do not supply a complete description of the process, since its objective nature is physical, and consciousness is only its "subjective side." But consciousness is not an *effect* of this physical process any more than the surface of an object is an effect of *it*. Nor is it a detachable part. Philosophers of mind do not at present have much to say about the hypothesis that a neural process could appear to its subject as a conscious process, without producing subjective *effects*, simply in virtue of its own subjective qualities. This seems to me a question worth pursuing.

Let me turn to the last of the three questions posed above. Does Freud's view provide a justification for *theorizing* about the central nervous system in mentalistic terms? This question is not, I think, settled in the affirmative by the discussion so far. We have argued that Freud's account explains

[16]See Saul A. Kripke, *Naming and Necessity* (Harvard University Press, 1980), esp. pp. 144–55.

how mentalistic terms, with or without the implication of consciousness, may in principle *refer* to physical processes of which no explicitly physical conception can be formed at present. This does not mean, however, that a useful theory of these matters can be constructed using the mentalistic concepts, as may be seen if we return to the analogy with the role of visual imagery in physics.

Visualization is useful in thinking about molecular or atomic structure, but most of the important quantitative concepts used in physical or chemical theory are not represented visually, but more formally. Even our understanding of the visible world depends on concepts such as weight, energy, and momentum that can be represented in visual terms only crudely. Physical theory depends on the development of nonphenomenal concepts.

Why then should it be expected that our understanding of the brain can be advanced by theorizing with phenomenal concepts of a mentalistic type? Desires and aversions, pleasures and pains, intentions, beliefs, and thoughts certainly provide very useful explanations of what people do. But is there any reason to expect that further refinement and systematization of these explanations will yield a theory of how the central nervous system operates? Freud argues persuasively that a complete theory is not to be expected if we restrict ourselves to describing the connections among states that are actually conscious. But is it enough to expand our field of investigation to include unconscious psychical states, that is, those that are analogous, in structure and causes and effects, to conscious psychical states? That would be like trying to do physics entirely in terms of visible substances and phenomena plus invisible substances and phenomena structurally and causally analogous to them. The result would be some kind of mechanism. Is not psychologism a correspondingly narrow view about the brain?

The idea that we may expect to discover something about the brain by developing mentalistic theories in psychology and linguistics has been revived recently in connection with the mentalism of Noam Chomsky.[17] It is not necessary to offer this as one of the justifications for mentalistic linguistics, which is after all the only promising method currently available for investigating how natural languages function. We can at least try to discover phonetic, syntactic, and semantic rules that people talk as if they were following. Linguists have had considerable success with this mode of description of grammar. But it is important to recognize that if people do not *consciously* follow certain statable rules in some area of activity, there is no *guarantee* that rules can be discovered that they may be said to be

---

[17] See Noam Chomsky, *Aspects of the Theory of Syntax* (M.I.T. Press, 1965), p. 193.

unconsciously following—rules they behave *as if* they were following, and to which their judgments of correct and incorrect usage conform.

This should be evident to anyone who reflects on the failures of conceptual analysis in philosophy, for conceptual analysis is a type of mentalistic theory that tries to formulate rules for the application of concepts, which users of those concepts speak *as if* they were following. Wittgenstein's *Philosophical Investigations* devotes much energy to combating the assumption that such stable rules must always be discoverable behind our intuitions of correctness and incorrectness in the use of language.

Moreover, even if a mentalistic theory of the *as if* type succeeds reasonably well in accounting for human abilities or competence in some domain, as has been true of grammar, there remains a further question: what significance is to be attached to the claim that people don't merely talk *as if* they were following certain rules, but that they actually *are* (unconsciously) following them? The grounds for this further assertion are unclear.

Chomsky suggests, without making it a central part of his view, that when a mentalistic theory of some domain like grammar is successful, it may come to have physical significance. His cautious but interesting comment on this possibility, at the end of *Language and Mind,* is as follows:

> I have been using mentalistic terminology quite freely, but entirely without prejudice as to the question of what may be the physical realization of the abstract mechanisms postulated to account for the phenomena of behavior or the acquisition of knowledge. We are not constrained, as was Descartes, to postulate a second substance when we deal with phenomena that are not expressible in terms of matter in motion, in his sense. Nor is there much point in pursuing the question of psycho-physical parallelism, in this connection. It is an interesting question whether the functioning and evolution of human mentality can be accommodated within the framework of physical explanation, as presently conceived, or whether there are new principles, now unknown, that must be invoked, perhaps principles that emerge only at higher levels of organization than can now be submitted to physical investigation. We can, however, be fairly sure that there will be a physical explanation for the phenomena in question, if they can be explained at all, for an uninteresting terminological reason, namely that the concept of "physical explanation" will no doubt be extended to incorporate whatever is discovered in this domain, exactly as it was extended to accommodate gravitational and electromagnetic force, massless particles, and numerous other entities and processes that would have offended the common sense of earlier generations.[18]

This is consonant with the outlook we have found in Freud, but it raises the question how a mentalistic theory would have to develop before its

[18] Noam Chomsky, *Language and Mind* (Harcourt, 1968), pp. 83–84.

subject matter was admitted to the physical world in its own right. A theory from which the mentalistic character can be removed without explanatory loss is not essentially mentalistic. One might, for example, construct a mentalistic version of Newtonian mechanics, describing the attractions of bodies to one another and their stubbornness in moving in a straight line unless acted upon by an external force (all these psychic states being unconscious, of course). But the explanatory content of such a theory could be given in clearer, more formal, quantitative, and nonmentalistic terms.

If, on the other hand, a theory is essentially mentalistic in that its explanatory value cannot be recaptured by a nonanthropomorphic version, then it may be doubted whether the things it describes will be admitted to the domain of physics. This is because mentalistic descriptions, connections, and explanations have to be understood by taking up, so far as is possible, the point of view of the subject of the mental states and processes referred to. Even where the mental states are unconscious, the understanding such a theory gives us requires that we take up the subject's point of view, since the form of explanatory connection between unconscious mental states and their circumstantial and behavioral surroundings is understood only through the image of conscious mental processes, with all the appeals to meaning, intention, and perception of aspects that this involves.

Since it appears to be part of our idea of the physical world that what goes on in it can be apprehended not just from one point of view but from indefinitely many, because its objective nature is external to any point of view taken toward it, there is reason to believe that until these subjective features are left behind, the hypotheses of a mentalistic psychology will not be accepted as physical explanations. The prospects for such an objectification of psychology are obscure, as is the form it might conceivably take. But this is a difficult topic that cannot be pursued here.

It should be mentioned that some psychoanalysts have maintained that Freud's theories are already far advanced toward objectivity—that his psychodynamics are impersonal and scientific, that the anthropomorphic terminology is only metaphorical and plays no essential theoretical role.[19]

---

[19] For example, H. Hartmann, E. Kris, and R. M. Loewenstein, "Comments on the Formation of Psychic Structure," in *The Psychoanalytic Study of the Child* 2 (1946), pp. 11–38. Also in *Psychological Issues* 14 (International Universities Press, 1964), pp. 27–55. The claim that Freud's theories are essentially mechanistic is sometimes also offered as a criticism. See, for example, A. C. MacIntyre, *The Unconscious* (Routledge, 1958), p. 22: "Although Freud abandoned finally and decisively the attempt at neurophysiological explanation . . . it is my contention and the most important contention in this part of my argument that Freud preserved the view of the mind as a piece of machinery and merely wrote up in psychological terms what had been originally intended as a neurological theory."

But these claims have been very persuasively challenged in a paper by William I. Grossman and Bennett Simon,[20] which is also an excellent guide to the psychoanalytic literature on this subject. Subjective anthropomorphic thinking seems indispensable to the understanding of such statements as this:

> The analytic physician and the patient's weakened ego, basing themselves on the real external world, have to band themselves together into a party against the enemies, the instinctual demands of the id and the conscientious demands of the super-ego.[21]

Psychoanalytic theory will have to change a great deal before it comes to be regarded as part of the physical description of reality. And perhaps it, and other mentalistic theories, will never achieve the kind of objectivity necessary for this end. Perhaps finally the physical explanations of the phenomena in question will not be reached by progressive refinement and exactness in our mentalistic understanding, but will come only in a form whose relation to mentalistic theories cannot be perceived by us.[22] Now, as in 1896, it is too early to tell.

[20] "Anthropomorphism: Motive, Meaning, and Causality in Psychoanalytic Theory," in *The Psychoanalytic Study of the Child* 24 (1969), pp. 78–111.

[21] *S.E.*, vol. 23, 173.

[22] A similar view is found in Donald Davidson, "Mental Events" (1970), reprinted in Davidson, *Essays on Actions and Events* (Oxford University Press, 1980).

2

Freud's Permanent Revolution

This was a review of Richard Wollheim's The Mind and Its Depths *(Harvard University Press, 1993) and Paul Robinson's* Freud and His Critics *(University of California Press, 1993), originally published in the May 12, 1994, issue of* The New York Review of Books. *The addendum is a response to Adolf Grünbaum's comments on the review, which appeared in the August 11, 1994, issue.*

Great intellectual revolutionaries change the way we think. They pose new questions and devise new methods of answering them—and we cannot unlearn those forms of thought simply by discovering errors of reasoning on the part of their creators, unless we persuade ourselves that the thoughts are identical with the errors. There is something strange about recent debates over the evidence on which Freud based his theories. His influence is not like that of a physicist who claims to have discovered a previously unobserved particle by an experiment that others now think to be flawed. Whatever may be the future of psychoanalysis as a distinctive form of therapy, Freud's influence seems to me no more likely to be expunged from modern consciousness than that of Hobbes, for example, or Descartes. Such thinkers have an effect much deeper than can be captured by a set of particular hypotheses, an effect that would not go away even if, in a wave of Europhobia, their writings should cease to be read.

I

The correct interpretation of Freud's influence, and the way we should evaluate it, is a common theme of the two books under review, and *The Mind and Its Depths* provides in addition a leading example of that influence. It is a collection of essays on art, morality, and the mind written by Wollheim during the period when he also published *The Thread of Life*[1] and *Painting as an Art*,[2] books whose subjects overlap with the essays. In *The Mind and Its Depths* we encounter one of the most psychoanalytic of contemporary thinkers. Wollheim has a strong sense of the reality and pervasive influence of the unconscious, and of the impact of infantile sexuality on the rest of mental life.

He holds that what Freud achieved was a vast expansion of psychological insight, rooted in commonsense psychology and employing some of its concepts, but going far beyond it. Psychological insights are not unusual, since we spend our lives trying to understand ourselves and each other, but the scope and imaginative character of Freud's methods of understanding create a special problem of interpretation and evaluation.

The problem is this. As Wollheim observes, commonsense explanations are a form of understanding "from within"; even when they provide insights into the mind of another, they depend, in part, on self-understanding, since they interpret the other person as another self. To understand someone else's thought, feelings, or behavior requires that we make sense—even if only irrational sense—of his point of view, by using our own point of view as an imaginative resource. Imagination enables us to make internal sense of beliefs, emotions, and aims that we do not share—to see how they hang together so as to render the other's conduct intelligible. But Freud's extension of this form of insight to unconscious thoughts, motives, and fantasies, and into the minds of infants, threatens to deprive ordinary psychological concepts, like belief, wish, and desire, of their familiar empirical support in the common experience and understandings of everyday life.

Some, like Sartre, have felt there was an outright contradiction in the idea of a thought of which one is not aware, but Freud could deal with that objection. In metaphysical outlook he was a sophisticated materialist; he believed that even conscious mental processes were also physical events in the brain, though we know almost nothing about their physical character. If that is true, then it makes sense to ask whether there may not also be other brain processes that are analogous to the conscious ones in physical

[1] Harvard University Press, 1984.
[2] Princeton University Press, 1987.

structure, that have recognizably psychological causes and effects, but that are not conscious. Their reality would be physical, even though we could know about them only through their psychological manifestations, just as we can at present, with very limited exceptions, refer to conscious brain processes only in psychological terms.[3] So the main problem about the unconscious is not metaphysical. The problem, rather, is whether the evidence supports such a vast extension, by analogy, of mental concepts to the unconscious, and the concomitant growth of psychological explanation.

Commonsense psychology allows us to identify the experiences or deliberations that have led to a belief, or the emotions expressed by a particular reaction, or the aims or values behind a course of conduct. Causal judgments of this kind are largely automatic; they fill our lives and our relations with others and are heavily supported by their usefulness, although they can also lead us astray. When we interpret other people in this way by making sense of their point of view, we are not merely imagining things, as when we see animals in the clouds or ascribe malice to a defective toaster. Rather we are trying to understand, within the limits of a nonscientific psychology, what really makes people tick, and we often hope to be confirmed by the person's own self-understanding.

Freud extended the range of such explanation to unheard-of lengths, to cover not only memory lapses and slips, but jokes, dreams, neurotic symptoms, and the substructure of erotic life and family ties—with forays into morality, politics, art, and religion. About some of these phenomena, no adequate psychological understanding was available at all; about others, he proposed to add a deeper level of understanding than that provided by conscious psychology. And he did it in many cases not by offering insights that others could easily evaluate from their own experience and observation, but by appealing to evidence gathered under the highly unusual conditions of psychoanalytic treatment, evidence that could be understood only by those familiar with the process.

Yet the entire system remained psychological in the sense Wollheim has specified. It sought to provide an understanding of human beings "from within," so that we could put ourselves in their shoes and make sense of their symptoms and responses by attributing to them beliefs, desires, feelings, and perceptions—with the difference that these were aspects of their point of view of which they were not consciously aware. What reason is

[3] This theme appears at various points in Freud's writings, including the *Project for a Scientific Psychology* (1895), "The Unconscious" (1915), and the *Outline of Psychoanalysis* (1938).

there to believe that such a vast extension of psychological interpretation is not merely a fantasy, like seeing animals in the clouds, rather than genuine knowledge?

It is a familiar fact that people can be unaware of their true motives, and that we often understand others better than they understand themselves. (Anyone knows this who has listened with embarrassment to a flagrant name-dropper making what he thinks is just amiable conversation.) But Freud carried this idea so far that he could not defend it just by appealing to common sense. He insisted on the scientific character of his findings and their support by clinical observation—meaning not controlled experiments, but the data that emerge in the analytic process. The analyst's sustained and unique interaction with the neurotic patient supplies him with much more extensive and systematic evidence for interpretation than is available to someone who merely observes the patient's symptoms—even someone who knows the patient well in the ordinary way.

Freud's confidence can best be understood, I think, as the belief that exposure in a great many cases to the various extremely detailed accounts of experience that emerge in analysis enabled him to see a deeper psychological coherence in phenomena that, taken in isolation, seem meaningless and inexplicable. No doubt such coherence can be misleading. One can imagine, for example, that a drug-induced mental disorder might produce elaborate patterns of thought and feeling that seem to point to a psychological, not a chemical, cause. In general, it is important to keep in mind the real possibility that a syndrome that makes psychological "sense" may nevertheless have a purely physiological explanation. But that means only that psychoanalytic evidence, like most evidence, is not conclusive.

Richard Wollheim's most direct comments on this matter appear in an essay called "Desire, Belief, and Professor Grünbaum's Freud." It is a response to Adolf Grünbaum's *The Foundations of Psychoanalysis,*[4] a book that takes the scientific claims of psychoanalysis seriously but interprets them in a curiously external way, neglecting the distinctively inner char-

---

[4] University of California Press, 1984. Grünbaum argues that Freud rests his case for the theory of repression on the superior therapeutic effectiveness of psychoanalysis in treating neuroses, and that such evidence is not available. His reading of Freud, and of the evidence, clinical and extraclinical, has been extensively criticized, notably by David Sachs, "In Fairness to Freud," *Philosophical Review* 98, No. 3 (July 1989), and by various commentators in *Behavioral and Brain Sciences* 9 (June 1986). More recently he has published *Validation in the Clinical Theory of Psychoanalysis* (International Universities Press, 1993), a further discussion of these issues, which includes both new material and versions of previously published essays, some predating *The Foundations of Psychoanalysis.*

acter of psychological insight. Toward the end of the essay Wollheim remarks tellingly, "If . . . psychoanalytic theory is an extension of commonsense psychology, perhaps we should begin by asking, How is commonsense psychology tested?" I take it the answer is that the evidence for commonsense psychology, instead of being the result of controlled experiments, is complex and widely dispersed. Wollheim charges Grünbaum with having an impoverished conception of how psychological explanation works, and with neglecting the essential role of psychological structure—that is, the need to use psychological categories of *some* kind— in both psychoanalytic and commonsense understanding.

> If what the patient says or does is to be brought to bear upon the hypothesis under consideration so that it, the hypothesis, can then be said to have been tested on the couch, the patient's material will in most circumstances have to be subsumed under categories deriving from psychoanalysis. . . . In saying or doing what he does, the patient has to be identified as, say, presenting *anal material* on a massive scale; resorting to *phantasies of omnipotence; assaulting,* or *fragmenting,* or *idealizing,* the analyst's interpretation; *acting out;* and so on. In other words, the patient's material must be subsumed under transference categories: that is, categories which capture what the person is doing *vis-à-vis* the analytic situation as he phantasizes it. (p. 108)

Each of these categories, or hypotheses explaining the patient's behavior, has to find its empirical support in countless other applications to other patients in other settings. In other words, psychoanalysis makes use of a complex network of interpretations, just as commonsense psychology does when it allows us to understand someone's reactions by referring to an interconnected network of desires, beliefs, emotions, memories, obsessions, inhibitions, values, and identifications. And Wollheim observes that even where Grünbaum proposes a more or less commonsense alternative to psychoanalytic explanation, namely, that the apparent clinical evidence for psychoanalysis is the result of suggestion by the analyst, he sees no need to make the dynamics of such suggestion psychologically comprehensible or to explain the mental processes through which it operates. The hypothesis of "suggestion," after all, is an alternative *psychological* explanation and has to be evaluated by the same standards as the explanations it is called on to refute.

How do we know whether a psychological explanation is correct? Although statistical analysis is not needed to prove that someone put on a sweater because he felt cold, one could easily imagine an idiotic psychological experiment statistically confirming the likelihood of a causal link in such cases. But the more interesting the case, the harder it is to reproduce it. What experimental evidence, for example, would help us to answer the question why Mikhail Gorbachev began the dismantling of the Soviet empire? Anything we can say about this will have to depend on the application of general methods for the motivational interpretation of intentional conduct to the unique circumstances of the case.

Much of human mental life consists of complex events with multiple causes and background conditions that will never precisely recur. If we wish to understand real life, it is useless to demand repeatable experiments with strict controls. (The same problem arises with regard to historical explanation, since historical events are, if anything, even less reproducible.) That doesn't mean that explanation is impossible, only that it cannot be sought by the methods appropriate in particle physics, cancer research, or the study of reflexes. We may not be able to run controlled experiments, but we can still try to make internal sense of what people do, in light of their circumstances, by trying to see how it might appear justified from their point of view—a technique supported by its usefulness in countless other cases, none of them exactly the same.

Explanations that refer to unconscious mental processes should be evaluated by the same standard. There may be some psychoanalytic explanations so simple that they can be tested by experiment or statistical analysis, but most are certainly not like that—rather they are applications of psychological insight in highly specific circumstances, which go beyond the bounds of consciousness. When we come to a brilliant and circumstantially rich conjecture like Freud's attribution of the forgetting of the word in a Latin quotation to the subject's anxiety that his mistress might be pregnant,[5] statistical confirmation is completely impossible, and we simply have to decide whether this is an intuitively credible extension of a general structure of explanation that we find well supported elsewhere, and whether it is more plausible than the alternatives—including the alternative that there is no psychological explanation.

The same problem arises for more general proposals, like Freud's hypothesis that in cases of melancholia an object-loss (such as the departure of a lover) is transformed into an ego-loss (the sense that one is worthless or despicable) through identification of the ego with the object of love by which it has been abandoned; the self-hatred that results can be understood as abuse by the ego of the internalized object. There seems no way to evaluate such a proposal experimentally—yet it is an empirical hypothesis about a psychic process that certainly appears to shed light on what goes on in some cases of acute depression.[6]

[5] The Psychopathology of Everyday Life (1901), Chapter 2.
[6] See "Mourning and Melancholia" (1917). Freud emphasizes that his proposal applies only to some cases of melancholia, and that others appear to be somatic in origin.

For most of those who believe in the reality of repression and the unconscious, whether or not they have gone through psychoanalysis, the belief is
based not on blind trust in the authority of analysts and their clinical
observations but on the evident usefulness of a rudimentary Freudian
outlook in understanding ourselves and other people, particularly erotic
life, family dramas, and what Freud called the psychopathology of everyday life. Things that would otherwise surprise us do not; behavior or
feelings that would otherwise seem simply irrational become nevertheless
comprehensible. You feel miserable all day, and then discover that it is the
forgotten anniversary of the death of someone who was important to you;
you find yourself repeatedly becoming absurdly angry with certain women
in your professional life, and come to realize that your anger is a throw-
back to a childhood struggle with your mother. In the end, if we are to
believe that Freud was getting at the truth, we must be able in some degree
to make use of his approach ourselves. Since controlled and reproducible
experiments are impracticable here, the kind of internal understanding
characteristic of psychoanalysis must rely on the dispersed but cumulative
confirmation in life that supports more familiar psychological judgments.

The question is not whether Freud got it exactly right, or whether
strong criticisms cannot be made of some of his case histories, but whether
the types of explanation he introduced substantially amplify the understanding of ourselves and others that commonsense psychology provides.
I believe that the pervasive Freudian transformation of our modern working conception of the self is evidence of the validity of his attempt to
extend the psychological far beyond its conscious base. Common sense has
in fact expanded to include parts of Freudian theory. This in turn makes it
credible that more extensive and systematic insights of the same type can
be developed by analysts who probe far more deeply and uncover far
more material for interpretation. To many of us it certainly *feels* as if,
much of the time, consciousness reveals only the surface of our minds and,
for many, this feeling is confirmed by their dreams.

II

Grünbaum's view is quite distant from the basic Freudian outlook that
is such a familiar feature of modern culture. Wollheim, by contrast, is
at home in a rich undergrowth of psychoanalytic categories, some developed by Melanie Klein. He puts special and interesting emphasis on the
phenomenology of the unconscious—that is, the subjective feelings and
fantasies the unconscious includes, which he argues are essential to its
explanatory power. For example, Wollheim puts forward the thesis of

the "bodily ego," according to which we conceive, when we are very young,

> of mental states on the model of corporeal entities, . . . of a thought as a piece of food in the mouth, or as faeces, and we conceive of accepting the thought as swallowing the piece of food, or of rejecting the thought as excreting faeces. (p. 87)

Because they incorporate these fantasies, the Freudian mechanisms of defense are not abstract forces but have a highly specific subjective (though unconscious) character.

It is difficult for an amateur to evaluate such claims; even when the subject matter is more familiar, the difficulty remains. The psychoanalytic understanding of morality is an interesting example. The story of the formation of the superego, "the internal version of the father in the Oedipal drama," has passed into popular psychology. But Wollheim resists this conception of morality, holding with Melanie Klein "that the injunctions or fulminations of internal figures not lying at the core of the ego play at best an unreliable, at worst a deleterious, role in the moral life." He thinks of the superego, in other words, as a threatening, punitive, and alien incorporated object, rather than as a better self with which the person comes to identify. Instead of basing moral development on the internalization of the disapproving father, Wollheim, following Klein, bases it on the reconciliation of much earlier feelings. After the first year of life the infant discovers that the object it loves and the object it hates are both its mother; the infant then struggles to repair, preserve, or revive the loved object it has injured in omnipotent fantasy. In time the infant will be led to integrate the good self and the bad self, the one that loves and the one that hates.

Wollheim describes the process, which is considerably more complicated than my brief sketch here, in an essay called "The Good Self and the Bad Self," which compares Klein with the philosopher F. H. Bradley,[7] who also held that morality must offer a form of harmonious self-realization. Wollheim is a naturalist about morality, in the sense that he believes that to have a claim on us it must be rooted in our earliest and most basic feelings. He urges us to avoid "the phantasy that morality marks the spot where human beings discard human nature." This appears to mean that we should not try to understand morality as a radical transcendence of infantile needs and wishes, and of the mental structures established before the age of two. Unless morality is rooted in those very needs and wishes, it will be superficial.

I cannot evaluate the Kleinian theory of infantile development even if I

[7] Bradley is the subject of Wollheim's first book, *F. H. Bradley* (Penguin, 1959).

am an instance of it, but apart from that, I do not see how a theory of this kind could by itself explain more than the very beginnings of the complex system of restraints on aggression and self-interest, acknowledgment of formal obligations and of the rights and claims of others, that make up a fully developed morality. The same could be said of the more familiar Freudian superego theory. Even if it starts with a family drama, morality in the strict sense requires forms of thought that are much more impersonal than fear of, love for, or identification with particular external or internal "objects," whether fathers or mothers. It aims to supply objective standards in the realm of conduct, which will allow us to justify ourselves to one another and to agree on what should be done.[8]

Wollheim's attitude toward morality is far more radical than Freud's and closer in spirit to Nietzsche's. His naturalism is applied in a startling way in an essay called "Crime, Punishment, and 'Pale Criminality,'" which suggests that human beings have a disposition "bound up with what is deepest in us, to do what is forbidden, and to do it for that reason"; and that if this is so, then the criminal justice system is based on a flawed understanding of human nature: what it forbids, it makes more attractive. Many social institutions, such as the criminal law, "imply a particular psychology," Wollheim writes, and if that psychology is false about human beings, "then the institution is at fault because instead of facilitating, it impedes, self knowledge."

This, he says, raises a further question:

> How much security from criminal behavior are we entitled to expect? How much protection can we rightly claim from those with whom we share our psychology? If, not criminality, but the seeds of criminality, are, in some identifiable way which the science of mind can make clear, present in all of us, how far are we right to distance it from us? . . . How far, if the need arose, should we be prepared to sacrifice security for self-knowledge? (p. 130)

But how is that need going to arise? Perhaps the human disposition to do what is forbidden causes some prohibitions to heighten the appeal of crime, but that only means that if we want security, we should take this into account in designing the criminal law. Where is the sacrifice of self-knowledge in this? I suspect that Wollheim is talking about something

---

[8] A recent collection of essays on Wollheim's work contains two valuable discussions of this question by Marcia Cavell and Samuel Scheffler. Both of them argue that a more objective and less "self"-centered conception of morality may be consistent with a psychoanalytic theory of moral development. See Jim Hopkins and Anthony Savile, editors, *Psychoanalysis, Mind and Art: Perspectives on Richard Wollheim* (Blackwell, 1992). Scheffler develops his ideas on the subject further in *Human Morality* (Oxford University Press, 1992), and Cavell sets out her position in *The Psychoanalytic Mind: From Freud to Philosophy* (Harvard University Press, 1993), which includes a plausible critique of Freud's theory of morality.

deeper than self-knowledge. He asks for a form of self-affirmation that is incompatible with rejecting anything at the core of the self; and this explains his distrust of conventional morality.

Art is different. Wollheim writes,

> It seems to me natural to think that art is more deeply rooted in human nature than morality, and I am surprised that philosophers make little of the fact that, though good art is more likeable than bad art, virtuous people do not enjoy this same advantage over those to whom we are drawn primarily for their charm, or their gaiety, or their sweetness of nature, or their outrageousness. (p. x)

A number of Wollheim's essays discuss artistic expression, perception, and style, and here too Wollheim is committed to psychological naturalism: "The broad characteristics of art, including expressiveness, originate outside art." Wollheim emphasizes the psychological importance of the phenomenon of "projection," the infusion of our perceptions of the outer world with inner mental states, which he believes is at the heart of the aesthetic response. Art gives meaning to our lives by its expressiveness, which creates a fit between our deep inner feelings and our external perceptions, and makes us at home in the world. Here again, as with the analysis of morality, a question arises whether such a personal theory doesn't make aesthetic response too subjective and idiosyncratic—but that will depend both on how objective we take such responses to be and how universal are the mental structures responsible, according to this theory, for the projections called forth by art. Wollheim himself believes that there is a universal human nature that all art, "or at any rate all great art," presupposes.

Both art and nature can be targets of projected feelings: both a real and a painted landscape can be seen as melancholy, for example. But with a work of art, Wollheim believes that the right response is determined by the artist's intention: the work has been created in order to evoke certain projections, and if the intention is fulfilled, that is what the spectator will see in it. Wollheim rejects the view "that criticism is at liberty to project on to a work of art whatever it wishes." He argues that the artist's own projective response to the work as he is creating it—his dual role as creator and spectator—has an essential part in the creative process: "the central fact about art [is] that it is an intentional manifestation of mind."

Painting as an Art contains many applications of this idea. For example, Wollheim attributes the uncanny effect of Caspar David Friedrich's great landscape, *The Large Enclosure near Dresden,* to the presence of an invisible "spectator in the picture," whose viewpoint does not have a natural relation to the landscape. When we look at the picture we are led to identify with this disembodied spectator inside it; we find ourselves both standing before the picture and floating above the landscape, which extends under the invisible spectator, and we are drawn into the attitude of detached but absorbed contemplation of nature expressive of Friedrich's early nineteenth-century Pietism. (On the only occasion when I saw it, the picture induced a strange spiritual disorientation, as if I had lost my self and were viewing the world *sub specie aeternitatis,* so I found Wollheim's account convincing.)

How much background knowledge we need in order to see the work as it was intended to be seen by the artist is another question. To perceive the meaning of a work of art generally requires some prior knowledge beyond what is needed to find a natural landscape beautiful: even to perceive a work's formal and nonrepresentational properties requires that the work "be perceived as part of an aesthetic tradition." But if the work is successful, understanding it will consist not in a deliberate act of inference and interpretation but simply in perceiving it as it was intended to be perceived. The essence of aesthetic understanding is to be found in experience, not theory. It is not to be found in social or economic explanation or in symbolic decoding.

The appeal of Wollheim's position lies in its insistence that what is important about a work of art is directly perceptible in it. What is harder to accept is his claim that the goal of aesthetic perception is always to experience the projection intended by the artist. This implies that a work of art cannot mean more than the artist intended it to mean, or knew that it meant, and that historical and symbolic and formal interpretation cannot produce a perceptual understanding of the work that interprets it as more than a product of the artist's purposes. A view contrary to Wollheim's might even include the possibility that the meaning of a work may develop over time, as the background of interpretation changes. I am drawn to Wollheim's emphasis on aesthetic experience. However, his theory may go too far in reducing aesthetics to psychology. The dominant role it gives to both intention and projection means that the work of art is not a free-standing creation whose aesthetic characteristics transcend both those psychological facts. I doubt that even great artists always know in all respects what they're doing, even if it is no accident that their works produce the effects they do.

III

Wollheim's diverse and unusual writings on many different subjects exemplify the influence of psychoanalytic modes of thought beyond therapy, and such influence is emphasized by Paul Robinson in his forceful response to three recent commentators on Freud: Frank Sulloway, Jeffrey Masson, and Adolf Grünbaum.[9] *Freud and His Critics* contains interesting general reflections on the significance of recent reactions to Freud as well as a dissection of these three writers. Robinson argues persuasively that none of the three makes a good case for their most distinctive claims about Freud and, further, that they all miss the real significance of Freud's intellectual contribution.

Sulloway is a historian who presents himself as a reintepreter of Freud, not as one of his critics. But Robinson believes he diminishes the interest and originality of Freud's ideas by exaggerating their biological content at the expense of the psychological. Freud's conviction that the mind, being a function of the brain, is a product of biological development, and that its structure is subject to evolutionary influences should be evident to any reader of his writings, and Sulloway provides a very detailed account of the biological and neurological background to Freud's intellectual development. But to treat this as the essence of a Freudian understanding of the mind is to read Freud much too reductively. The mind may be a biological product, but biological concepts can provide us with only a superficial understanding of its content and workings. Sulloway magnifies the influence on Freud of the crackpot theories of his early confidant Wilhelm Fliess, even though they left their traces. It is true that Freud corresponded with Fliess about the effects on the mind of biological calendars, the sense of smell, and the evolution of upright posture. But it is not possible, Robinson argues, to replace psychological insight—an understanding "from within" of the type that engaged Freud's real genius—with such hypotheses.

Robinson turns next to the egregious Masson, who accuses Freud of being a liar and a coward because he abandoned the claim that his early patients had been victims of real sexual abuse as children, and explained their symptoms instead by the theory of infantile sexuality and fantasy. Masson believes Freud thus missed the chance to be a great crusader against child molestation and that his theory became a means for blaming innocent victims. Robinson demonstrates that Masson's claims that the patients had in fact been sexually abused are simply unsupported assertions. And he adds: "The most powerful objection to Masson's thesis of moral cowardice is that Freud abandoned the seduction theory only to embrace an idea that was even more offensive to the prejudices of his

---

[9] In addition to Grünbaum's 1984 book, he discusses Sulloway's *Freud, Biologist of the Mind* (Basic Books, 1979) and Masson's *The Assault on Truth: Freud's Suppression of the Seduction Theory* (Farrar, Straus and Giroux, 1984), drawing also on some of the responses these works have attracted.

culture, the theory of infantile sexuality." Freud always recognized the existence of child abuse. His doubts had to do with its extent. But the claim that some accusations of childhood seduction are the product of fantasy provokes extreme resistance, and not only from Masson. I believe this insistence on the innocence of childhood and the evil behavior of adults covers up deeper feelings, which then surface in an emotionally delicious blend of prurience and moral outrage. The recent popular obsession with child molestation owes a good deal to such feelings.[10] Robinson persuasively identifies Masson as a representative of the new puritanism that emerged in the 1980s as a reaction to the sexually expansive 1960s. Masson's view of sex as joyless and charged with aggression belongs to an antiliberal tendency that has been gaining strength recently. It fits well with the outlook of those who see in pornography only an instrument for the subjection of women. Freud is a natural target for such enemies of self-knowledge.

Robinson's criticism of Grünbaum takes issue with the importance he assigns to therapeutic success as the empirical ground on which Freud's theories must stand or fall. Freud at various times denied that effective therapy was the ultimate test of his theories.[11] The theory of repression is an explanatory one, and the evidence for it comes from a variety of sources. I agree with Robinson that by insight and imagination it is possible, and sometimes even easy, to extrapolate from the conscious and familiar, and to discover unconscious psychological explanations in complex individual cases where statistical verification is impossible.

Only particular examples can provide evidence for this claim—examples that leave no credible alternative. Though some may find Freud's famous case histories persuasive, I believe they are too complex and ambiguous to serve this purpose. It is not surprising that they have generated so much interpretive and historical controversy. The best evidence for skeptics is smaller in scale. Einstein once wrote, in a letter to Freud:

> Until recently I could only apprehend the speculative power of your train of thought, together with its enormous influence on the *Weltanschauung* of the present era, without being in a position to form a definite opinion about the amount of truth it contains. Not long ago, however, I had the opportunity of hearing about a few instances, not very important in themselves, which in my

[10] It has resulted in some dreadful persecutions of the innocent. For example *The New York Times* of November 21, 1993 (p. 29), reported the acquittal of a Sunday school teacher charged with lurid rapes and tortures on the basis of testimony elicited from his pupils, who were three or four years old at the time.

[11] For example in his 1917 *Introductory Lectures* (*S.E.*, vol. 16, 255).

judgment exclude any other interpretation than that provided by the theory of repression.[12]

But how could Einstein tell? What is it about a concatenation of circumstances that "exclude any other interpretation"?

Not knowing what Einstein's instances were, I can only describe an episode I witnessed myself. At a dinner party, an elderly man of independent means, who had spent his life as a private scholar without an academic position, challenged a psychiatrist who was present to explain why, whenever he listened to the news on the radio, he fell asleep just at the point when the stock market report came on. The psychiatrist, knowing these facts, replied that it probably expressed difficult feelings about his father. "My *father!*" said the man incredulously, "My father has been dead for fifty years!" The conversation then went on to other things, but the next day, the man telephoned the psychiatrist to report that later in the evening the memory had come flooding back to him that when, in his youth, he had resisted going into the family business, his father had made him promise at least to listen to the stock market report on the radio every day.

Many people have been exposed to equally obvious examples—though most are not so cut and dried, and the material produced in psychoanalysis is much more complex and strange. Grünbaum is inhospitable to the use of psychological insight to extend familiar and basic forms of psychological explanation to radically unfamiliar situations. But this may be partly because he himself has a rather wooden psychological imagination. As Robinson points out, when Grünbaum tries to propose an alternative interpretation to Freud's for the same data, the interpretation falls flat. (And his idea of a slip of the tongue that might be caused by a concealed but conscious thought is "the man who turns from the exciting view of a lady's exposed bosom muttering, 'Excuse me, I have got to get a *breast* of *flesh* air!'")

Robinson concludes with an excellent statement of Freud's true intellectual legacy, which these critics fail to recognize:

> He is the major source of our modern inclination to look for meanings beneath the surface of behavior—to be always on the alert for the "real" (and presumably hidden) significance of our actions. He also inspires our belief that the mysteries of the present will become more transparent if we can trace them to their origins in the past, perhaps even in the very earliest past. . . . And, finally, he has created our heightened sensitivity to the erotic,

[12]Quoted in Ernest Jones, *The Life and Work of Sigmund Freud* (Basic Books, 1957), vol. 3, p. 203.

above all to its presence in arenas . . . where previous generations had neglected to look for it. (pp. 270–71)

The book is flawed, however, by one serious confusion, which crops up occasionally, as in the following passage: "One would simply never know from reading Sulloway, Masson, and Grünbaum that many of their contemporaries entertained profound doubts about science, objectivity, truth, and the possibility of achieving stable, irrefragable knowledge of the self and society." Robinson describes all three writers as "positivists," because of their innocent attachment to outmoded ideas of truth and objectivity, and he regards this attitude as itself a rejection of Freud's outlook:

> Modernism entailed a loss of confidence in the stability and transparency of the self. It also entailed the recognition that all human knowledge is subjective and indeterminate. Freud's theory of the unconscious, which denies that the self is aware even of its own ideas, was the most powerful articulation of this modernist sensibility. (p. 16)

Robinson is referring to the facile subjectivism that now blights many of the humanities and social sciences. According to this view, anyone who thinks that some questions have right and wrong answers, which can be confirmed or refuted by evidence and argument, is an epistemological caveman.

Robinson incorrectly attributes such a view to Freud. There is a vast difference between holding that we are not transparent to ourselves and must discover our real mental nature by difficult and indirect investigative methods, and holding that there is no such thing as truth or objectivity. The unconscious does not abolish objectivity, even if it makes it more difficult to achieve. In Robinson's sense, Freud was certainly a "positivist" and a believer in the pursuit of truth by the correct assessment of evidence.

That does not imply that what we believe to be true is immune to revision in the light of later evidence or argument, nor does it imply that everything can be known. But it does imply that, even though like any science psychology relies on imagination to frame its hypotheses, its aim is to discover objective truths about the human mind, and that if all Freud succeeded in doing was to develop a new way of talking or seeing things, he failed. That is what he meant by his repeated insistence that what he was doing was science. Freud would have been delighted to tangle with Grünbaum and would have had no patience whatever with the attacks on objectivity that Robinson depressingly describes as "the most visible intellectual current of the age." It is no service to Freud to defend him by appealing to this slothful outlook, let alone to ascribe it to him.

Addendum

A fundamental problem in making progress with this dispute is that there is no agreement over what should be regarded as Freud's distinctive contribution, specifically for the purpose of assessing its validity, value, or degree of empirical support. Grünbaum identifies it with a set of general psychological principles; I identify it with a form of understanding, which manifests itself in countless individual interpretations and explanations. We both agree that psychoanalytic hypotheses are causal and require empirical confirmation, but we differ as to the kind of evidence that is most important. I don't deny the importance of possible future epidemiological and experimental tests of the sort that he thinks crucial. My central disagreement with Grünbaum is about whether there is now, in advance of all such experiments, substantial reason to believe in the unconscious and psychoanalytic explanations that refer to it—reasons of a kind that were also available to Freud.

I don't think the crucial question for evaluating Freud's legacy is whether he was right (to take Grünbaum's example) in proposing that repressed homosexuality is a necessary causal condition of paranoid delusions. Even apart from the likelihood that paranoid delusions often have nonpsychological causes, this universal generalization seems thoroughly implausible on its face, and no doubt Freud's writing are filled with general hypotheses that are just as false. But the core of his contribution lies elsewhere, in a form of insight that depends not on the application of specifically psychoanalytic laws but on the extension of the familiar forms of psychological explanation beyond their traditional, rational domain.

I make a point of the continuity between psychoanalytic and common-sense explanations because I believe that psychoanalysis can borrow empirical evidence for its most important general foundations from the ubiquitous confirmation of the system of ordinary psychological explanation in everyday life. (Here I follow not only Richard Wollheim but two other philosophers, Donald Davidson and James Hopkins, who develop this point of view much more thoroughly than I can do here.[13]) Commonsense psychology depends not just on causal generalizations of the kind Grünbaum cites (that insults anger people, that good tidings create joy, etc.); a list of such laws wouldn't take you very far in understanding people. Much more important is the general scheme by which we try to make sense of

[13] See Hopkins's "Introduction: Philosophy and Psychoanalysis" in Hopkins and Wollheim (eds.), *Philosophical Essays on Freud* (Cambridge University Press, 1982); Davidson's "Paradoxes of Irrationality" in the same volume; and Hopkins's "Epistemology and Depth Psychology: Critical Notes on *The Foundations of Psychoanalysis*" in S. Clark and C. Wright (eds.), *Psychoanalysis, Mind, and Science* (Blackwell, 1988).

others as more or less rational beings—each with a complex system of beliefs, assumptions, preferences, desires, values, aims, and dispositions to make inferences—and interpret their conduct as purposive and intentional in the light of these conditions.

The fundamental causal principle of commonsense psychology is that, in most cases, you can discover causally relevant conditions (conditions that make a *difference* in precisely Grünbaum's sense) for a human action or thought or emotion by fitting it into a rationally coherent interpretation of the whole person as an intentional subject of this type—by seeing how from the person's point of view it is in some way *justified*. Interpretation reveals causation because that's the kind of system a human being is. And this principle is so well supported in endless simple cases, in which it can be confirmed by the possibilities of prediction and control, that we are fully warranted in applying the same principle to identify psychological causes in unique and unrepeatable cases: by trying to make intentional and purposive sense of them.

That's what I mean by intuitive plausibility, and it necessarily applies in the first instance to specific explanations, rather than to general principles. I believe the essence of Freud's method was to extend the reach of this explanatory system to areas of human behavior and feeling where it had previously not seemed that sense could be found. In this way he increased our understanding of the influence of the mind, but confirmation goes from the particular to the general: the general theory of repression and psychosexual development has to be supported by its indivdual instances, rather than the reverse.

I don't have the sort of experience that would enable me to form a judgment on the conflicts between different post-Freudian theories at the level of general principles. But the general Freudian method of extending the familiar interpretive scheme of psychological explanation to the unconscious in particular cases, the method on which all such theories depend for evidence, is something that all of us should be able to confirm from our own experience: it is simply a matter of making sense of irrational or unintentional or involuntary conduct, when it fits into the same type of pattern so familiar from ordinary psychology, with some of the blanks filled in by thoughts or wishes of which the subject is not aware.

The case of the stock market sleeper, standing for countless others, was supposed to illustrate the point; Grünbaum's reaction to it shows how far apart we are. First he says that Freud was wrong to think that there is a tendency to forget painful experiences. I entirely agree that this is not a universal tendency; the opposite is true for me. But the point is irrelevant, because no generalization of this kind enters into the grounds for the explanation, which depends only on the particulars of the case. Next,

Grünbaum says I don't allow for "the psychiatrist's rash creation of a mind-set in the gentleman, when he told him, without *any* additional information, that his falling asleep during the stock market news probably expressed difficult feelings about his father." Grünbaum seems to have missed the significance of the crucial background evidence, known to the psychiatrist, of the man's ambivalence toward his inherited wealth, as shown by his unusual life as a private scholar on the periphery of the academy. That is what prompted the interpretation, since in light of the background, the otherwise puzzling symptom *makes expressive sense.* The recovered memory, vividly evoked by the interpretive suggestion, falls into place like another piece cut from the same jigsaw puzzle and strongly reinforces the "sense" of the symptom—though this is obviously just the beginning of the story: we don't know what blend of defiance, fear, love, and guilt characterized the man's actual feelings about his father.

But Grünbaum won't have any of this. His reference to "creation of a mind-set" implies, I take it, that the memory was probably false and planted by the suggestion of the psychiatrist. To prefer this alternative to one that makes sense of the symptom reveals, I think, both Grünbaum's deep-seated allergy to the admission of unconscious motives and his readiness to call on suggestion as an all-purpose alternative explanation with the slimmest excuse. I don't know whether the symptom ceased after this episode, but no doubt if it had, Grünbaum would have attributed that to suggestion too.

In appealing to the pervasive influence of Freudian ideas on modern self-consciousness, I meant that we all employ these forms of understanding constantly, that experience continually presents us with circumstances where they are appropriate. Evidently this is not true of Grünbaum; perhaps he regards it all as so much vulgarization. Let me try to answer his final question, however.[14] Religious superstitions, ethnic canards, witchcraft, and slavery are very different examples of entrenched error, but I'll focus on witchcraft, which is often brought up in these debates. Neither of us believes in witchcraft, but the interesting question is, Why? Would Grünbaum appeal to controlled experiments establishing that curses issued by fully certified witches have no statistical effect on the death rate of their victims? I wouldn't be interested in such data even if they existed; my reason for dismissing witchcraft, even though countless people have believed and still believe in it, is that we know on much more general

---

[14]Grünbaum had asked, "If pervasive cultural influence were evidence of validity, then religious superstitions and ethnic canards or stereotypes, which are far more prevalent than Freud's ideas, as well as earlier witchcraft and slavery ought to possess a high degree of validity. Does Nagel apply his cultural criterion to them as well? If not, why not?"

grounds that the world doesn't work that way. There are no supernatural forces that can be invoked by sticking pins in a doll. This simply follows from a general knowledge of physics and biology.

But psychoanalysis is not a theory of supernatural forces. It is an extension of psychological explanation to further phenomena *within* the domain of its original application, that is, the lives of human beings with minds. This is not in any way incompatible with the rest of our scientific understanding of how things work. It is part of our idea of the natural order that people's behavior is influenced by their mental condition; that the influence should be larger and more various than we originally thought should not surprise us.[15]

A final comment on therapeutic efficacy, which is indirectly relevant to the issue of confirmation. I have had no first-hand experience of psychoanalysis or psychotherapy, but I know many people who have. While I don't know whether psychoanalysis is more or less effective in eliminating unwanted symptoms than medication or behavior therapy, for example, I am quite sure that it has a different *kind* of effect on patients from more "external" forms of treatment. My observation is that psychoanalysis can confer a valuable form of self-knowledge that is deep though essentially perceptual and not theoretical, and that this self-understanding, whether or not it cures neuroses directly, can be *used* by those who have it to anticipate, identify, and manage forms of irrationality that would otherwise victimize or even disable them. It also permits a subtler response to neurotic irrationality in others, through the enhancement of psychological imagination. For this reason I believe it will survive the development of simpler symptomatic cures, even though, because of its cost in time and money, the traditional form will always be an option for only a small minority.

---

[15] Incidentally, the extended reach of the mind is also revealed in a completely different way—by the recent discovery that physiological processes ordinarily completely involuntary, like heartbeat and blood pressure, can be brought under conscious, voluntary control with the right kind of training.

3

Wittgenstein: The Egocentric Predicament

This was a review of David Pears, The False Prison: A Study of the Development of Wittgenstein's Philosophy, *vol. 2 (Oxford University Press, 1988). The main question for interpreters of Wittgenstein is how to understand the role he assigned to the empirical conditions of meaning—conditions of natural agreement and shared form of life, within which all justifications, corrections, and criticisms must take place. His writings encourage an "idealistic" reading: these forms of life are* the given, *on which everything else is grounded. But this yields such a radical and obviously false view of truth in various domains that I think it can't be correct as an interpretation, even though I don't have an alternative. It is also too much of a general philosophical theory about the nature of reality to be attributed to the later Wittgenstein. Whatever may have been his response, Wittgenstein's recasting of the Kantian criticism of philosophical thought that tries to transcend the conditions of its own significance remains the deepest philosophical insight of the twentieth century.*

In the 1950s, when I was an undergraduate at Cornell, it was the only American university where Wittgenstein's later work was the object of intensive study. He had died in 1951, and *Philosophical Investigations* was published in 1953. I remember in those pre-Xerox days sharing with some fellow students the typing of *The Blue Book* and *The Brown Book* in multiple

---

Reprinted with permission from *The London Review of Books,* May 18, 1989.

carbons, from a set available in Ithaca—pre-*Investigations* texts dating from the mid-1930s that circulated in samizdat until they were finally published in 1960 as part of the still continuing stream of volumes from the *Nachlass*.

The atmosphere surrounding the study of Wittgenstein was both thrilling and stifling: philosophy was agony, and it was necessary to immerse yourself in problems so deep you could hardly breathe. Superficiality was the great danger; nothing could be achieved without struggle, either in approaching the problems or in understanding what Wittgenstein said. Above all, there was the sense that it was almost impossibly difficult to express the truth—witness Wittgenstein's own failure to publish all but a fraction of the huge volume of material he wrote after returning to philosophy at the age of 40, so that, except for the *Investigations*, he stands in a peculiar relation of diminished responsibility to it.

I still think this attitude is basically right. There is no way to approach Wittgenstein except by getting mired up to your ears in apparently insoluble philosophical problems, and then seeing whether the places where he suggests you put your feet actually enable you to walk. Today Wittgenstein's name is dropped everywhere as the symbol of an easygoing conceptual relativism, and references to the Private Language Argument and Forms of Life are almost as common as references to the Heisenberg Indeterminacy Principle. But that is a cultural curiosity: Wittgenstein's work is scarcely more accessible now than it was thirty-five years ago. It is too easy to embrace the solutions without understanding the problems. As David Pears observes, "when we read one of Wittgenstein's discussions of philosophical illusions, there are two things which we may not find it easy to hold together in our minds simultaneously, his success in dispelling them and the depth and difficulty of the problems that produced them." In this second volume of a formidable two-volume study, Pears tries to provide access to Wittgenstein's later work through the deep traditional problems to which it is a response—the response of trying to find a way out. This means that the book is difficult. Pears is not an agonizer either temperamentally or stylistically, but he is true to his subject, and while there are things to disagree with, those who work through it will gain a sense of Wittgenstein's depth and radicalism.

In line with his title, Pears traces the development of Wittgenstein's thought largely in relation to a theme that has been central in Western philosophy since Descartes, and which Wittgenstein found in Schopenhauer: the suspicion that we are trapped inside our own minds and that nothing we can do in the way of language, thought, imagination, or perception will enable us to reach beyond them. Descartes thought of this as a problem about what we can know. He assumed that we could at least form the conception of an external world: the issue was whether we could know anything about it or not. But in the development of modern philosophy through Kant, this evolved into an even more radical doubt about what we can think. Even if there is a world beyond our minds, there seems no way for anything in our experience to make contact with it or represent it as it is in itself, so that the reach of our thought is limited to our own actual or possible experiences, including the experiences of "external" perception.

This position is unstable, however. If even our thoughts cannot reach beyond our minds, the idea of an unreachable world beyond is a conceptual illusion: no such thought is possible; anything we take for the thought of what is unthinkable by us must be something else, or gibberish. We cannot say that we can think of the world *only* as it appears to us, because the implied contrast is meaningless.

In Wittgenstein's first book, the *Tractatus Logico-Philosophicus* (1921), this result is embodied in the position that solipsism coincides with pure realism. Everything in the world is equally real—from my sense impressions to the stars—but still the world is *my* world. This shows itself in the fact that however objectively I describe the world (including gaps to be filled in by the things that I don't know, and even if that objective description affords no privileged position to the particular person I am), I can always add redundantly: "And it is I who am saying and thinking this." "Everything in the world" is an expression of my language. Yet I cannot think that I am trapped, for that would require, impossibly, forming the thought of what was unthinkable by me.

The *Tractatus* offered a general theory of language and thought and of their relation to the rest of reality. Wittgenstein's later writings reject the possibility of any such theory, in favour of piecemeal description of samples from the great variety of linguistic and mental activities of which humans are capable.[1] But the egocentric predicament remains a central occupation. Wittgenstein continually raises and attempts to dissolve doubt about the adequacy of our language and thought to reach the world it aims to grasp. The details of his response depend on the particular kind of thought he is discussing—about the physical world, other minds, mathematics, action, sensation, meaning. But the general strategy is to make clear an unintelligibility in such doubts that is quite simple: if they are expressible, they must be wrong. If I say, "How is it possible that by merely saying the word 'Aristotle' I should be able to refer to *Aristotle*?" I seem to have forgotten the beginning of the sentence by the time I get to the end—

[1] While the *Tractatus Logico-Philosophicus* was a genuine treatise, Wittgenstein's later writings are more like a distilled version of the bizarre, disconnected activity of philosophical thought and discussion itself, which in most writers results in a highly structured product unrecognizably different from the process that produced it.

since the second occurrence of the name has to refer to Aristotle for the question to have any sense. I can't grab hold of Aristotle himself by some kind of superlinguistic reference, against which it is then possible to criticize the ordinary natural conditions of application of the name as inadequate to their purpose.

The same problem of intelligibility arises if I ask how by using the word "plus" I can capture the operation of *addition,* which is a function defined over all of the infinite possible pairs of numbers, only a small sample of which I shall ever encounter, or the question of whether my ascription of pain to other people really picks out *pain,* as opposed to some other sensation, or nothing at all. How are the second halves of these questions supposed to be understood, if the questions are serious?

According to Wittgenstein, the philosophical problem arises in each case when we wrench language, mental pictures, or other vehicles of thought apart from the conditions that give them significance—as if we could really grasp reality only by transcending those limits. We then use those transcendent "thoughts" to call into question the adequacy of mundane thoughts with their mundane conditions to express what they purport to express. Our actual thought and language come to seem deficient by reference to an unreachable ideal. Pears quotes a passage from "Notes for Lectures on Private Experience and Sense Data,"[2] which ends: "Isn't what you reproach me of [sic] as though you said: 'In your language you're only *speaking!'*" Pears adds, "Language cannot very well ingest its subject-matter," and: "If we think of it as something sublime, spoken from nowhere, the demands that it makes on the world will be too exorbitant to be satisfied and the outcome will be scepticism."

Much of Pears's book is devoted to analysis of the development from 1929 on of Wittgenstein's critique of skepticism about the possibility of conceiving of any mind other than one's own (a kind of logical as opposed to epistemological solipsism) and, less radically, about the possibility of ascribing sensations like one's own to other subjects of experience on the basis of the merely external observations of those subjects to which one is restricted (the apparent essential privacy of sensation language).

To understand Wittgenstein it is necessary to be able to take these problems seriously. You begin by trying to understand your own system of language and thought from within. You are pulled toward the conclusion that in that system other "persons" are merely objects of your external perception and that inner experiences, in the sense in which you have

---

[2] *Philosophical Review,* July 1968. Pears rightly stresses the importance of these notes, written by Wittgenstein in English between 1934 and 1936, which appear to contain the first appearance of the Private Language Argument.

them yourself, cannot intelligibly be ascribed to those others. You can't imagine *feeling* someone else's pain, since if you did it wouldn't be his but yours. So in application to others, the idea of pain is not really that of a feeling but of an externally observable syndrome, composed of circumstances and behavior. Your idea of real feelings, and of a real self, cannot intelligibly be applied to any but your own case. Use of the same words about "others" is a kind of pun. This is the concept of mind that Wittgenstein was fighting against in the 1930s.

Pears shows how the attack on solipsism prefigures the later attack on private language. In both cases Wittgenstein turns the tables on the skeptic by arguing that the thoughts each of us has about his own case—"I" or "The way red looks to me"—which in the skeptical thought are supposed to provide the secure starting point from which we try and fail to generalize, become unintelligible if we try to understand them in isolation from their second- and third-person analogues: other people's identification of a person and of the character of his experiences.

What could be more perfectly secure and transparent, one might think, than my idea of myself—of my ego—and my use of the word "I" to designate it? If I feel a pain in my hand, I know immediately and without need for observation of any kind that it is I who feel it: so my subjective identification of myself is entirely self-contained and independent of the identification of my body or anything else in the world. But Wittgenstein argues that this is an illusion, produced by abstracting language from those connections between experience and its external manifestations that allow us to ascribe experience to one another and therefore allow us to learn to ascribe it to ourselves.

The possibility of the thought of myself depends on familiar natural facts. As Pears puts it, "it is a familiar fact that, when a person's right hand is hurt, there is a line running into the seat of his consciousness and out again to his mouth. He says, 'I am in pain,' and though the word 'I,' as used by him, does not mean 'this body,' it does presuppose the integrity of this personal line. There has to be a connection running back from the mouth that speaks through the seat of the consciousness of pain to the injured part of the body." And my infallibility in identifying myself as the subject of my pain—which seems to show a pure ego independent of the body—can in fact be explained, in Wittgenstein's words, by this: "The man who cries out with pain, or says that he has pain, *doesn't choose the mouth which says it.*" My infallible identification of myself as the subject of an experience is merely a linguistic extension of this, rather than the identification of the "ego." It is not, in other words, the application of a purely first-person concept at all.

Wittgenstein was not a behaviorist, as Pears makes clear, but he believed that what Pears calls the "personal line" plays an indispensable role as a condition for the possibility of mental concepts and mental language, and that we cannot use that language to describe circumstances too radically removed from those conditions. This is true not only of the idea of how red looks, or pain feels, to me. He opposed what Pears calls the "Dogma of Far-Reaching Sense," which leads us to think that words carry their meaning with them anywhere.

Passing from the self to the contents of experience, let us consider the irresistible philosophical problem of the inverted spectrum: even if solipsism is false, how can I have any evidence whatever that colors appear to others as they appear to me? Since I can never look into their minds, I can never have any reason to believe that blood doesn't look to someone else the way grass looks to me, and vice versa—even if there is *no* behavioral or anatomical difference between us. But the intelligibility of this hypothesis seems to depend on some alternative basis of significance for the ascription of sensory qualities to others, which survives intact even if the usual connections with anatomy, circumstances, and discriminatory and linguistic capacities are imagined to be evidently unusable. And what can this be?

Clearly it is supposed to be a direct projection into the mind of the other of the immediate connection between the word "red" and a particular sensory quality that I experience in my own case, without having to rely on any of these external connections. I stare at the ketchup bottle and ask the simple question: "Is what he has or is it not the same as *this?*"

We should be able to see Wittgenstein's answer coming. "The same as *this*" is an attempt to stretch an ordinary piece of language beyond the ordinary conditions of its application—to express a supercomparison by reference to which the usual criteria of comparison can be seen as inadequate. But compelling as it seems, it hasn't been given an alternative basis of significance. As Wittgenstein says, "when it is said 'Either he has this experience, or not'—what primarily occurs to us is a picture which by itself seems to make the sense of the expressions *unmistakable:* 'Now you know what is in question'—we should like to say. And that is precisely what it does not tell him."

Not only that, but even your ascription of sensory qualities to your *own* experiences, which seem from the inside completely independent of the outward connections to circumstances, behavior, and standard objects of perception, are according to Wittgenstein dependent for their significance on the existence of such connections in general. If you say, "By 'red' I mean 'the same as *this*,'" you are assuming that your subjective idea of a sensation-type is well defined independently of its connection with anything else. But in fact your first-person identification of color impressions as the same or different was learned in connection with capacities for discrimination that show up first in relation to external standard objects and that can be identified by other speakers who teach you the language.

You may imagine that this is only a device that sets up a connection between words and sensation-types in your mind, a connection in which those external relations have no part. The reply to this proposal brings us to the Private Language Argument and the much-debated subject of rules.

In order for a word to be more than a noise or a scribble or a flicker in the mind—in order for it to mean something—there must be a distinction between its correct and its incorrect application. What is it that determines that distinction? It cannot be whatever the speaker says, for then he wouldn't be *saying* anything. The word must carry something else along with it. What is that, and how does the speaker make a connection with it when he uses the word with that meaning?

This is an enormously difficult question. Wittgenstein saw that the background conditions of meaning become invisible to us because words themselves seem drenched with meaning when we use them all the time. So it is difficult even to understand the question, "In virtue of what does my word 'red' mean a particular type of sensory impression?" One wants to reply: "In virtue of its meaning *red*." But that simply repeats what we want explained, as much as if we had said: "In virtue of its meaning *this type of color impression*."

Wittgenstein does not offer an analysis of meaning, but he does try to identify certain attempts to use language that cause it definitely to lose its moorings, so that the distinction between correct and incorrect application of the term in question no longer exists, and all we have left is the *word* (usually in italics). He believed that the mythical private language of experience, completely detached from anything in our behavior and circumstances that could be observed by others, which is used to express radical skepticism about the experience of others, is an example of this. We fail to see it because we unconsciously rely on our understanding of the experiential concepts of the public language, whose conditions of meaning are concealed in their subjective application to ourselves.

If no one else could in principle tell whether I was using the word "red" (as a term for a type of visual impression) in the same way on two occasions, then neither could I, and there would be no distinction between my using it in the same way and my using it differently. To make sense of the distinction it is not enough, according to Wittgenstein, simply to use the word over again, saying: "It's the difference between applying it to an impression that really is red and applying it to one which isn't." Of course, *if* there is a difference, that is how we will describe it. But something more has to be said about what that distinction might conceivably amount to.

The problem in these cases is that we tend to employ a picture whose

usual application is blocked here: we imagine two color patches side by side, looking different, for example. But what does this image mean in application to the case where I apply the same word to two temporally separated color impressions, and there is no conceivable way of any kind to compare them apart from my conviction, in particular, none of the evidence we could usually employ from the public domain—the objects I was looking at, my physical condition, and the correlation between my general identification of color impressions and other people's? To raise these questions is not simply to assume a verificationist position, for particular unverifiable claims could be shown to have sense in this way. But it is to require that a type of picture or expression have some conceivable basis of application if we are to believe that the sense of understanding it gives us is not illusory.

Whether my application of a word in a particular case is correct depends on what I mean by it. But what I mean by it is also something about me. So if we are to make sense of the possibility of correcting what I actually say by reference to what I ought to say in light of what I mean, we have to find a comparison between my actual convinced use and something else about me—about what in some larger sense I am doing. It is this crucial distance that vanishes if the application of my language to my experience is imagined logically isolated from everything else as in the mythical private language. We are left with *nothing but* my successive applications of a term, without anything to compare them with that can count as the rule for its application—the criterion that determines whether I have applied it correctly in each case.

The question of what Wittgenstein thought supplied this need in natural language is a central issue of Wittgenstein interpretation, stirred up recently by Saul Kripke's proposals and the response to them[3]—which Pears now joins. Pears explains Wittgenstein's argument that the rule for the application of a term cannot be captured by an "instant mental talisman," for no such thing could by itself determine the distinction between correct and incorrect for an indefinite series of possible future applications: since any such talisman could be interpreted in more than one way, we would still have to explain what makes one of them correct.

All we can do along these lines, in Wittgenstein's view, is to describe possible grounds of correction for an individual's use of a term—grounds the individual himself might recognize as valid. According to Pears, there are two main types of grounds: comparison with the use of others, and

[3] Saul Kripke, *Wittgenstein on Rules and Private Language* (Harvard University Press, 1980).

calibration on standard external objects of perception that can be reidentified independently of the subject's application of the term in question. In emphasizing the importance of standard objects, Pears agrees with Colin McGinn.[4]

The possibility that this basis for correction might be sufficient for the existence of a rule suggests that a language that was private in the sense that it was invented and used entirely by a solitary being would not be logically impossible, but it would not be *logically* private, either, since others could in principle learn it, and if they did, comparison with their usage would become a further check on whether the inventor was continuing to use the terms of the language correctly.

If an account of this kind is correct, then we see that the final appeal for the correctness or incorrectness of a particular use of a term is simply more use, of that and other terms, by the user and other persons—not something of a fundamentally different kind. If the challenges we are able to understand have run out, and we have answered every actual challenge by comparisons that do not themselves give rise to further challenge, we are entitled to regard the application as correct. But there is no ultimate, Platonic standard available by which to validate all the judgments to which we appeal in confirming the original one. Beyond a certain point we obey the rules of our language "blindly," as Wittgenstein says, and if we did not, the idea of the valid use of a term would be impossible. It must rest ultimately, if not in the first instance, on judgments we cannot help making. As Pears says, "my obedience is 'blind' not because I shut out considerations that might have influenced me . . . but because, when I have worked my way down to the foundations . . . there are no more considerations, doubts, or justifications. I do not even have to listen to the rule, because it speaks through my application of it."

One issue raised by Kripke's discussion is whether this position—that the only standard of judgment is a wider circle of judgment—is a form of skepticism. In describing Wittgenstein's position as a "skeptical solution" to the problem of rules, logic, and meaning, Kripke did not mean that Wittgensten himself would accept such a designation. As Pears says, Wittgenstein thought that skepticism is produced by the demand for a superior standard of correctness of an impossible, Platonic kind, whereas the naturalistic standard of what we and others cannot help doing is all we can have and all we need.

This does not, as Pears thinks, settle the question. We can call someone a skeptic who wouldn't accept the description himself, if we believe that his account of the basis of a form of thought does not supply an adequate foundation for its actual claims, which reach farther than that basis would warrant. And we may say this whether we are able to supply an alternative basis or not. Thus someone who thinks ethics claims a certain kind of objectivity will regard emotivism as a skeptical theory about ethics, even if it is presented as an analysis of ordinary ethical statements, and even if he cannot himself offer an alternative foundation for the objectivity of ethics. The same might be said of phenomenalism as an analysis of statements about the external world.

The issue in this case is whether Wittgenstein's view that there is no content to the idea of correctness in the application of any universal term beyond use, broadly conceived, undermines the full strength of the claim to objectivity implicit in our understanding of such terms and what we take ourselves to be doing when we think with them. I believe that it does, that if Wittgenstein is right, our language is not what we thought it was. What we had thought was that, by picking up on a shared use, we could come to mean a particular arithmetical function by "plus" or a particular color by "red," and that this "meaning," whatever it is and however we manage it, determines the difference between correct and incorrect application of the term over a range of possible cases infinitely beyond all uses to which the term will be put by us or anyone else, and determines it in a way that is independent of all actual future uses. In other words, meaning reaches vastly beyond conceivable conditions of application, and the limited criteria by which we check use merely provide evidence for meaning.

Wittgenstein's reply is that this thought is only apparently intelligible, and that his account does not undermine anything possible, let alone anything real. But even it he is right in this, the issue whether his solution is skeptical depends on whether this illusion of far-reaching sense is internal to our language, or results from imposing on it an unreal external standard that is a philosophical artifact. One might ask what evidence there could be that our language makes stronger claims than it can sustain. This raises the question of whether the apparent naturalness of skeptical problems in philosophy itself supplies such evidence. The dissatisfaction and sense of diminishment that Wittgenstein's arguments often produce in those who find them compelling provide some evidence for the pessimistic view. But Pears, in a striking image, says: "they are like people who have been hypnotised and told that they are not standing on firm ground but on a narrow foot-bridge across a gorge, and then the only way to get them to walk is to tell them that there are high parapets on each side of them."

At the end of the book, Pears expresses some sympathy with the feeling that in application to logic and mathematics, Wittgenstein's account of rules is paradoxical. I see no difference between the cases of logic and experience. That the supposedly infinite applicability of a descriptive term should rest on nothing more than finite agreement in use is just as paradoxical as the dependence of the infinite expansion of a mathematical series on something similar. Our belief in the determinate reality of the infinite expansion or the endless range of cases seems to get no support from the natural human phenomena that Wittgenstein argues so persuasively are all we have got. Pears remarks on the parallel, but I think he errs in finding the position in philosophy of mind and general philosophy of language easier to swallow than the comparable position in philosophy of mathematics.

But the book is a real achievement. There is a commendable emphasis on the continuity over a lifetime of Wittgenstein's underlying philosophical concerns. Above all, there is a sense of traditional philosophical motivation. This remarkable figure will occupy us for a long time to come, and Pears's study is a very important contribution to the effort to achieve a command of his ideas and what led to them.

4

Chomsky: Linguistics and Epistemology

This was written for the volume that emerged from a New York University Institute of Philosophy symposium held April 12–13, 1968. I had been preoccupied with Chomsky's ideas on the philosophy of psychology since about 1960, when I arrived at Harvard as a graduate student and found that the most exciting courses being offered in the Boston area were Chomsky's at M.I.T.

I now have doubts about the end of this paper, which seems to suggest that a priori knowledge can't depend on the contingencies of our mental makeup. But this clearly involves a confusion between two kinds of "dependence." From the fact that the possibility of justification depends on certain contingencies, like intersubjective agreement, it doesn't follow that those contingencies form part of the justification. They may merely be conditions of understanding, where what is understood is not contingent but necessary, and once understood, self-evident. Our ability to do logic is contingent on many conditions, physical and mental, which do not make logic any less a priori. However, this doesn't change the picture for the case of grammar: I still think the innate language-learning capacity isn't a form of innate knowledge, both because it can't be brought to consciousness and because the correctness of its results requires empirical confirmation.

Reprinted with permission from *Language and Philosophy*, Sidney Hook, editor (New York University Press, 1969).

There is some reason to believe that Chomsky's views about the innate contribution to language acquisition have a bearing on epistemological issues: on disputes over the existence of a priori knowledge, for example. Certainly if he is right, grammar provides a striking example of strong innate constraints on the form of human thought, and a natural object of philosophical fascination.

I am not going to discuss the correctness of Chomsky's view concerning the importance and size of that innate contribution, or the adequacy of the support offered for it. The object of this paper is to investigate what epistemological consequences Chomsky's empirical hypotheses about language learning have, if they are *correct*. The discussion will divide into two parts. First, I shall consider how Chomsky's hypotheses are most appropriately formulated, and specifically how the concept of knowledge can enter into their formulation. Second, I shall consider the bearing of these hypotheses on the epistemological status of our knowledge of natural languages, and also what they suggest about other kinds of knowledge, particularly those sometimes thought to be a priori.

I

The following, from page 58 of *Aspects of the Theory of Syntax,*[1] gives a clear, brief statement of Chomsky's position:

It seems plain that language acquisition is based on the child's discovery of what from a formal point of view is a deep and abstract theory—a generative grammar of his language—many of the concepts and principles of which are only remotely related to experience by long and intricate chains of unconscious quasi-inferential steps. A consideration of the character of the grammar that is acquired, the degenerate quality and narrowly limited extent of the available data, the striking uniformity of the resulting grammars, and their independence of intelligence, motivation, and emotional state, over wide ranges of variation, leave little hope that much of the structure of the language can be learned by an organism initially uninformed as to its general character.

I believe Chomsky means to assert that we have here a genuine case of innate knowledge. His sympathetic references to the Rationalists suggest that he does. Moreover, the alternative to an organism initially *uninformed* as to the general character of the structure of natural languages would seem to be an organism initially *informed* as to that general character. And elsewhere (p. 27) he speaks of ascribing tacit knowledge of lin-

[1] M.I.T. Press, 1965.

guistic universals to the child. In any case, Chomsky's contentions about language acquisition will suggest to most students of epistemology, as they suggest to me, that we are presented here with an example of innate knowledge. It is this natural philosophical interpretation that I want to examine, so the remainder of this essay will be concerned not with Chomsky's philosophical views, but only with the philosophical implications of his linguistic views.

The first question, then, is whether the initial contribution of the organism to language learning, alleged by Chomsky, is properly described as knowledge at all. Let us begin with a natural but bad argument for a negative answer to the question. The argument has the form of a reductio.

Why wouldn't the decision to apply the concept of knowledge in this case also commit us to ascribing innate knowledge, perhaps even a priori knowledge, to the human digestive system (or perhaps rather to human beings in virtue of the behavior of their digestive systems). For without having to be trained, instructed, or conditioned, the individual is able to adjust the chemical environment in his stomach to break down the digestible food that is introduced, while rejecting, sometimes forcibly, what is indigestible. This formidable task of classification and variable response is carried out even by infants, so it cannot be learned entirely from experience.

Admittedly the infant is not consciously aware of the principles that govern his gastric secretions, nor is the adult, unless he has studied physiology. But neither a child nor an adult who has not studied linguistics is consciously aware either of the grammatical rules of his language or of the principles by which he arrives at the ability to speak the language governed by those rules, on the basis of his exposure to a subset of the sentences of that language. The reasons that can be offered in support of innate knowledge of the general character of linguistic structure would count equally well in favor of the view that there is innate knowledge of the proper chemical means of digesting various kinds of food. Either both are examples of innate knowledge, or neither is. And the latter possibility is more plausible. We could say that in both cases there is an extremely important innate *capacity*—to discriminate among and digest foods, or to acquire command of natural languages having a certain type of structure—but it would not be called innate *knowledge* in either case.

The trouble with this argument is that it ignores the difference between the operations that we have in the two cases the capacity to perform. In the case of digestion, the operation is not an action at all. Nor do the data on which the operation is based, that is, the various foods introduced into the stomach, have to be brought to the awareness of the organism. In the case of language learning, on the other hand, conscious apprehension of the data (limited as they may be) is essential, and what the individual can do as a result of his linguistic capacity is to speak and understand sentences.

Moreover, the exercise of the capacity involves *beliefs:* for example, that a certain combination of words is, or is not, a sentence of the language. Someone who regurgitates a bad oyster, by contrast, is not thereby said to believe that it is indigestible. Though we may not possess an adequate analysis of the distinction, it is clear that certain methods of response and discrimination warrant the attribution of beliefs and attitudes, while others do not. Only of the former category is it appropriate to consider whether they give evidence of knowledge.

It is clear that such cognitive concepts are applicable to linguistic capacity and performance on particular occasions. The question is whether the concepts of knowledge and belief can be applied at higher levels of generality and abstraction in the description of the individual's linguistic capacity, and ultimately in the description of his capacity to acquire that capacity.

We may distinguish two theses: (1) that the general capacity to produce a set of performances, each of which provides an instance of knowledge, is itself an instance of more general knowledge; (2) that the general capacity to acquire other capacities, each of which is an instance of knowledge, is itself an instance of still more general knowledge. The first thesis is more plausible than the second, but both are needed to warrant the inferential ascent from cases of linguistic knowledge revealed in particular utterances to the ascription of a knowledge of linguistic universals on which language learning is alleged to depend.

To go step by step: It seems obvious that we can speak of linguistic knowledge whose object is not merely the grammaticality or meaning of a particular utterance, but something more general. (In fact, it is doubtful that we could speak of knowledge in the particular case unless we could also speak of it on a more general level.) For example, we can ascribe to the ordinary speaker of English, on the basis of countless particular performances and responses, the knowledge that the plural form of a noun is usually formed by adding "s," and that among the exceptions to this is the word "man," whose plural is "men." Now we *might* verify this ascription by finding that the individual can actually state the rule, but someone can possess general knowledge of the rule without being able to state it. He may never have heard the words "plural," and "noun," for example, and may be unable to formulate the principle in any other way. When we come to the more complicated principles to which grammatical English speech conforms, that will be the usual situation. Only professional grammarians will be able to state those rules, and sometimes even that may not be true.

Under what conditions can knowledge of a language governed by certain rules be described as knowledge of those rules? Consider another type of knowledge that cannot be explicitly formulated by its possessor, namely, unconscious knowledge in the ordinary psychoanalytic sense. This is, of course, a very different phenomenon from knowledge of the rules of grammar, but it has an important feature that, as Saul Kripke pointed out to me, may bear on the linguistic case. The psychoanalytic ascription of unconscious knowledge or belief—or unconscious motives, for that matter—does not depend simply on the possibility of organizing the subject's responses and actions in conformity with the alleged unconscious material. In addition, although he does not formulate his unconscious knowledge or attitude of his own accord and may deny it upon being asked, it is usually possible to bring him to *see* that the statement in question expresses something that he knows or feels. He is able eventually to acknowledge the statement as an expression of his own belief, if it is presented to him clearly enough and in the right circumstances. Thus what was unconscious can be brought, at least partly, to consciousness. It is essential that his acknowledgment *not* be based merely on the observation of his own responses and behavior and that he come to recognize the rightness of the attribution from the inside.

It seems to me that where recognition of this sort is possible in principle, there is good reason to speak of knowledge and belief, even in cases where the relevant principles or statements have not yet been consciously acknowledged, or even in cases where they will never be explicitly formulated. Even though knowledge of the rules of a language is in other ways quite unlike the unconscious knowledge revealed by psychoanalysis, accurate formulations of grammatical rules often evoke the same sense of recognition from speakers who have been conforming to them for years that is evoked by the explicit formulation of repressed material that has been influencing one's behavior for years. It can happen even if the grammatical principles are formulated in a technical vocabulary that may require a certain amount of effort to master.

So long as it *would* be possible with effort to bring the speaker to a genuine recognition of a grammatical rule as an expression of his understanding of the language, rather than to a mere belief, based on the observation of cases, that the rule in fact describes his competence, it is acceptable, I think, to ascribe knowledge of that rule to the speaker. It is acceptable, even though he may never, in fact, be presented with a formulation of the rule and consequently may never come to recognize it consciously.

If the condition of recognizability cannot be met, however, the ascription of knowledge and belief seems to me more dubious. And this casts doubt on the possibility of carrying the ascription of knowledge to any level of generality or abstraction higher than that involved in the specification of grammatical rules for a particular natural language. Even some of those rules are highly abstract. But when we consider the alleged innate contribution to language learning, we pass to quite another level; it is doubtful that the principles of such a linguistic acquisition device, when they have been formulated, could evoke internal recognition from individuals who have operated in accordance with them.

The rules of a particular grammar deal in part with recognizable expressions, and retain some connection, in their formulation, with the speaker's conscious experience of his language. The connection in the case of linguistic universals, of the kind that Chomsky suggests are innately present, is more remote. One example that he offers is the proposal that the syntactic component of a grammar must contain transformational rules. This highly abstract condition is supposed to apply to *all* languages and to determine the way in which a child acquires knowledge of the grammar of his native language by being exposed to samples of speech. But is it supposed that he could in principle be brought some day to recognize such a principle as the proper expression of an assumption he was making at the time (once the proper principle has been formulated and its meaning conveyed to him)? This may be a possibility, but the conditions of explanatory adequacy that Chomsky accepts seem not to demand it. Explanatory adequacy is in itself, of course, a very strong requirement. But a hypothesis could be shown to satisfy it on the basis of external observation of the language-learning feat itself. The additional test of asking the language learner whether he can recognize the principle as one that was activating him all along seems irrelevant. It seems not to be required that such internal recognition should *ever* be available or possible, no matter how much effort is expended on it.

So I am uneasy about extending the concept of knowledge, and the related concepts of belief and assumption, to the description of those innate capacities that enable a child to acquire knowledge of a language—any natural language—on the basis of rather minimal data. Not every innate capacity to acquire knowledge need itself be an instance of knowledge, even though its structure may be quite complex.

II

The difficulties raised so far are really about the ascription of innate *beliefs* or *assumptions* on the basis of language-learning ability. But the epistemologically more interesting question is whether the other main condition for knowledge—namely, the justification condition—could be met in such cases. There is disagreement over the exact nature of this condition, but it should be possible to discuss the present issue without entering that maze.

The problem is that we can imagine almost any belief to be innately present, or that there is an innate tendency to develop that belief as the result of certain minimal experiences, but that is not a sufficient basis for ascribing knowledge. Not just any belief that one cannot help arriving at is ipso facto justified, even if it should be true.

Even if someone discovered that he was able on request to specify the square root of any integer to four decimal places, without reflection or calculation, the innateness of his ability would not guarantee the validity of his answers. The grounding of his knowledge of square roots would be rather that he and other persons could verify by calculation in case after individual case that the number he unreflectively believed to be the square root of a given integer in fact was the square root. In virtue of this further evidence, his unreflective belief in any given case could be taken as strong evidence of its own truth.

The phenomenon of language learning that Chomsky describes is different because it reveals an innate capacity that we all share. All speakers of English reach agreement in an obedience to certain grammatical rules and attain it naturally and without calculation after a certain amount of exposure to the language. Now, no one individual's innate propensity to arrive at these rules of itself guarantees that they are the rules of the language he is speaking. That depends on a more general conformity to those same rules by all speakers of the language, and this is guaranteed by the universality of those same innate propensities. Thus, if any given individual knows that his own linguistic intuitions about sentences that he has not encountered before, as well as his own original linguistic productions, are in conformity with the linguistic intuitions of other speakers of his language, then he can regard his innate tendencies as providing strong evidence for their own accuracy. I am not suggesting that we actually *do* step back from our linguistic intuitions in order to validate them in this way. I am suggesting only that it is because such a justification is available that we can plausibly describe what our innately governed linguistic propensities provide as *knowledge* of the language.

In each case, the fact that the tendency to arrive at a certain belief was innate did not by itself make it a case of knowledge. In the special case of language, where the actual rules are simply those by which competent speakers generally are governed, a universal innate tendency to arrive at certain rules is enough to guarantee their accuracy, but any one individual must still know that he is in conformity with the universal tendency in order to know that his linguistic intuitions are correct. And that is an empirical matter; in any individual case the alleged innate contribution to language learning can itself be assessed for its accuracy as a source of knowledge of the language. It may be that no one ever engages in this sort of assessment and that the innate tendency to construct the grammar of one's language also includes an innate tendency to assume that other speakers will construct it in the same way; in fact, this seems likely. But that assumption too is open to epistemological assessment by other means.

So the innate factor, which Chomsky argues must underlie our language-learning capacity, bears no resemblance to the sort of unquestionable, epistemologically unassailable foundation on which some philosophers have sought to base human knowledge, and which is generally referred to as a priori or innate knowledge. What has been sought under this heading is something that is not itself open to the usual varieties of epistemological assessment and doubt, something whose opposite is unimaginable.

What Chomsky offers is a system of innate propensities that we are conveniently stuck with. It is perfectly imaginable that we should be differently constituted, but we are not. A mere innate tendency to believe certain things or perform in certain ways, no matter how universal, is not a priori knowledge. Even Hume thought that we all share a natural propensity to believe that the sun will rise again tomorrow. To point out the natural phenomenon of human agreement, innately determined, is simply to turn aside the epistemological demand that motivates the search for a priori knowledge.

In fact, such a move is closely related to Wittgenstein's position, the main difference being that Wittgenstein applies it much more generally and not just to language learning. He argues that if one follows any chain of epistemological justification far enough, one comes in the end to a phenomenon of human agreement—not conventional agreement, but natural, innately determined agreement—on which the acceptance of that justification depends. He supposes this to happen whether the justification is empirical or deductive. If he is right, the procedures by which we subject one innate contribution to epistemological assessment will themselves simply depend on another innate contribution. And if at every stage what we have reached is only a contingent feature of our constitution, then there is no unquestionable a priori foundation on which our knowledge rests. It depends on a network of innate responses and propensities, and they are simply there.

If this is so, then epistemology may be essentially impossible. Insofar as Chomsky's contentions about language suggest that similar innate contributions underlie other cognitive phenomena as well, they suggest that all knowledge is in similar straits: it lacks an unassailable foundation. Sometimes, as in the case of language, one can take further steps to justify one's confidence in the yield of one's innate mechanism. Evidence of this kind is available to any speaker who successfully uses the language to communicate with others. But the admission of such evidence may in turn depend on innate principles that, without guaranteeing their own justification, form part of one's basic constitution, so the task of justification may be incompletable.

Though this is epistemologically unsettling, it has practical compensations. If we had to learn by trial and error, or by training, how to digest food, we should have a much harder time surviving. But fortunately we don't need to *know* how to digest food, for we do it automatically. Language learning may be similar. We do not need to *know* how to construct the grammar of a natural language on the basis of our early childhood exposure to samples of it. We simply *arrive* at a command of the language after a certain period of exposure and find ourselves convinced that other speakers are following the same rules.

It may be true in many areas of human activity and experience that if we had to rely on what we could come to know, by either empirical or rational means, we should be unable to survive. But if in these areas we are fortunate enough to possess an innate endowment that suits us to deal with the world awaiting us, we do not require the knowledge that it would be so difficult, or perhaps impossible, to obtain. We can be guided by our innate ideas instead.

5

Fodor: The Boundaries of Inner Space

This was part of an American Philosophical Association symposium held December 26, 1968. I was responding to Jerry Fodor's paper, "The Appeal to Tacit Knowledge in Psychological Explanation," which appeared in The Journal of Philosophy 65 *(1968), p. 627. I am slightly surprised by the aggressiveness of the tone, but it still seems to me that the impossibility of reducing intentionality to any sort of mere regularity remains an obstacle to the use of computer simulation as the key to the essence of mind. While there may be much to learn from such programs, something is lost, and it is the most difficult aspect of the problem.*

Many things happen in our bodies and our minds to which we do not have introspective access. With suitable training, the range of our nonobservational, introspective awareness can be extended, but we are very complicated organisms, too complicated to oversee every detail of our own operation. Fortunately an enormous amount of what we and our bodies do does not require attention and is the result of minimal learning or none at all. This is true not only of completely involuntary processes like healing, blood clotting, spermatogenesis, and ovulation, but also of those alterations in individual nerve and muscle cells that form the substructure of ordinary intentional action, from tying our shoes to playing spiccato passages on the cello. We take care of the pounds and let the micrograms take

Reprinted with permission from *The Journal of Philosophy* 66 (1969).

care of themselves. As Fodor's interesting paper points out, the same is true of mental operations (whatever their relation to brain function may be). Depth perception depends on factors most perceivers never think about, and the precise relation between other experiences and the perception of depth or the estimation of size has to be determined by psychological experiment. It is no more accessible to introspection than is the mechanism by which scar tissue is formed.

Facts such as these raise a general question. How much of all that a man's body and mind do, can *he* be said to do? How many of the responses and operations that his body, his brain, and his mind so compliantly perform, and without which he could do nothing, are things he is able to do or knows how to do? If we begin with something that anyone would describe as an action, a man's tying his shoes, for example, we can break it down bit by bit until we have passed beyond the fingers and muscles and perceptions of overlap, to the level of changes in the permeability of cell walls and in the potential gradient at nerve synapses, down beyond that to alteration in the large molecules at the nucleus of the cell, or to the subatomic events on which that depends. At some point it will be clear to everyone that by traveling deep enough inside the person we have lost him and are dealing not with the means by which he ties his shoes but with the physiological and mental substructure of his actions. If there is a line between a person and the rest of that elaborately organized organic system in which his life proceeds, where does the line fall, and what kind of line is it? I am going to discuss Fodor's paper in the light of this question and the answer to it implicit in his remarks.

Two things seem clear about the sort of case that Fodor wants to explain partly in terms of tacit knowledge. First, if I understand him rightly, this sort of case must involve a terminal performance or operation that is more or less conscious and that provides grounds for ascribing to the performer nontacit knowledge as well: knowledge of how to tie his shoes, for example, or knowledge of the relative distances of things in his visual field. The tacit knowledge in these cases underlies a more widely recognized explicit knowledge or ability. This means that tacit knowledge is not ascribable to an individual in explanation of the many unconscious and involuntary operations that his body accomplishes, from the regulation of heart rate to increases in the white blood cell population.

Second, even where the manifest operation is clearly of the right type, it cannot be broken down indefinitely far to reach the tacit knowledge that explains it. We may be able to break down someone's tying his shoes into the movements and combinations of individual atoms and, using Fodor's image, represent the individual as a huge army of little men, one for each atom, obeying instructions that reach them through an elaborate chain of commands originating with one little man who is more or less in charge. Yet I assume Fodor would have no inclination to ascribe tacit knowledge at the level of atomic structure, because we cannot be said to move the atoms in our bodies; these movements are not operations we perform, by means of which we do more elaborate things.

Fodor marks the inner boundary of action and, hence, of knowledge by means of the concept of an *elementary operation*. "An elementary operation," he says, "is one which the normal nervous system can perform but of which it cannot perform a proper part. Intuitively speaking, the elementary operations are those which have no theoretically relevant internal structure" (p. 629). This is not a clear definition. It is unclear, for example, whether it excludes an operation, some proper part of which can occur as a component of a different operation, although none of its proper parts can occur alone. Let us suppose that what is meant is the possibility of performing the operation in isolation and the impossibility of performing any of its proper parts in isolation, and let us ignore for the moment problems about what "performance" means here. I wish to argue that there is no reason whatever to believe that operations that are not elementary for an organism consist of sequences or groups of operations that are elementary for that organism.

To begin with, an operation may fail to be elementary because one of its proper parts can be performed separately, though what remains when that part is subtracted cannot be performed separately. Second, there may be more than one way of dividing up a nonelementary operation exhaustively into elementary parts. In that case, how are we to decide in what "way" the agent has actually performed the operation? Third, even if there is one and only one exhaustive set of elementary operations covering the ground of some action, the way in which the elementary movements are brought about as part of the larger action may have nothing to do with the way they are brought about when they occur in isolation.

Let me introduce a few facts. In the ball of the thumb there is a muscle called the *abductor pollicis brevis,* which plays a vital role in the tying of shoelaces, the performance of spiccato passages on the cello, and other matters. (It produces the movement by which one depresses the space bar on a typewriter.) This muscle consists of several thousand muscle fibers, and it is innervated by approximately three hundred motoneurons, each of which controls a distinct subset of the fibers. The system comprising a motoneuron and the muscle fibers that it innervates is called a *motor unit.* Activation of these motor units in subtle combinations permits one to produce the proper tone in a Beethoven sonata or the characteristic shape of the first letter of one's signature.

Recently the neuroanatomist J. V. Basmajian discovered that human subjects could be trained to activate selected individual motor units in the abductor pollicis brevis at will.[1] They were able to produce the appropriate picture on an oscilloscope set up to register the discharge of particular motor units. Later some of the subjects were able to do so without looking at the oscilloscope. They were able to activate adjacent motor units separately, and even to beat out rapid and elaborate drum rhythms, though ordinarily such units do not discharge in isolation. When asked how they did this, the subjects could not say, just as we cannot say how we manage to move our thumbs.

This road has been traveled even further recently. Fox and Rudell, two psychologists at the University of Iowa, have employed standard reinforcement techniques to train cats to produce specific brain events in response to a visual signal.[2] An arbitrary cortical response is selected for reinforcement—one that is detectable by implanted electrodes and that has a low probability of occurrence prior to the training. It is then brought under operant control; that is, the cat learns to use it to obtain food when hungry. The experimenters were unable to correlate any gross motor behavior with the cat's production of the neural event. The experiment has not, to my knowledge, been tried on humans.

I have introduced these examples to show that extremely minute components of the physical structure of an act may, on their own, achieve the status of intentional action. But even if, after months of training, I were to acquire individual control over each of the motor units of the abductor pollicis brevis, this would not imply that when I depress the space bar on my typewriter, I do so by activating all three hundred of those motor units at once. No doubt when I depress the space bar, all or most of the motor units are activated at once. But I may be completely unable to *activate* them all at once. I may be unable even to attempt that feat, or, if I do attempt it, nothing may happen, or I may produce a dreadful cramp in my thumb. Of course, it is conceivable that I should succeed, but what reason is there to believe that the method by which the ordinary thumb movement is produced bears any interesting relation to the method by which it might be produced through the summation of three hundred simultaneous intentional motor unit innervations? So far as I am able to gather, the weight of current neurological information provides no support for such an atomistic view of behavior. Moreover, there is a good deal of

[1] *Science* 141 (1963) pp. 440–41. See also C. G. Phillips, "Changing Concepts of the Precentral Motor Area," in J. C. Eccles, ed., *Brain and Conscious Experience* (Springer, 1966), p. 40.

[2] *Science* 162 (1968), pp. 1299–1302.

evidence in the opposite direction, evidence that the brain (in some way not yet formulated) encodes complex general behavior patterns rather than collections of particular component movements. (Something analogous seems to be true of the perceptual recognition of universals.) It is not *necessarily* false that we tie our shoes or play musical instruments or speak by the composition, conscious or unconscious, of distinct individual finger and tongue motions (not to mention individual motor unit innervations). It is just false. An answer to the question "What happens when one says 'Beethoven'?" is not ipso facto an answer to the question "How does one say 'Beethoven'?" If I understand him correctly, Fodor's model of the little man with his battalion of underlings does not represent a promising direction for current neurological theory.

To return to the question of knowledge, it seems to me pointless to apply that term to the integrative capacity that permits the production of a complicated sequence of movements, each of which could be produced separately but are in fact produced in a different way when they occur as part of the sequence. This is even clearer if the sequence *cannot* be adequately produced via sequential distinct production of the individual component movements. Knowledge need not be verbally expressible, but it should be either consciously exercised or capable of reaching consciousness upon adequate reflection.[3]

I realize that the expression "tacit knowledge" is a technical barbarism and that there is something peculiar about bringing ordinary linguistic intuitions to bear on the question of its application. Still, there seems to me a point in objecting to the terminological debasement that it represents, much as one might object to the designation "Salisbury steak." Besides, if one applies the term "knowledge," however qualified, to capacities of the sort to which Fodor applies the term "tacit knowledge," then one adds to the obscurity of an important philosophical question that is already quite obscure enough: where to draw the inner boundaries of the self.

It may be impossible to do this at all, but, if we make the attempt, the concept of knowledge will be one of our important resources, and it is therefore desirable to try to reach an understanding of that concept in its natural habitat before extending it to a wider range of phenomena. The concept of intentional action is another concept that has to be examined in

---

[3] I have elaborated this contention in "Chomsky: Linguistics and Epistemology," Chapter 4 in this volume. But let me observe that a reference to consciousness, or perhaps to intention, in the conditions for ascribing knowledge to a person, merely sets the problem and does not solve it. Precisely those concepts must be explained if we are to understand what it is to ascribe a capacity to a person rather than to his body or brain alone.

such an investigation. Both knowledge and action are ascribed to individual persons, and they definitely exclude much that the organism can do but that we do not ascribe to the person. Now it may be that these concepts and the distinctions they draw are not theoretically interesting. It may be (though I doubt it) that the idea of a person, with which these other concepts are bound up, is a dying notion, not likely to survive the advances of scientific psychology and neurophysiology. Perhaps we shall have to fall back on the idea of an organism or an organic system. But we cannot know this without having tried to understand the other concept first.

Fodor, of course, is not out to scrap the concept of a person. He wants to extend the range of organic processes and capacities that can be ascribed to the person as subject, by extending the concepts of knowledge, action, and judgment. But by giving the homunculus too much to do, he may have obscured the special character of what humans can actually be said to do. If I knew what this character was, I would tell you, but I do not. Neither does Fodor, but he uses the idea nevertheless, for he appeals to tacit knowledge only to explain human *performances* and *operations,* not to explain just any organic function, even a highly integrated one like metabolic control, which would presumably be as amenable to computer simulation as shoelace tying is. But if he admits the relevance of a notion like performance at the terminal level, why can't he admit it at the level of the integration that makes a complex performance possible? In other words, if the integration of movements in shoe tying is not itself a conscious or intentional performance, why not withhold the term "knowledge" from the capacity to produce that integration, just as one would withhold the term "knowledge" from the capacity to tie shoes if shoe tying were itself not a conscious or intentional performance?

Let me remark in closing that I do not understand what purpose is served by Fodor's introduction of a machine into the argument. One has to know how the organism's behavior is produced to know whether a given computer simulation is optimal; if one knows that, one has all the support one is likely to get for a description of the individual as applying tacit knowledge or following rules. I cannot imagine what a computer simulation will add, even supposing the notion makes sense and even if the etiology of the machine's output can be represented by a sequence of English sentences. Though it is alarmingly easy to get the contrary impression from his paper, I presume Fodor is not arguing that, since the machine evidently has tacit knowledge of the rules by which it operates, we may legitimately infer, from like effects to like causes, that the person has tacit knowledge of the same rules. What then *are* we permitted to conclude from the case of this imaginary computer? It might be thought that at least we can infer from the computational character of the machine to the computational character of the organism. But since a close analogy on this score is already a condition of optimal simulation, I cannot see what purpose the whole procedure serves.[4]

---

[4] In the discussion, however, Fodor pointed out that *evidence* for the optimality of a computer simulation need not come only from a direct comparison of the ways in which the behavior and its simulation are produced. On the basis of other evidence, one might therefore conclude that a simulation was optimal and, thus, infer that the behavior and the machine output had the same etiology.

6

Armstrong on the Mind

This was a review of David M. Armstrong's A Materialist Theory of the
Mind (*Routledge and Kegan Paul / Humanities Press, 1968*). *In addition
to the expected criticisms of Armstrong for failing to address problems posed
by the subjectivity of the mental, the essay contains what was then a preview
of Kripke's ideas on identity and necessity, which I knew from lectures and
conversation. I'm struck by the fact that I expressed some sympathy for
eliminative materialism—a position I now regard as ridiculous.*

I

Much of the recent materialist literature has defended a materialism of
common sense: the view that identification of the mental and the physical
requires no adjustment or alteration of our plain psychological concepts.
It is held that materialism is not paradoxical and does not require us to
abandon the ordinary conception of man. Armstrong's weighty, lucid, and
readable book carries the defense of this position considerably further
than it has been taken before. It does this partly by improving and clarify-
ing arguments that have already appeared elsewhere; partly by a number
of original moves, some of them extremely penetrating; and partly by
sheer bulk. I believe that the resulting philosophy of mind has certain
defects inherent in the attempt to portray materialism as an undisturbing
doctrine. But let me outline the position before embarking on criticism.

First published in *The Philosophical Review* 79 (1970).

Armstrong's task is set for him in the following way:

> The object that we call a "brain" is called a brain in virtue of certain physical characteristics: it is a certain sort of physical object found inside people's skulls. Yet if we say that this object is also the mind, then, since the word "mind" does not mean the same as the word "brain," it seems that the brain can only be the mind in virtue of some *further* characteristic that the brain has. (p. 78)

He concludes that this further characteristic, or set of characteristics, must also be physical, if materialism is true. The solution is to provide a causal analysis of the mental concepts, according to which they pick out "states of the person apt for bringing about a certain sort of behavior." (To avoid circularity this must be purely "physical behavior" rather than "behavior proper.") Secondarily, some mental states are also states of the person apt for being brought about by a certain sort of stimulus. The word "apt" is meant to cover a multitude of relations.

An essential feature of this analysis is that it tells us nothing about the intrinsic nature of mental states. They fall under the concept of mind because of their role as intermediaries in the causal chain between stimulus and response, but beyond that the mental concepts tell us nothing about them: those concepts are topic-neutral. Therefore, if the causal analysis can be carried forward purely in terms of physical stimuli and physical behavior, the way will be clear for an identification of the states, processes, and events so specified with states, processes, and events in the central nervous system. And no additional, nonphysical attributes will have been presupposed by the application of mental concepts. The resulting identification will be similar in many ways to the identification of the gene with the DNA molecule.

The truth of materialism can be established only by neurophysiology, to which Armstrong defers frequently in the course of the book. But the possibility of materialism requires that a reductionist analysis of mental concepts be correct. A complete reduction to physical terms, such as behaviorism, is unacceptable because it does not preserve the logical possibility of disembodied minds, something Armstrong feels must be allowed by a correct theory. His causal analysis admits this possibility while preserving the connection between mind and behavior, for the analysis does not entail that the causes of behavior are physical; hence it leaves open the possibility that they should be phenomena of a sort that could exist apart from the body. To be precise (though Armstrong does not put it quite this way), the topic-neutral analysis leaves it logically possible that what falls under a mental concept should be something whose disembodied existence is possible. But of course it is also logically possible that mental states should turn out, as Armstrong maintains, to be phenomena whose disembodied existence is not possible.

The first third of the book raises difficulties for various alternative theories of mind and outlines the case for central-state materialism. It includes a lengthy attack on incorrigibility, which Armstrong believes would be fatal to his position. Almost all of the remainder is taken up by Part Two, *The Concept of Mind,* which is described as the intellectual center of the book. There Armstrong provides causal analyses of an enormous number of mental concepts. Many of them are causal reworkings of behaviorist or dispositional analyses. Indeed, he says:

> We can be very sanguine in advance about the success of our programme, because we shall inherit all the astonishing progress made by Analytical Behaviourism in unfolding the nature of mental concepts, without having to accept the doctrine that proved the downfall of Behaviourism: the denial of inner mental states. (p. 118)

Much of the resulting theory is impressive, although I am inclined to think that the attempt at comprehensiveness is a mistake. (In the section on emotions, for example, embarrassment gets six lines, disgust five, and despair three.)

One notion to which Armstrong devotes a good deal of attention is that of purpose. It is fundamental not only to his account of the will but also to his account of perception. The model for purposive behavior is the feedback control of a homing rocket, with the important qualification that the feedback cause must be information supplied by perception or some other form of awareness. Perception in turn is analyzed in terms of the capacity for discriminatory behavior. Armstrong maintains that perceptions are not the *basis* of perceptual judgments, but are simply the acquirings of those judgments themselves. Their causal analysis depends on their providing a necessary precondition for appropriate discriminatory behavior, should the organism want to do something that requires this. But then the threat of circularity arises, for, on the one hand, the discriminatory behavior referred to in the analysis of perception must be purposive, and, on the other hand, purposive behavior is distinguished from a merely mechanical adjustment (like alteration of body temperature) by the former's dependence on perception as a feedback cause. Armstrong's suggestion for dealing with this problem is that the two concepts of perception and purpose cannot be independently applied—that both become applicable only when the feedback mechanism is enormously complex, and that the quantity, subtlety, and temporal scope of the information responded to in genuine purposive behavior, as well as the complexity of the resulting behavioral modifications, provide a sufficient distinction between this and the simpler feedback mechanisms that we do not characterize in the same terms.

Chapter 11, in which he develops this view, is described by Armstrong as the central chapter of the whole book. But I believe that its most important and original philosophical contribution appears in the succeeding chapter, on secondary qualities. He describes his position as a realistic reductionism, and it is much more persuasive that the behavioristic reductionism developed by J. J. C. Smart to accommodate these same recalcitrant concepts to a materialist view. Armstrong simply employs the same device in the analysis of secondary qualities that he has already employed in the analysis of mental states: he analyzes them as states possessing certain external, causal properties, but whose intrinsic nature is left unspecified by this identification. Redness, for example, is a property common to various familiar objects and substances, which normal observers can detect by means of their eyes. In addition, it is one of the determinates falling under a single determinable, in a familiar order with other colors. But this analysis of the concept carries no implications about what that property or that determinable is—just as the causal analysis of a mental state implies nothing about the intrinsic nature of that state. And just as the mental state can therefore be contingently identical with a physical state of the central nervous system, so the color or other secondary quality can be contingently identified with a physical property of objects or their surfaces, if we discover what is responsible for our ability to make the relevant discriminations and classifications just by looking.[1] Armstrong later applies the same method of analysis to bodily sensations. Pain, for example, is described as the perception of a bodily disturbance of a type that characteristically evokes a desire that the perception should cease, but nothing more about the intrinsic nature of the disturbance is implied by this, so

---

[1] At one point (p. 275) Armstrong suggests that the analysis of the concept of redness provides us only with *contingent* truths about redness. Although he does not put it quite this way, one might add that what is necessarily true of redness, its intrinsic nature, can be discovered only by empirical investigation. This suggests the possibility of a more general attack on the traditional association of necessity with analyticity and a priori knowledge. Such a program has in fact been carried out by Saul Kripke, but his results are not published. [They subsequently appeared as *Naming and Necessity* (Harvard University Press, 1980).] They also suggest, however, that we should not regard central-state materialism simply as a contingent thesis, but should say instead that if Armstrong's version of materialism is true, it is necessarily true of the mental states that they are physical states, but only contingently true of them that they are mental states, since that depends on their effects rather than on their intrinsic nature. What is analytically true of something under a certain description may not be necessarily true of it, since that description may fit the thing only contingently. On the other hand, a nonanalytic statement about it may be necessarily true, if, for example, it says what the thing is.

it can be "contingently" identified with the stimulation of pain receptors.

In view of his analysis of secondary qualities, I do not understand Armstrong's remarks about the possibility of inverted spectra, a possibility he wants to defend. He says that half of the population might have one inner state when they looked at red objects and another when they looked at green objects, while the other half had the reverse. And he claims (p. 258) that even if their behavior did not differ, at least one of the groups would have false beliefs about the world. But what false beliefs could they be? On Armstrong's analysis, the content of ordinary perceptual judgments would remain unaffected if both groups were affected in their different ways by a common property of red objects. The judgment "This is red" would have the same analysis for both. If that is true, how can one group be right and the other wrong? Moreover, if Armstrong is correct in maintaining that perceptions are merely the acquiring of perceptual judgments, then the two groups will not have different perceptions, although the same perception will be a different physical state in each group.

It is not possible to discuss here most of the analyses Armstrong offers. Mental states are accounted for in terms of many different relations to behavior, including direct cause, necessary condition, and mere resemblance to other mental states that stand in causal relations to behavior. He analyzes introspection as the inner perception of one's mental states. Like outer perception, its behavioral manifestations involve the capacity to discriminate, control, and take into account the circumstances of which it is a perception, these being themselves states of the person apt for the production of certain behavior.

The book contains a discussion of knowledge based on (a) a causal theory of inferring and (b) a definition of noninferential knowledge that employs the notion of a belief being *empirically sufficient* for its own truth. Except for adding the qualification *"in this particular situation,"* Armstrong leaves the notion of empirical sufficiency unexplained, and I find it opaque. Does it imply anything, for example, about the causal relation (in either direction) between the belief and the circumstance that makes it true? And how is "this particular situation" defined? Since the situation as it is includes the truth of the belief, some interpretation is necessary. Despite the book's length, its effort to cover so much ground sometimes results in skimpy treatment of large issues.

II

I now wish to raise some general questions about the type of materialism whose possibility Armstrong defends and about the causal analysis of mental concepts. My first problem is this: why should a materialist theory of the operation of human beings correspond closely enough to any mentalist picture to permit identification of items from the two theories? Even if some form of materialism is true, it will not automatically be expressible in the framework of commonsense psychology. Currently available data about the central nervous system do not seem to me to encourage such a hope, and some of them positively discourage it; for example, the fundamental left-right bifurcation of cerebral function, to which nothing in the commonsense psychology of perception and action corresponds.

There is an important respect in which Armstrong's analogy between materialism and the equation of the gene and the DNA molecule fails. Premolecular genetics was an exact scientific theory: the concept of the gene was introduced in the service of scientific explanation, and subsequent work in molecular biology that makes the equation plausible has had the same aim. But the psychology of common sense, embodied in the ordinary concepts of belief, desire, sensation, perception, emotion, and so forth is not a scientific theory. The mental states for which Armstrong offers causal analyses are picked out by a system that has evolved naturally, and whose form may depend significantly on its extrascientific functions. Our dealings with and declarations to one another require a specialized vocabulary, and although it serves us moderately well in ordinary life, its narrowness and inadequacy as a psychological theory become evident when we attempt to apply it in the formulation of general descriptions of human behavior or in the explanation of abnormal mental conditions.

The crude and incomplete causal theory embodied in commonsense psychology should not be expected to survive the next hundred years of central nervous system studies intact. It would be surprising if concepts like belief and desire found correspondents in a neurophysiological theory, considering how limited their explanatory and predictive power is, even for gross behavior. The physical behavior that, on Armstrong's analysis, a given intention is apt to cause may be the product of causes whose complexity cannot be brought into even rough correspondence with the simple elements of a present-day psychological explanation.

If that is so, then a physicalist theory of human functioning will not take the form of identifications between old-style psychological states and microscopically described physical states of the central nervous system. It will be couched instead in the concepts of a more advanced theory of human higher functioning. Moreover, it cannot be assumed that these concepts will be drawn from among those now available for the description of the brain. Neurophysiology may uncover phenomena with which we are not familiar and that do not simply reduce to multiple occurrences of phenomena with which we are familiar. (Armstrong recognizes this possibility, and even the possibility that the materialism that turns out to be correct will not be a physicochemical materialism.) I therefore doubt that the terms for expressing the two sides of a physicalist identity are at present available, and the development of physiological psychology could leave us with terms so tied to a common theory that any true identities we tried to formulate would be tautological. None of this is an objection to materialism, but it suggests that the formulation of that doctrine needs to progress beyond the terms of the traditional identity theory.

I want to ask next what the exact status of Armstrong's causal analyses is and whether they are successful in what they set out to accomplish. On pages 84 and 85, he says he is not attempting to provide *translations* of mental statements, but only to *do justice* to the nature of mental states by means of purely physical or neutral concepts. But on page 90 he refers to the enterprise as a logical analysis of the mental concepts and as a conceptual thesis. I take it that he regards his analyses as partial—as rough indications of the kinds of physical phenomena to which our mental concepts are tied. In fact, he relies largely on our ordinary nonverbal knowledge of the behavior characteristic of conscious beings and does not provide much detailed physical analysis at all. But there is no need, for his purposes, to provide any analysis in physical terms *independent* of the psychological vocabulary. If the mental concepts are applied to conditions causally related to certain behavior, it is unlikely that we possess the vocabulary for an independent description of precisely that behavior, without reference to the kind of mental state it typically manifests. It cannot in general be assumed that a physical feature to which we respond uniformly, and whose name we can therefore learn, will be analyzable in terms of component physical features for which we also happen to possess (or could come to acquire) a vocabulary. Most of our nonartificial concepts may be in this sense logically primitive.

But if that is so, there is no need to seek *analyses* of the mental concepts in other terms. Armstrong's causal theory can state truths about our mental states, even if it does not provide adequate analyses of the mental concepts. A materialism of the type Armstrong favors would require that mental states *do in fact* enter into the causation of behavior. But as regards the *analysis* of mind, it need impose only a negative requirement: that mental concepts not entail the involvement of any nonphysical substance or attribute.

Even Armstrong's defense of this negative thesis, however, raises serious difficulties. It leads him to the unusual claim that the intrinsic nature of our mental states plays no part in our mental concepts and, indeed, will not be known to us until it is discovered what the causes of our behavior are. It is a striking feature of Armstrong's book that he does not regard this as a claim that one might find it difficult to accept. He never takes seriously the natural objection that we must know the intrinsic nature of our *own* mental states, since we experience them directly.[2]

Consider, for example, how he accounts for the conceivability of disembodied existence. Armstrong believes that this is taken care of by the topic-neutral element in his causal analysis, which allows for the possibility that the causes of our behavior may be nonphysical. But note that this is not the same as allowing the possiblity of disembodied existence: it is only allowing the possibility of that possibility. This is not a trivial distinction. Armstrong is content to maintain that we do not know that the disembodied existence of the mind is inconceivable. But some philosophers would maintain that we know that the disembodied existence of the mind *is* conceivable. The latter, stronger thesis is the basis of Descartes's proof that the mind and the body are distinct. He did not hold merely that the mind might, for all we know, be something distinct from the body and therefore in principle capable of independent existence. Rather, he held that we can without difficulty conceive of its independent existence, and therefore it must be something distinct from the body.

This is a powerful argument. To oppose it one must maintain, as Armstrong does, that in being subject to his own mental states Descartes is not aware of their intrinsic nature, so he has no grounds for claiming that he can conceive, for example, *this set of sensations* occurring even though his body does not exist. Clearly it would not content Descartes to be told that he cannot be certain that the disembodied occurrence of those sensations is *in*conceivable, for he is certain that it *is* conceivable, having conceived it.

Descartes's argument also has the following turned-around version, which to my knowledge he never employed. The existence of the body without the mind is just as conceivable as the existence of the mind without the body. That is, I can conceive of my body doing precisely what it is doing now, inside and out, with complete physical causation of its behavior (including typically self-conscious behavior), but without any of the mental states I am now experiencing, or any others, for that matter. If that is really conceivable, then the mental states must be distinct from the body's physical states, and Armstrong's causal analysis of mental concepts cannot be correct, for on that analysis the presence of appropriately complex physical causes of appropriately complex behavior would *entail* the existence of conscious mental states.

The conceptual exercises on which these arguments depend are very

---

[2] Though his attack on incorrigibility presupposes a rejection of the idea of direct acquaintance with our own mental states: he contends, as it were, that we know them only by description.

convincing. If Armstrong is right, they are illusory. But then what am I doing when I conceive of my mind without my body, or vice versa? I am certainly not just imagining that the causes of my bodily behavior are states of a nonphysical substance, which can therefore be conceived separated from that body. The type of possibility involved here has nothing to do with analyticity. What is being claimed is not that under a certain description (namely, a mental one) there is no contradiction in supposing that my mental states should exist apart from my body. Rather, it is being claimed that in virtue of what they *are*, their separability is conceivable.[3] The real issue is whether one can know that one has conceived such a thing, and whether one's immediate acquaintance with the contents of one's own mind puts one in a better position to do this than to conceive of the Morning Star persisting and the Evening Star being destroyed. (That is not conceivable, since they are the same. And its conceivability cannot be proved by arguing that it is not a contradiction, for that only shows that those descriptions do not *entail* that it is inconceivable.) What must be shown, to defeat the Cartesian argument, is that when we try to conceive of our minds without our bodies, or vice versa, we do not succeed in doing that, but instead do something else, which we mistake for it. We may, for example, conceive of other beings psychologically similar to ourselves, but having a different psychophysical constitution; this would not be to conceive of our own mental states proceeding without bodies of the sort we now have. Either Descartes is mistaken in thinking that we can conceive of their separate existence, or else some kind of dualism is correct.

One sign of something seriously wrong is that Armstrong regards it as a *virtue* of his theory that it makes short work of the problem of other minds. He says:

> Suppose a human body exhibits the right sort of behaviour. Given our analysis of the nature of mental states we need only three premises to infer the existence of a mind that this behaviour is an expression of. (*i*) The behaviour has *some* cause; (*ii*) the cause lies in the behaving person; (*iii*) the cause is an "adequate" cause—it has a complexity that corresponds to the complexity of the behaviour. Given only these quite modest assumptions, the existence of another mind is necessary. (pp. 124–25)

But this "solution" to the problem leaves it a complete mystery why it has ever bothered anyone. The problem arises precisely at the point where Armstrong's three premises are satisfied, and we discover that the exis-

---

[3] Here again I have been led by Kripke's work on possibility and necessity to see that there is more to the Cartesian argument than a mere confusion between synonymy and identity. It is based on the recognition that if a mental event *is* a physical event, then it is not possible for the former to occur without the latter.

tence of a mind can still be doubted. A theory of mind that overrules this doubt without accounting for its source has left some serious philosophical work undone.

I suspect that these are not difficulties for materialism per se, but rather stem from features of the first-person application of mental concepts that have not been revealed by Armstrong's straightforward causal analysis. This may bear on the usefulness of Armstrong's theory as a formulation of materialism. But there is also a question of whether our ordinary mental concepts, however analyzed, will prove to have any exact connection with a true physical theory of the operation of those organisms that we describe as human. If not, the assumption that we are persons may have to be reexamined.

7

Dennett: Content and Consciousness

This was a review of Daniel C. Dennett's first book, Content and Consciousness *(Routledge and Kegan Paul/Humanities Press, 1969). Like most of Dennett's writings, I found it highly enjoyable and packed with fascinating scientific information, but totally unconvincing with regard to its main thesis.*

Although it does not solve the mind-body problem, this is a valuable and interesting book. Dennett begins with the accurate observation that no one would find the identity theory plausible if it were not for the unpalatability of the alternatives. As he puts it, the motive for identification is to avoid ontic bulge. If there really are mental phenomena, they must be either identical or nonidentical with physical phenomena. If dualism is to be avoided, and if behaviorism is not a viable way of avoiding it, one seems to be thrown into the arms of a neural identity theory.

Dennett's attempt to show that such a theory cannot be right suffers from his assumption that the identities would have to be general, rather than holding between particular mental and particular neural events—an assumption not shared by all defenders of the theory. Nevertheless, he is right about the negative motivation that is its most powerful support and that has led philosophers to expend so much ink and energy trying to make it work. His promise of a new alternative therefore commands considerable interest.

Dennett suggests that mental phenomena may be neither identical nor

Reprinted with permission from *The Journal of Philosophy* 69 (1972).

nonidentical with neural phenomena, because most mental terms are non-referential. This is a radical proposal, for if terms like "pain," "thought," "mental image," and "belief" do not refer, then in a sense there are no such things.

The standard example of a nonreferential term is "sake." There are no sakes, but there are truths statable in terms of "sake." Mental terms are not locked firmly into single idioms as "sake" is, but Dennett discusses the term "voice" as an intermediate example. Voices do not really exist, he says, because one can describe the circumstances in virtue of which any statement containing the word "voice" is true, without referring to a voice (by that or any other name). One refers instead to sounds, vocal chords, frequency manifolds, and the like. This is not just drawing attention to a category difference; it is reduction without identification. "No amount of talk of categories and category mistakes will keep us from the snares of dualism unless we are prepared to grant ontological priority to one category at the expense of the other" (p. 13).

Dennett argues that a similar method of analysis may be fruitful for the mental vocabulary. If we fuse mental terms into their contexts and remain ontologically neutral about their reference, we can seek "a scientific explanation of the differences and similarities in what is the case in virtue of which different mental language sentences are true and false" (p. 18). "Our task will involve at least this much: framing within the scientific language the criteria—the necessary and sufficient conditions—for the truth of mental language sentences" (p. 19). These truth conditions are presumably not supposed to give the *meaning* of the mental language sentences, and it has remained unclear to me exactly what kind of conditions they are supposed to be and how one can tell whether they have been successfully described. Since this new method of analysis is the backbone of the book, more discussion of its logical character would have been appropriate.

Having formulated his task, Dennett declares that the main apparent obstacle to its successful completion is the Intentionality of the mental. Essentially, he makes what I believe to be the mistake of regarding the mind-body problem as a special case of the question how a physical mechanism can be an Intentional system. The question will be answered, he says, if we can find a way of ascribing significance to internal states of the mechanism. We are able to do this with computers, but that is parasitic on the Intentionality of the uses to which computers are put by human beings: a computer's internal states have no significance in themselves.

The significance of brain states, however, cannot be explained in the same way without simply pushing the problem back a step. The explanation must not covertly place a little man in the brain, whose interpretation of its states gives them their significance. Dennett suggests that a non-anthropomorphic explanation of the desired kind may be formulated by reference to evolution and natural selection, which support ordinary ascriptions of function and could well support more complex ascriptions of significance, if applied to the states of an evolved organism that responds in complex ways to information from within and without.

Unfortunately, in demonstrating how such a task is to be executed, Dennett reveals a strong behaviorist streak. As an example of the type of analysis be has in mind, he discusses the case of pain. On what he calls the *personal* level, pain explains avoidance and distress behavior, and that is where the explanation stops. To provide a physiological explanation of the same events is to abandon the personal for the *subpersonal* level. It is nevertheless possible on the subpersonal level to explain the significance of ordinary pain behavior. (Dennett imagines the process by which such compulsive responses to injury or threatened injury might have evolved.) But if an account of *this* is all that is required to describe in scientific language those facts in virtue of which it is true that we feel pain, then the position is shamelessly behaviorist. In fact Dennett asks:

> Could any sense be made of the supposition that a person might hit his thumb with a hammer and be suddenly and overwhelmingly compelled to drop the hammer, suck the thumb, dance about, shriek, moan, cry, etc., and yet *still* not be experiencing pain? That is, one would not be acting in this case, as on a stage; one would be compelled. One would be physically incapable of responding to polite applause with a smiling bow. Positing some horrible (but otherwise indescribable) quality or phenomenon to accompany such a compelled performance is entirely gratuitous. (pp. 94–95)

A curious word. It may be gratuitous, but there is certainly a *difference* between that kind of behavior with pain and the same behavior without it. An organism that displayed the compulsive avoidance behavior without the inner feeling is perfectly imaginable, and Dennett's subpersonal account would apply to it as well as to us. Therefore, although he may have described in scientific language the basis of certain Intentional or functional features of pain, he has not captured what pain is, any more than someone who describes the conditions under which something is a name has said what ink is. Dennett says, of course, that "pain" does not refer. But he cannot claim this until he has more plausibly exhausted the conditions for the truth of statements about pain, on the model of his earlier dissection of voices.

A similar assault on the phenomenon of consciousness follows, but again it turns out that what is explained on the subpersonal level is not consciousness, but only certain patterns of behavior that are characteristic of consciousness but also compatible with its absence. Dennett proposes to analyze consciousness, a complex notion, in terms of two types of awareness:

(1) A is aware$_1$ that p at time t if and only if p is the content of the input state of A's 'speech centre' at time t.

(2) A is aware$_2$ that p at time t if and only if p is the content of an internal event in A at time t that is effective in directing current behavior. (pp. 118–19)

The definitions are further explained in terms of information storage and retrieval. It is acknowledged that awareness$_1$ may characterize certain complex machines. Such an analysis of consciousness may lead to a solution of the mind-body problem for machines, but that is an issue different from the traditional mind-body problem. Dennett claims that the various cases collected under the ordinary word "consciousness" consist of capacities to be aware$_1$ or aware$_2$ in different degrees, and that there is no room "for a concept of awareness$_3$, which would apply only to people and rule out all imaginable machines" (p. 121). But this claim is not established: it is not even supported. Because he assumes that the Intentionality of mental states is the main obstacle to an escape from dualism, Dennett's alternatives to dualism leave the core of the problem untouched.

Dennett goes on to discuss perception, imagination, thought, action, and intention. He is motivated throughout by the aim of accounting for these phenomena in ways that do not simply reintroduce the analysandum into the analysis, by assuming in one way or another a little man or committee of men in the brain. He observes:

> If an image is to function as an element in *perception*, it will have to function as the raw material and not the end product, for if we suppose that the product of the perceptual process is an image, we shall have to design a perceiver-analogue to sit in front of the image and yet another to sit in front of the image which is the end product of perception in the perceiver-analogue and so forth *ad infinitum*. (p. 134)

Much of what he says about mental concepts is imaginative and convincing. But his fundamental enterprise is to reduce our ontological commitment to the mental by explaining on the subpersonal level, "where people, thoughts, experiences and introspective reports are simply not part of the subject matter" (p. 113), how there can be truths that are nonreferentially "about" these things on the personal level. This enterprise remains unfulfilled, and the conditions of its success remain cloudy. It is possible to say a great deal that is true about the mind and its relation to the body, while leaving the mind-body problem fundamentally undisturbed.

8

Dennett: Consciousness Dissolved

This was a review of Daniel C. Dennett's Consciousness Explained (*Little, Brown, 1991*). *It is noticeable how little Dennett's view has changed; nor, of course, has mine. Dennett's view is essentially Gilbert Ryle crossed with Scientific American—an eternal optimism about the possibility of clearing up the mind-body problem by some sensible observations on the behavioral criteria for mental ascriptions, plus lots of empirical facts. I continue to think that this misses the real problem from the start. The disagreement between us will presumably end only in the grave, if then.*

The deepest division among writers on the mind and the brain falls between reductionists and antireductionists: between those who think mental phenomena can someday be fully accounted for by the resources of physical science, and those who think that mental phenomena are so radically different from everything else that a comparably radical expansion of the forms of scientific understanding is required to explain how they arise from the physical operation of the brain.

In this dispute, conscious experience occupies a central role, because one of the toughest challenges for the reductionist is to explain to the antireductionist how it is conceivable that the subjective taste of chocolate, for example, should not merely be *caused* by certain neuron firings in the brain that are in turn caused by stimuli to the taste buds, but should consist of *nothing* but those or other physically describable events. Physical science

---

was developed, after all, to deal with what is outside the mind, independently of how it seems to us.

Daniel C. Dennett is a prominent and tireless defender of the reductionist position—the majority view among those working in the field. *Consciousness Explained* is his full-scale assault on the problem of consciousness. It is, to borrow his own words about another recent effort, an instructive failure—instructive both in itself and in its failure to create a convincingly complete explanation of consciousness out of the limited materials he allows himself.

The book is an exercise in utopian theorizing on the basis of available information—an admirable activity in a subject as undeveloped as this one. Its speculations are offered not as testable hypotheses, but as ways of thinking about the mind-brain relation that would fit consciousness comfortably into a world whose basic constituents were fully describable by physics—showing that "the various phenomena that compose what we call consciousness . . . are all physical effects of the brain's activities." The analogy of the relation of computer software to computer hardware plays a significant role in the story, and Dennett makes a commendable effort, given his lack of sympathy, to explain the leading antireductionist arguments and to destroy them—with the air of dispelling clouds of seductive illusion and superstition.

He is a witty and gifted scientific raconteur, and the book is full of fascinating information about humans, animals, and machines. The result is highly digestible and a useful tour of the field, but in the end it supports the conclusion that what Dennett wants to do can't be done.

His project is doomed by a methodological assumption that he simply states, but that should have been a primary focus of his argument: "Since you can never see directly into people's minds, but have to take their word for it, any such facts as there are about mental events are not among the data of science, since they can never be properly verified by objective methods." He goes on: "The challenge is to construct a theory of mental events, using the data that scientific method permits. Such a theory will have to be constructed from the third-person point of view, since *all* science is constructed from that perspective."

This dictates his strategy, which he calls "heterophenomenology." In fact, the procedure relies implicitly on our first-person understanding of consciousness, while pretending to do without it. What he will do is to construct a third-person theory, which, though it employs familiar psychological terms in the "as if" sense in which one might apply them to a robot, is based solely on the behavioral and physiological manifestations generally associated with consciousness, and does not assume that the beings he is talking about (humans, mostly) are conscious at all.

Such a theory would therefore be equally applicable to a sufficiently complex and animated but subjectively unconscious zombie, if there were such a thing. Once he has produced this third-person theory, however, Dennett asks the clinching question: Could a physical system that satisfied this description really fail to be conscious—would anything necessary for consciousness be missing? And his answer is: No—that's all that consciousness is.

The idea that mental events are not among the data of science was the premise that led to behaviorism, and Dennett's position is a sophisticated descendant of that view: both depend on the same confusion about objectivity. Objectivity in any area of thought requires some method of confirming or disconfirming the observations or judgments of one individual by reference to those of others. But the particular way we do this for physical data is determined by the nature of those data and should not be identified with objectivity in general.

It is not suitable for mental data, but that doesn't mean that the idea of objective data about mental events is meaningless: it means only that we need to use objective standards that combine the first- and third-person points of view, as they are in fact combined in the ordinary concepts for attribution of conscious states that we all employ without difficulty, and that we use to correct experiential descriptions by ourselves and others. A theory of consciousness that doesn't include mental events among the data is like a book about Picasso that doesn't mention his paintings.

Even if one rejects Dennett's large reductionist claim, the theory is of interest, for much of it could be true of consciousness even if it is not all there is to consciousness. Dennett is as opposed to what he calls Cartesian materialism as he is to Cartesian dualism. He believes there is no "Cartesian theatre" in the brain where the contents of consciousness are all on view even for a material self. As he puts it: "The pineal gland is not only not the fax machine to the Soul, it is also not the Oval Office of the brain, and neither are any of the other portions of the brain." Somehow consciousness has to be spread across the brain, but even more interestingly, it has to be smeared in time—physical time, that is. Some of the best discussion in the book concerns experimental results showing that the subjective appearance of temporal sequence or temporal simultaneity among conscious experiences cannot be understood in terms of corresponding relations of brain events in real time. Reflection on the nonlocalized and nonlinear character of consciousness leads Dennett to suggest a complex picture of the brain producing multiple drafts of versions of the world and its aspects, from many different subsystems, in competition with one another. Consciousness is a "virtual machine," resembling a von Neumann computer (which was in fact designed on the model of the stream of conscious thought), programmed through cultural evolution into the vast parallel-processing architecture of the brain. He thinks it is "too recent an innovation to be hard-wired into the innate machinery."

This last is a bizarre claim: Dennett seems to be confusing consciousness with *self*-consciousness. He identifies it with a capacity to make second-order judgments about our own discriminatory states, where those judgments need not themselves be conscious, but are verbally expressible. A creature that not only can sort red things from green, but also say, appropriately, that something looks or seems red to it, has conscious color perceptions. Neither the second-order judgment nor the first-order perception need have any further instrinsic experiential quality: there are no such qualities, only judgments, and they can be explained in terms of a third-person theory of the functioning, including verbal functioning, of the organism.

This definition implausibly implies that babies can't have conscious sensations before they can form judgments about themselves. But the main problem is that, understood in the purely third-person, hetero-phenomenological sense Dennett has given it, the formula doesn't imply anything at all about the consciousness of the subject. Of course, we would believe that anything that functioned physically and behaviorally like a grown human being was conscious, but the belief would be a conclusion from the evidence, rather than just a belief in the evidence. It is only Dennett's Procrustean conception of scientific objectivity that leads him to think otherwise.

9

O'Shaughnessy: The Will

This was a review of Brian O'Shaughnessy's The Will: A Dual-Aspect
Theory *(Cambridge University Press, 1980). Although it is mostly a description of the book, I include it out of sympathy with O'Shaughnessy's
approach to the relation between mind and body and with his defense of
conceptual analysis as an essential resource for understanding the world,
particularly the human world, at a basic level.*

A good philosopher must find his obsession, and it will drive him for the
rest of his life. Brian O'Shaughnessy's obsession has been with the most
intimate of those relations in which the self stands to the physical or
"external" world: its relation to that part of the physical world that it can
move directly and of which it has immediate awareness—the body.

There is an air of paradox in describing the body as part of the external
world simply because it is a physical object, and this shows how fruitful the
topic of human action must be as a key to understanding the place of the
self in the world. It is here, if anywhere, that the apparently radical divide
between mind and matter can be replaced by an intelligible, inner connection. For our bodies are not outside us, even though they are physical
objects. We are not aware of them only through their effects on our senses
(I can look at my hand to see its position on the keyboard, but I also know
without looking how far my left index finger is from the letter *t*). And we
do not move them only by pushing them around (if my left arm is asleep I

Reprinted with permission from *The Times Literary Supplement*, March 27, 1981.

can move it with my right, but then I do not move my right *with anything:* I just move it.)

But if my body is not outside me, then is my body part of my mind, so that a portion of the physical world is contained in the self? Strange as it sounds, that is O'Shaughnessy's answer: "Events occurring outside the brain can be parts, indeed essential parts, of *immediately experienced* psychological events." Perhaps indeed when we think from the inside out it is inconceivable that any self remotely like ours psychologically should not have a body in this very strong sense: not that it is *housed* in a body but that direct physical action and direct knowledge of its own physical posture and orientation are parts of its mental life. And this pervasion of the self by the body in action may infect the more "inner" psychological phenomena of sensation, perception, desire, belief, intention, thought, because of the closeness with which they are joined to action and bodily self-awareness in a single conceptual net.

This reversal of the usual direction of approach to the mind-body problem is a main feature of O'Shaughnessy's book. He is investigating the relation between mind and body from *within the mind itself*—not as it might appear to external observation of behavioral effects or physiological causes of psychological phenomena. He wants to understand that mysterious and essential aspect of the inner life of each of us: the condition of *being* a physical, animal organism.

To defend his view, he must resist a rival picture of the intimate relation between the self and the body: that we move our bodies directly by the causal effect of a special type of inner mental act, a volition, and are directly aware of our bodies through a body image that is a kind of passive sensory trace. According to this view, our bodies are much closer to our minds than any other physical object is, but the two remain ultimately distinct and their relation to one another is almost magical, as it would be magical if I could move the furniture simply by willing it to move. O'Shaughnessy opposes to this a nonmagical picture that is nevertheless not a reduction of the mental to the physical, and in the course of it he propounds a general and original theory of the structure of the mind.

Before describing the results, let me say something about the philosophical context. This work concerns the mind-body problem, but though it expresses a debt to Wittgenstein and to the writings of Elizabeth Anscombe, Stuart Hampshire, and Donald Davidson on the subject of action, its approach is quite different from most of the literature in analytic philosophy of the last thirty years. That literature has usually started from the assumption that persons and animals are physical organisms and has asked how it is possible to attribute psychological states to such organisms on the basis of observation of their behavior, and what the relation is between those psychological states and the brain states on which they depend. The approach has been largely from the outside in; for the most part, the results have been crude and superficial, the products of self-imposed blindness.

O'Shaughnessy's approach is from the inside out. He too believes we are (at least) physical organisms, but he wants to see what can be discovered about the relation between our psychological states and the operation of our bodies by starting from the point of view of the psychological subject, immediately aware in certain respects of what he is doing, feeling, and thinking. Instead of trying to construct the mind out of an ontology from which it has been excluded, he starts with the mind, explores it from within, and discovers that it inevitably opens out into the physical world in virtue of its inevitable possession of a body: particularly in action—"the very soul of the agent expanding as it were beyond its natural confines out into the world at large."

He describes his theory of the will as a dual aspect theory, because it holds that voluntary actions are essentially both psychological and physical events—not *combinations* of psychological and physical events, but Janus-faced—and that their psychological character requires that they also be physical, even though at the same time it cannot be reduced to or analyzed in terms of their physical character.

While he does not take up the relation between mental events and the brain in general, and does not argue for a general dual aspect theory of the mind, he explains why a view of this kind might have contemporary appeal:

> On the one hand, the steadily accruing achievements of physics and its bril-
> liantly successful application to the problem of Life in Molecular Biology,
> together with recent success in constructing artificial intelligences—create a
> climate of thought conducive to *materialism*. On the other hand, the increasing
> revulsion at crassly destructive and levelling reductionism, which is rapidly
> losing its charms along with its credibility—make for a climate in which a
> program of *ontological conservation* has great attractions.

"Of course," he adds, "one cannot in adopting such an historical perspective elevate oneself above the need for argument." A fine antihistoricist motto.

O'Shaughnessy's inquiry proceeds by a method of a priori reasoning that makes his work traditional in a way that Kripke's work is traditional. For it is based on the conviction that by taking apart certain natural and inescapable concepts through the kind of philosophical self-exploration that can be carried out only by their possessors, we can make fundamental discoveries about the nature of the reality to which those concepts apply.

There is a great deal that philosophy alone cannot discover, but we cannot hope to learn what is most important about some aspects of reality without uncovering those fundamental features by which they are grasped in thought—and we are likely to be confused in any further inquiry unless we understand these features first.

The mind is one such domain, and action a central example. Much can be discovered about it by empirical scientific methods. But "the ultimate constituents of physical action . . . are pre-scientifically, indeed *a priori*, given. In this sense, the concept of a physical action is an *a priori* concept, which stands nonetheless in need of *a posteriori* given application conditions." Science can discover the latter, for example, the physiological mechanisms that make action possible, but philosophy must discover what action *is*—its necessary and sufficient conditions. Then how did we acquire such a priori concepts, and why should we believe what they seem to reveal about reality? O'Shaughnessy's answer is (not unintentionally) obscure: *"Certain natural facts must nonargumentatively have guided pre-rational mankind in forming these crucial usages* in the dim pre-history of the species at the dawning point of self-consciousness. More exactly: the passage from pre-rational to rational *internally* involved the formation of *certain natural facts. . . .* This is how man came to know of *The World/Space/Truth/Self/Time/Consciousness:* the whole galaxy of Metaphysical Leading Lights." These are concepts that we could not, as self-conscious, rational beings, have lacked. They are determined by primal facts of inner and outer reality.

By contrast there are many concepts we might have lacked and that were initially acquired by ostension. Almost everything about those things has to be discovered by empirical inquiry, because the concepts contain so little.

> Whereas there is a philosophical analysis of the concept of physical action, there could hardly be a comparable philosophical analysis of the purely *a posteriori* idiosyncratic concepts of gold or tiger. Yet the divergence in the nature of the enterprises is by no means total; for they are from the point of view of *the word's extension* at one. For the philosophical analysis, from that point of view, does no more than indicate certain *a priori*–given constraints upon the extension of "immediately willed event." It leaves the final element in the determination of that extension up to science, and this last is precisely the position with "gold" and "tiger."

Just how much truth about reality is buried in those rich, obscure a priori concepts, waiting to be extracted by philosophy, is a controversial matter. Many contemporary philosophers suspect that these natural concepts are full of confusion and ignorance, so that we should rely on them only warily, not hesitating to replace them with others that are cleaner or more scientifically sound. I believe this is fundamentally wrong because science must build on a prescientific awareness and understanding of certain aspects of the world, which can never be thrown away no matter how much is added to it, because it is constantly being reused. It must be possible to explain technical jargon ultimately in natural terms; otherwise, the connection with the understanding is lost and the dangers of confusion or emptiness become really serious.

O'Shaughnessy's method may seem to some to place too much reliance on prescientific concepts, but it seems to me to be justified by its results as well as by its rationale.

Here are a few of the conclusions: Physical action is psychologically primitive and, like sensation, has a character independent of its intentional content. It need not be intentional under any description. Here O'Shaughnessy disagrees with Davidson. He argues convincingly that any general account of voluntary action must apply to idle tappings of the foot and movements of the tongue, of which we need not be aware and that we do not intend, but that are nevertheless not involuntary. These "subintentional" acts must contain the common core of all voluntary action. This does not consist of a mental act together with the physical movement that it causes. Rather, the observable physical movement "is the surface tip of an event that reaches all the way back into the brain. Namely: the act of the will." Every act, successful or not, is identical with an act of trying or striving, the activation of a pre-established physical "power line" from the brain to the muscles. Strivings are the direct and inevitable expressions of act-desire: "They are, so to say, nothing but buds on the tree of desire. And like any good bud, they will in propitious circumstances ripen into the flower from which they were never distinct."

They are psychological events because, like sensations, they are introspectively accessible to the attention. If I believe that I am trying to raise my arm, I cannot be mistaken even if my arm is not rising. But when I succeed in raising any arm, my raising it is identical with my trying to raise it. So an introspectively accessible psychological event is identical with an externally observable physical event.

Hence we arrive at a dual aspect theory of physical action. It cannot be replaced by a volition theory that breaks the action into psychological cause and physical effect—because trying to raise my arm is not an event of the inner world. When it succeeds it is an observable action, and when it fails it resembles some fractional beginning of that same action, extending from its origin in the brain to the forward limit of its blocked causal development.

The will as such is not free, but if it results from the intentions of a rational being whose commitments are perpetually open to review or renewal, it can manifest the freedom possible for those who are not omnipotent. (I shall not attempt to summarize the elaborate causal theory relating subintentional actions, desire, belief, decision, choice, consciousness, intention, commitment, and self-determination—and locating the sense in which our actions do not *happen to us.*)

"A necessary condition of willing change in a physical object is: that it be incorporated into the body image." But the body-image is not a three-dimensional sensuous entity, although sensations or sense data do play a part in external perception. "To be seemingly aware of an arm is not to be aware of a seeming arm." Rather, the body-image is the *body-ego,* the fundamental conception of what physically one is (and an absolute condition of knowing reality in the physical mode). There is both short- and long-term body image, and while they depend causally on kinesthetic and proprioceptive sensation, they are not sensory images, but something of a different mental type that allows us to locate our bodily sensations and gives our will something to act on. The long-term body-image "is that which expedites the transition from the given sensations of any instant to the range of possible postures and movements one may realistically attempt" (though it is not limited to that over which one has active power: think of a woman's breasts).

The influence of Freud on this book is evident not only in the references but in the ambition and hope of creating a rich theory of the self from within by using specialized and largely self-created tools to uncover what is constantly at work inside us. So is the related influence of Wittgenstein, a determination to allow "bizarre and wild outbreaks of the philosophical unconscious" (O'Shaughnessy's phrase) to operate as clues to the discovery of what is under our noses, in the subtle operation of concepts that present us with a smooth and simple surface.

The result is a theory of mind and body much richer than anything Wittgenstein would have allowed himself. But it shares with the *Philosophical Investigations* a view that while mental phenomena are *sui generis* and not analyzable in terms of behavior or anything else about the body, they are in their essence connected with the body as well as with each other. The closest we can come to defining them is to discover these essential connections. And that is not the same as reducing the contents of the mind to mere blanks in the network of bodily circumstances and manifestations to which they are epistemically or causally related. A headache is as real as a blow on the head.

10

Searle: Why We Are Not Computers

This was a review of John R. Searle's The Rediscovery of the Mind *(M.I.T. Press, 1992). Though Searle and I agree about a great deal, I don't think it's possible to distinguish his antireductionist solution from property dualism. And I do not believe it could be a brute fact of nature that the higher order mental properties of the nervous system should be produced by the details of its physicochemical operation. The relation between the levels must be more "internal" than that—a form of intelligibly necessary consequence rather than pure correlation. The irreducibility of the ontologically subjective to the ontologically objective continues to be an obstacle to the imaginability of such a connection.*

According to a widely held view, the brain is a giant computer and the relation of the human mind to the human brain is like that of a computer program to the electronic hardware on which it runs. The philosopher John Searle, a dragonslayer by temperament, has set out to show that this claim, together with the materialist tradition underlying it, is nonsense, for reasons some of which are obvious and some more subtle. Elaborating arguments that he and others have made over the past twenty years, he attacks most of the cognitive science establishment and then offers a theory of his own about the nature of mind and its relation to the physical world. If this pungent book is right, the computer model of the mind is not just doubtful or imperfect, but totally and glaringly absurd.

His main reasons are two. First, the essence of the mind is consciousness: all mental phenomena are either actually or potentially conscious. And none of the familiar materialist analyses of mind can deal with conscious experience: they leave it out, either by not talking about it or by identifying it with something else that has nothing to do with consciousness. Second, computers that do not have minds can be described as running programs, processing information, manipulating symbols, answering questions, and so on only because they are so constructed that people, who do have minds, can interpret their physical operations in those ways. To ascribe a computer program to the brain implies a mind that can interpret what the brain does, so the idea of explaining the mind in terms of such a program is incoherent.

I

Searle's book begins with a lucid critical survey of the different views now circulating about the relation of the mind to the body. The mind-body problem was posed in its modern form only in the seventeenth century, with the emergence of the scientific conception of the physical world on which we are now all brought up. According to that conception, the physical world is in itself colorless, odorless, and tasteless, and can be described mathematically by laws governing the behavior of particles and fields of force in space and time. Certain physical phenomena cause us to have perceptual experience—we see color and hear sound—but the qualities we experience do not belong to the light and sound waves described by physics. We get at the physical reality by "peeling off" the subjective effects on our senses and the way things appear from a human point of view, consigning those to the mind, and trying to construct an objective theory of the world outside our minds that will systematically explain the experimental observations and measurements on which all scrupulous observers agree. However radically the content of contemporary physics and its conception of the role of the observer may differ from that of classical physics, it is still in search of a theory of the *external* world in this sense.

But having produced such a conception by removing the appearances from the physical world and lodging them in the mind, science is faced with the problem of how to complete the picture by finding a place in the world for our minds themselves, with their perceptual experiences, thoughts, desires, scientific theory construction, and much else that is not described by physics. The reason this is called the mind-*body* problem is that what goes on in our minds evidently depends on what happens to and in our bodies, especially our brains, yet our bodies are part of the "external" world—that is, the world external to our minds—that physical science describes. Our bodies are elaborate physical structures built of molecules, and physics and chemistry would presumably give the most accurate description of everything they do or undergo.

Descartes famously thought that if you considered carefully the nature of outer physical reality and the nature of inner mental reality (as exemplified by your own mind), you could not help seeing that these had to be two different kinds of things, however closely they might be bound together: a mind and its thoughts and experiences just couldn't be constructed out of physical parts like molecules in the way that the heart or the brain evidently can be. Descartes's conclusion that mental life goes on in a nonphysical entity, the soul, is known as dualism—sometimes "substance" dualism, to distinguish it from "property" dualism, which is the view that though there is no soul distinct from the body, mental phenomena (like tasting salt or feeling thirsty) involve properties of the person or his brain that are not physical.

The power of Descartes's intuitive argument is considerable, but dualism of either kind is now a rare view among philosophers,[1] most of whom accept some kind of materialism. They believe that everything there is and everything that happens in the world must be capable of description by physical science. Moreover, they find direct evidence that this can be done even for the mind in the intimate dependence of mental on neurophysiological processes, about which much has been learned since the seventeenth century. And they find indirect evidence, from the remarkable success of the application of physics and chemistry to other aspects of life, from digestion to heredity. Consequently, most efforts to complete the scientific worldview in a materialist form have proceeded by some sort of reduction of the mental to the physical—where the physical, by definition, is that which can be described in nonmental terms.

A reduction is the analysis of something identified at one level of description in the terms of another, more fundamental level of description—allowing us to say that the first really is nothing but the second: water can be described as consisting of H_2O molecules, heat as molecular motion, light as electromagnetic radiation. These are reductions of the macroscopic physical to the microscopic physical, and they have the following noteworthy features: (1) They provide not just external information about the causes or conditions of the reduced phenomenon, but an internal account of what water, heat, and light really are. (2) They work only because we have distinguished the perceptual appearances of the macroscopic phenomena—the way water and heat feel, the way light looks—

[1] But see Geoffrey Madell, *Mind and Materialism* (Edinburgh University Press, 1988).

from the properties that are being reduced. When we say heat consists of molecular motion, we mean that heat as an intrinsic property of hot objects is nothing but the motion of their molecules. Such objects produce the feeling of heat in us when we touch them, but we have expressly not identified that feeling with molecular motion—indeed, the reduction depends on our having left it out.

Now how could *mental* phenomena be reduced to something described entirely in physical, nonmental terms? In this case, obviously, we cannot leave out all effects on the mind, since that is precisely what is to be reduced. What is needed to complete the materialist world picture is some scheme of the form, "Mental phenomena—thoughts, feelings, sensations, desires, perceptions, and the like—are nothing but . . . ," where the blank is to be filled in by a description that is either explicitly physical or uses only terms that can apply to what is entirely physical.[2] The various attempts to carry out this apparently impossible task and the arguments to show that they have failed make up the history of the philosophy of mind during the past fifty years.

Searle's account of that history begins with behaviorism, the view that mental concepts do not refer to anything inside us and that each type of mental state can be identified with a disposition of the organism to behave observably in certain ways under certain physical conditions. When this view began to look too much like a bald denial of the existence of the mind, some philosophers put forward *identity* theories, according to which mental processes are identical with brain processes in the same way that light is identical with electromagnetic radiation. But identity theories were left with the problem of explaining in nonmental terms what it means to say of a particular brain process that it is a thought or a sensation. After all, this can't mean only that it is a certain kind of neurophysiological process. And given the aim of these theories, it couldn't mean that the brain process has some mental effect. The proposed solution was a revival of behaviorism in a new form: thirst, for example, was identified not with a disposition to drink, but with a brain state, but that particular brain state's being identical with thirst was now said to consist simply in the fact that it was typically

___

[2] Another reductionist strategy, which I haven't the space to discuss here, is to substitute for a theory of what mental states *are* a theory of the externally observable grounds on which we *ascribe* mental states to people, and to claim that this system of "assertability conditions" is all the analysis the concepts need. One doesn't *identify* mental phenomena with anything physical, because one doesn't identify them with anything. But the conditions of applicability of mental concepts are, on this view, compatible with the world's being nothing but a material system. This is essentially Daniel Dennett's strategy in *Consciousness Explained* (Little, Brown, 1991) [discussed in Chapter 8 in this volume].

caused by dehydration and that it typically caused a disposition to drink. In this way it was thought that the identification of mental states with brain states could avoid all reference to nonphysical features.

These "causal behaviorist" analyses were eventually succeeded by a more technical theory called "functionalism," according to which mental concepts cannot be linked to behavior and circumstances individually but only as part of a single interconnected network. The behavior caused by thirst, for example, depends on the rest of a person's mental condition—his beliefs about where water is to be found and whether it is safe to drink, the strength of his desires to live or die, and so forth. Each mental state is a part of an integrated system that controls the organism's interaction with its environment; it is only by analyzing the role played by such states as thirst, pain, other kinds of sensation, belief, emotion, and desire, within the total system, that one can accurately describe their connection to behavior and external circumstances. Such a system may still permit mental states to be identified with brain states, provided the latter have causal or functional roles of the kind specified by the theory (still to be constructed) of how the integrated system works. Finally, functionalism led to what Searle calls Strong AI (Strong Artificial Intelligence)—the identification of mental states with computational states of a computer program that controls the organism's behavior—a program that is physically realized in the hardware (or wetware) of the brain.[3]

All these theories attempt to reduce the mind to one or another aspect of a world that can be fully described by physics—the world of particles and fields. They have not been worked out in detail; they are just hopeful descriptions of the kind of thing a theory of the mind would have to be, together with some extremely sketchy examples. While each new proposal has been criticized by defenders of alternative reductionist accounts, Searle argues that there is one big thing wrong with all of them: they leave out consciousness.

II

No theory that leaves out consciousness can claim to be a theory of the mind, and no analysis of consciousness in nonmental terms is possible;

---

[3] Behaviorism is more or less represented by Gilbert Ryle, identity theory by J. J. C. Smart, and functionalism by Hilary Putnam—but there are many writers and the literature is very large. See one of the excellent recent collections on the philosophy of mind: Ned Block, editor, *Readings in Philosophy of Psychology*, two volumes (Harvard University Press, 1980); W. G. Lycan, editor, *Mind and Cognition* (Blackwell, 1990); David Rosenthal, editor, *The Nature of Mind* (Oxford University Press, 1991). Putnam has now abandoned functionalism; see *Representation and Reality* (M.I.T. Press, 1988).

therefore, no materialistic reduction of the mental can succeed. Searle contends that none of these theories could possibly provide an account of what pain, hunger, belief, vision, and the like really are, because all they talk about is what is externally observable—the organism's behavior and its causal structure—and a description of something exclusively in those terms fails to guarantee that it has any consciousness at all: each of these behaviorist, functionalist, or computational theories could be satisfied by an unconscious zombie of sufficient physical complexity.

> The crucial question is not "Under what conditions would we *attribute* mental states to other people?" but rather, "What is it that people *actually have* when they have mental states?" "What are mental phenomena?" as distinct from "How do we find out about them and how do they function causally in the life of the organism?" (p. 23)

We attribute consciousness to other people and to animals on the basis of their behavior, but this is simply evidence of consciousness rather than proof of it, and it has to be supplemented by evidence of physiological similarity: since we believe in the uniformity of nature, we naturally infer that creatures who behave similarly to us and have sense organs and nervous systems physically similar to ours also have conscious experiences of some kind. But, Searle argues, no quantity of facts about physical behavior or functional organization by themselves entail that a system is conscious at all—and any theory that claims, for example, that vision is "nothing but" a certain state of the organism must, to be adequate, have the consequence that if the organism is in that state, it *can't fail* to be conscious. Otherwise, it will leave out the most important thing about vision and, whatever its other merits, won't qualify as an account of what vision is.

Not only do materialist reductions fail to imply that the system is conscious; it is clear in advance that no further development along the same lines, no added structural or behavioral complications, could do so. The reason is that there is a crucial difference between conscious phenomena and behavioral or physiological phenomena that makes the former irreducible to the latter: consciousness is, in Searle's terms, "ontologically subjective." That is, its essential features cannot be described entirely from an external, third-person point of view. Even the physiological description of what goes on inside the skull is external in this sense: it is described from outside. It is not enough to summarize the third-person observations, behavioral or physiological, that lead us to ascribe conscious mental states to others. The first-person point of view, which reveals what a conscious mental state is like for its subject, is indispensable.

This becomes clear when we ask, What is consciousness? Though we can describe certain of its features and identify more specific types of mental phenomena as instances, it is so basic that it can't be defined in terms of anything else. You, reader, are conscious at this very moment, and your conscious condition includes such things as the way this page looks to you; the feel of the paper between your fingers, the shirt on your back, and the chair on which you're sitting; the sounds you hear of music or surf or police sirens in the background; and your experience of reading this sentence. Searle's claim is that no amount of third-person analysis, whether behavioral, causal, or functional, could possibly tell us what these experiences are in themselves—what they consist of, as distinguished from their causes and effects. This is perfectly obvious because subjective facts about what it's like for someone to be in a certain condition—what it's like from his point of view—can't be identified with facts about how things are, not from anyone's point of view or *for* anyone, but just in themselves. Facts about your external behavior or the electrical activity or functional organization of your brain may be closely connected with your conscious experiences, but they are not facts about what it's like for you to hear a police siren.[4]

Searle believes that the persistence of materialistic reductionism in the face of its evident falsity requires explanation. He likens it to the constant repetition by a compulsive neurotic of the same destructive pattern of behavior, and he hopes that by bringing to light its underlying causes he can break the hold of the compulsion. It is evident, both from what they say and from what they do, that reductionists are convinced in advance that some materialist theory of the mind must be correct: they just have to find it. This assumption is part of a scientific worldview to which they can see no alternative. But underlying the assumption, according to Searle, are two crucial misconceptions. The first is that we have to choose between materialism and dualism:

> What I want to insist on, ceaselessly, is that one can accept the obvious facts of physics—for example, that the world is made up entirely of physical particles in fields of force—without at the same time denying the obvious facts about our own experiences—for example, that we are all conscious and that our conscious states have quite specific *irreducible* phenomenological [that is, subjective] properties. The mistake is to suppose that these two theses are inconsistent, and that mistake derives from accepting the presuppositions behind the traditional vocabulary. My view is emphatically not a form of dualism. I reject both property and substance dualism; but precisely for the reasons that I reject dualism, I reject materialism and monism as well. The deep mistake is to suppose that one must choose between these views. . . .
>
> Once you accept our worldview the only obstacle to granting consciousness

[4] To declare an interest: I am one of those cited as proponents of this line of argument, the others being Saul Kripke and Frank Jackson.

its status as a biological feature of organisms is the outmoded dualistic/materialistic assumption that the "mental" character of consciousness makes it impossible for it to be a "physical" property. (pp. 28, 91)

This radical thesis, that consciousness is a physical property of the brain in spite of its subjectivity, and that it is irreducible to any *other* physical properties, is the metaphysical heart of Searle's position. The point here, however, is that Searle contends that materialists are drawn to implausible forms of psychophysical reduction because they assume that if mental states cannot be explained in such terms, then the inescapable alternative is dualism: they would then have to admit that nonphysical substances or properties are basic features of reality. And the fear of dualism, with its religious and spiritualist and otherwise unscientific associations, drives them to embrace reductionist materialism at any intellectual cost: "Materialism is thus in a sense the finest flower of dualism."

To escape from this bind, says Searle, we have to free ourselves of the urge to ask whether there are one or two ultimate kinds of things and properties. We should not start counting in the first place.

He is absolutely right about the fear of dualism (indeed, I believe he himself is not immune to its effects). Its most bizarre manifestation is yet another theory, called "eliminative" materialism. This is the view that, because mental states can't be accommodated within the world described by physics, they don't exist—just as witches and ghosts don't exist. They can be dismissed as postulates of a primitive theory customarily referred to as "folk psychology"—about which P. F. Strawson has remarked that it is the province of "such simple folk as Shakespeare, Tolstoy, Proust, and Henry James."[5] Searle patiently pulverizes this view, but his real point is that the entire materialist tradition is in truth eliminative: all materialist theories deny the reality of the mind, but most of them disguise the fact (from themselves as well as from others) by identifying the mind with something else.

The second crucial misconception behind the compulsive search for materialist theories, according to Searle, is a simple but enormously destructive mistake about objectivity:

There is a persistent confusion between the claim that we should try as much as possible to eliminate personal subjective prejudices from the search

[5] Eliminative materialism was first proposed by Paul Feyerabend and Richard Rorty; versions of the view are defended by Steven Stich, *From Folk Psychology to Cognitive Science: The Case against Belief* (M.I.T. Press, 1983); Paul M. Churchland, *Matter and Consciousness: A Contemporary Introduction to the Philosophy of Mind* (M.I.T. Press, 1984); and Patricia S. Churchland, *Neurophilosophy* (M.I.T. Press, 1986). Strawson's comment is in *Skepticism and Naturalism: Some Varieties* (Columbia University Press, 1985) p. 56.

for truth and the claim that the real world contains no elements that are irreducibly subjective. And this confusion in turn is based on a confusion between the epistemological sense of the subjective/objective distinction, and the ontological sense. Epistemically, the distinction marks different degrees of independence of claims from the vagaries of special values, personal prejudices, points of view, and emotions. Ontologically, the distinction marks different categories of empirical reality. (p. 19)

This seems to me entirely convincing, and very important. Science must of course strive for epistemic objectivity—objective knowledge—by using methods that compensate for differences in points of view and that permit different observers to arrive at the same conception of what is the case. But it is a gross confusion to conclude from this that nothing that has or includes a point of view can be an object of scientific investigation. Subjective points of view are themselves parts of the real world, and if they and their properties are to be described adequately, their ontologically subjective character—the subjectivity of their *nature*—must be acknowledged. Furthermore, this can be done, in the epistemic sense, objectively: although only you are now experiencing the look of the page in front of you, others can know that you are, and can know a good deal about what that experience is like for you. It is an objective truth that you are now having a certain subjective visual experience.

If we accept this distinction, the question becomes, How can we form an epistemically objective scientific conception of a world that contains not only the familiar ontologically objective facts described by physics, chemistry, and biology, but also the ontologically subjective facts of consciousness? And that brings us, finally, to Searle's own view, which he calls "biological naturalism," and which combines acceptance of the irreducible subjectivity of the mental with rejection of the dichotomy between mental and physical: "Consciousness . . . is a biological feature of human and certain animal brains. It is caused by neurobiological processes and is as much part of the natural biological order as any other biological features such as photosynthesis, digestion, or mitosis" (p. 90).

And in spite of his antireductionism, he also writes as follows:

Consciousness is a higher-level or emergent property of the brain in the utterly harmless sense of "higher-level" or "emergent" in which solidity is a higher-level emergent property of H_2O molecules when they are in a lattice structure (ice), and liquidity is similarly a higher-level emergent property of H_2O molecules when they are, roughly speaking, rolling around on each other (water). Consciousness is a mental, and therefore physical, property of the brain in the sense in which liquidity is a property of systems of molecules. (p. 14)

If this view could be clarified in a way that distinguished it from the alternatives, it would be a major addition to the possible answers to the mind-body problem. But I don't think it can be.

Suppose we grant that states of consciousness are properties of the brain caused by, but not reducible to, its neural activity. This means that your brain, for instance, has a point of view of which all your current experiences are aspects. But what is the justification for calling these irreducibly subjective features of the brain *physical*? What would it even mean to call them physical? Certainly they are "higher order" in the sense that they can be ascribed only to the system as a whole and not to its microscopic parts; they are also "emergent" in the sense of being explained only by the causal interactions of those parts. But however great the variety of physical phenomena may be, ontological objectivity is one of their central defining conditions; and as we have seen, Searle insists that consciousness is ontologically subjective.

Searle doesn't say enough about this question. Perhaps he believes that if brains are made up of physical particles, it follows automatically that all their properties are physical. And he quotes a remark of Noam Chomsky that as soon as we come to understand anything, we call it "physical." But if "physical" is in this sense merely an honorific term (another way I've heard Chomsky put the point), what is the metaphysical content of Searle's claim that mental properties are physical, and his emphatic rejection of property dualism? He says, after all, that the ontological distinction between subjective and objective marks "different categories of empirical reality." To say further that we are "left with a universe that contains an irreducibly subjective physical component as a component of physical reality" merely couches an essentially dualistic claim in language that expresses a strong aversion to dualism.[6]

Perhaps we could adopt Searle's use of the word "physical," but the basic issue is more than verbal. It is the issue of how to construct an intelligible and complete scientific worldview once we deny the reducibility of the mental to the nonmental. As Searle points out, we cannot do so by continuing on the path that physical science has followed since the seventeenth century because that depended on excluding the mind of the observer from the world being observed and described. To propose that conscious-

[6] Searle identifies me as a defender of property dualism. I prefer the term "dual aspect theory," to express the view deriving from Spinoza that mental phenomena are the subjective aspects of states that can also be described physically. But all I would claim for the idea is that it is somewhat less unacceptable than the other unacceptable theories currently on offer. I share Searle's aversion to both dualism and materialism, and believe a solution to the mind-body problem is nowhere in sight.

ness is an intrinsic subjective property of the brain caused by its neural activity is the first step on a different path—the right one, in my opinion. But there are large problems ahead, and they are not just empirical but philosophical.

Even if we learn a great deal more than we know now about the physiological causes of consciousness, it will not, as Searle is aware, make the relation of consciousness to the behavior of neurons analogous to the relation of liquidity to the behavior of H_2O molecules. In the latter case the relation is transparent: we can *see* how liquidity is the logical result of the molecules "rolling around on each other" at the microscopic level. Nothing comparable is to be expected in the case of neurons, even though it is empirically evident that states of consciousness are the necessary consequences of neuronal activity. Searle has an interesting discussion of this difference, which he says results only from a limitation of our powers of conception: we can represent the necessary relation between the macro and micro levels of water since we picture them both from the outside, but we can't do this with subjectivity, which we have to imagine from the inside, whether it is ours or someone else's. I agree, but I believe this means we do not really understand the claim that mental states are states of the brain: we are still unable to form a conception of *how* consciousness arises in matter, even if we are certain that it does.[7]

III

Searle's second set of arguments against the computer model of mind depends on the specific nature of computers and is more distinctively Searle's own: it grows out of his long-standing concern with the theory of meaning and the "intentionality" of mental states—their capacity to mean something or refer to something outside themselves, and their consequent susceptibility to judgments of truth or falsity, correctness or incorrectness.[8]

How is it possible for computers to answer the questions we put to them—arithmetical questions, for example? The explanation has two parts. First, it is possible to formulate each of those questions by using a

[7] Colin McGinn, in *The Problem of Consciousness* (Blackwell, 1991), suggests that we are constitutionally incapable of arriving at such an understanding. Though he could be right, I think his pessimism is premature.

[8] See Searle's essay "Minds, Brains, and Programs," in *Behavioral and Brain Sciences* 3, No. 3 (September 1980) pp. 417–24. See also *Intentionality: An Essay in the Philosophy of Mind* (Cambridge University Press, 1983).

string of symbols—letters or numerals—selected from a short list and distinguished by their shapes, and to devise a finite set of rules for manipulating those symbols, which has the following property: if you start with the string corresponding to the question, and follow the rules for moving, removing, and adding symbols, you will arrive, after a finite series of uniquely determined steps, at a point where the rules tell you to stop; and the last string you have produced will correspond to the answer:[9] you only have to read it. But to follow the rules for manipulating the symbols, you don't have to know what they mean, or whether they mean anything: you just have to identify their shapes.

Such rules are called rules of *syntax* (as opposed to rules of *semantics*, which you need to interpret a string as meaning something). The beauty of it is that we could train someone to do long division, for example, completely mechanically, using a set of rules and tables, without his knowing that the symbols he was writing down represented numbers or anything at all; but if he followed the syntactic rules, he would come up with what we (but not he) could read as the answer.[10]

The second part of the explanation is that there are, besides writing on paper, different ways of encoding arithmetic in a set of symbols and syntactic rules, and, for some of those ways, it is possible to design physical machines to carry out mechanically all the steps in juggling the symbols that the rules prescribe. Instead of a person following the syntactic rules mechanically without knowing what the symbols mean, a physical mechanism can carry out the same operations on the symbols automatically. But note, not only does this mechanism not know what the symbols mean, it doesn't even know, as our semantically deprived scribe did, that it is following rules for their manipulation, syntactic rules. It doesn't know anything—in fact, it isn't following rules at all, but is just functioning in accordance with the laws of physics, in ways that clever engineers have designed to permit us to interpret the results both syntactically and semantically.

Searle's well-known "Chinese room" argument described a conscious person who, without knowing Chinese, follows rules for manipulating Chinese characters and puts together sentences intelligible to people who know Chinese. The point being made against the computer model of mind was that syntax alone can't yield semantics.[11] In *The Rediscovery of the Mind*, he extends the argument to show that physics alone can't yield syntax. Following rules, even purely syntactic rules, is an irreducibly men-

[9] Such a procedure is called an "algorithm."
[10] The general theory of this type of computability was developed by Alan Turing.
[11] See his "Minds, Brains, and Programs."

tal process—an "intentional" process in which the meaning of the rules themselves must be grasped by a conscious mind. It is not just a matter of regularity in physical behavior:

> A physical state of a system is a computational state only relative to the assignment to that state of some computational role, function, or interpretation . . . *notions such as computation, algorithm, and program do not name intrinsic physical features of systems:* Computational states are not *discovered* within the physics, they are *assigned to* the physics. . . .
>
> *The aim of natural science is to discover and characterize features that are intrinsic to the natural world. By its own definitions of computation and cognition, there is no way that computational cognitive science could ever be a natural science, because computation is not an intrinsic feature of the world. It is assigned relative to observers.* (pp. 210, 212; italics in original)

Searle's distinction between what is intrinsic to the thing observed and what is relative to an observer or interpreter is a fundamental one. He argues that intrinsic intentionality—that is, the capacity for grasping the meaning of statements and consciously following rules—occurs only in minds. Words on a page or electrical resistances in a computer chip can be said to mean something, or to obey rules of grammar or arithmetic, only in the derivative sense that our minds can interpret them that way, in virtue of their arrangement. This means that the claim that the brain is a computer would imply that the brain has intentionality and follows rules of computation not intrinsically but only relative to the interpretation of its user. And who is the user supposed to be? If the brain is a computer, it does not have intrinsic intentionality. If it has intrinsic intentionality, it must be more than a computer. Searle chooses the second alternative. He also argues that those theories which try to construe the brain as a computer always surreptitiously assume a mind or "homunculus" as its interpreter.

There is a lot more to this argument, and though I find its negative conclusions persuasive, questions I have not touched on could be raised about Searle's positive theory of intrinsic intentionality, which is meant to be consistent with his biological naturalism. As with consciousness, it remains extremely difficult to see how intrinsic intentionality could be a property of the physical organism. But instead of pursuing these questions here, I will turn to Searle's views about the unconscious and its relation to consciousness, for these serve to bring together the two parts of the argument.

Searle has put great weight on the claim that subjective consciousness is not reducible to anything else. But most of our mental states are not conscious. Take all the beliefs and hopes and intentions you may have but are not thinking about right now—the belief that there's a leaning tower in Pisa, for example. It just became conscious, but you've probably believed it for years. If such beliefs can exist unconsciously, then consciousness is not an essential feature of mental life, and it must be possible for intentional mental states to be embodied in a purely material brain. So it could be argued that even for those mental states which are conscious, their subjective, experienced character is not essential for their intentionality. Perhaps consciousness is just a kind of subjective "tint" that sometimes gets added to the truly functional black and white of mental states so that a theory of mind could dismiss consciousness as inessential.

Here is Searle's reply to the suggestion:

> We understand the notion of an unconscious mental state only as a possible content of consciousness, only as the sort of thing that, though not conscious, and perhaps impossible to bring to consciousness for various reasons [such as repression], is nonetheless the *sort of thing* that could be or could have been conscious. (p. 156)

He calls this the "connection principle"; his argument for it is that even unconscious mental states must have a distinctively subjective character to qualify as beliefs, thoughts, desires, and so on. To be about anything, and therefore true or false, right or wrong, a state must belong at least potentially to the point of view of some subject. Searle acknowledges that it was a neurophysiological state of your brain that made it true two hours ago that you believed that there was a leaning tower in Pisa, but he argues that neurophysiology alone cannot qualify that state as a belief, because no physiological description by itself implies that the brain state has any intentionality or meaning at all—even if we add to the description on account of the physical behavior it might cause. His conclusion is that neurophysiological states can be assigned intentionality only derivatively, in virtue of the conscious states they are capable of producing: "The ontology of the unconscious consists in objective features of the brain capable of causing subjective conscious thoughts." This has the surprising consequence that a deep, allegedly psychological mechanism like Chomsky's Language Acquisition Device, which allows a child to learn the grammar of a language on the basis of the samples of speech it encounters at an early age, is not a set of unconscious mental rules at all, but simply a physical mechanism—for it is incapable of giving rise to subjective conscious thought whose content consists of those rules themselves. So in Searle's view, the child's conformity to the rules in learning language is not an example of intrinsic intentionality, but only intentionality assigned by the linguist-observer.

In sum, consciousness is the essence of the mental, even if most mental states are not conscious at any given time. One cannot study any aspect of mental experience without including it or its possibility in the definition of what one is trying to understand. In particular, intentionality is inseparable from it.

The Rediscovery of the Mind is trenchant, aggressive, and beautifully clear, in Searle's best "What is all this nonsense?" style. It is a valuable antidote to one of the dominant illusions of our age.

II

ETHICS AND POLITICAL
PHILOSOPHY

11

Aristotle on *Eudaimonia*

This derives from a reply to a paper by John M. Cooper, "Intellectualism and Practical Reasoning in Aristotle's Moral Philosophy," presented at a meeting of the Society for Ancient Greek Philosophy, December 28, 1969. His paper wasn't published, but some of the material appeared later in his book, Reason and Human Good in Aristotle *(Harvard University Press, 1975).*

The *Nicomachean Ethics* exhibits indecision between two accounts of *eudaimonia*—a comprehensive and an intellectualist account. According to the intellectualist account, stated in Book 10, Chapter 7, *eudaimonia* is realized in the activity of the most divine part of man, functioning in accordance with its proper excellence. This is the activity of theoretical contemplation. According to the comprehensive account (described as "secondary" at 1178 a 9), *eudaimonia* essentially involves not just the activity of the theoretical intellect, but the full range of human life and action, in accordance with the broader excellences of moral virtue and practical wisdom. This view connects *eudaimonia* with the conception of human nature as composite, that is, as involving the interaction of reason, emotion, perception, and action in an ensouled body.

The *Eudemian Ethics* exhibits a similar indecision, less elaborately expressed. Most of the work expounds a comprehensive account, but the following passage appears at its close:

Reprinted with permission from *Phronesis* 17 (1972).

Therefore whatever mode of choosing and of acquiring things good by nature—whether goods of body or wealth or friends or the other goods—will best promote the contemplation of God, that is the best mode, and that standard is the finest; and any mode of choice and acquisition that either through deficiency or excess hinders us from serving and from contemplating God— that is a bad one. This is how it is for the soul, and this is the soul's best standard—to be as far as possible unconscious of the irrational part of the soul, as such. (1249 b 17–24)

Although this passage is admittedly somewhat isolated, it seems to support the conclusion that Aristotle was tempted by an intellectualist (or perhaps spirtualist) account of the ends of life in the *Eudemian Ethics*. In fact, considering the emphasis on the divine element in our nature at the end of the *Nicomachean Ethics* (1178 b 7–33), it does not seem out of line to bring God into the matter at the end of the *Eudemian*. "Intellectualist" may be rather too dry a term for the almost Augustinian sentiments that can be detected in both works.

Since the philosophical issue between these two positions arises in virtue of the ambivalence of the *Nicomachean Ethics* alone, I shall discuss it largely in that setting. I shall also comment on its relation to the psychology of the *De Anima*. There is a connection between intellectualist tendencies in the *Ethics* and Aristotle's view of the relation between *nous* and the rest of the soul. But the latter view appears to me to contain as much indecision as the former. It is because he is not sure who we are that Aristotle finds it difficult to say unequivocally in what our *eudaimonia* consists, and how the line is to be drawn between its constituents and its necessary conditions. Moreover, I shall argue that intellectualism has strong defenses even without a two-substance theory of human beings.

Aristotle's program is compactly set out in *Nicomachean Ethics* Book 1, Chapter 7, beginning at 1097 b 22. If we are not to stop with the truism that the supreme human good is *eudaimonia*, we must inquire into the *ergon* of man, since if something has an *ergon*, that thing's good is a function of its *ergon*. The *ergon* of a thing, in general, is what it does that makes it what it is. Not everything has an *ergon*, for there are things to be which is not to do anything. But when something has an *ergon*, that thing's good is specified by it. The proper *ergon* of man, by which human excellence is measured, is that which makes him a man rather than anything else. Humans do a great many things, but since some are done equally well, or better, by plants, fish, and animals, they are not among the things to do which is to be human.

This lands us immediately in difficulty, for the inference seems unsound. If the feature of life unique to humans could exist in the absence of those features that humans share with the beasts, the result would be not a human being but something else. And why should we take the highest good of a rarefied individual like that as the ultimate end for complicated and messy individuals like ourselves? One would expect at the very least that the *interaction* between the function that differentiates us from animals, and the functions that we share with them, would play a role in the definition of *eudaimonia*. This would mean including the *practical* exercise of the rational faculty as well as the contemplative.

Suppose we pursue this line of criticism further, however, by asking whether we should not demand the inclusion of still more functions in the definition of human *ergon* and hence of human good. What about health, for example, or fertility? It will be objected that these fail to meet an essential condition for inclusion: the condition of autonomy.[1] This condition states that the fundamental elements of human good cannot be due simply to luck. And health, for example, can be the result of sheer good fortune, rather than a man's own efforts.

But the basis of this objection must be examined. It stems, presumably, from the condition that good is tied to *ergon* or functioning, and what simply *befalls* a thing, whether that thing be a man or a plant, is not an instance of its functioning or malfunctioning. Therefore, if I contract cholera, the intrusion of the hostile bacilli is a calamity, but not a malfunction of mine, hence not to be weighed in counting me *eudaimon* or not. Its *effect* on me, however, is certainly a malfunction. And why should this purely physical malfunction not be *in itself* a deviation from my human well-being (rather than just because of its deleterious effects on the life of reason)? If it is excluded on the ground that sweating, throwing up, and shuddering with fever are not things that *I do*, then the question has been begged. For the issue is precisely whether the account of what a person is and does should include or exclude the bodily functions that he shares with animals and even plants. If digesting, for instance, is something a clam does, why is it not something a human does as well—and something to do which is part of being human, even though it does not require *effort*?

In neither the *De Anima* nor the *Nicomachean Ethics* is the nutritive element excluded from the human soul, yet it is not one of the aspects of human functioning that Aristotle is willing to regard as a measure of *eudaimonia*. This position has considerable intuitive appeal. If we could see why nutrition is assigned such a low status, we might have a clue to the train of thought that tempts Aristotle to pare away everything except

[1] Cooper points out the importance of this condition. His paper cites three textual statements of it: *EE* 1215 a 12–19, *NE* 1099 b 18–25, and most explicitly *Politics* 1323 b 24–29.

the intellect, till the only thing that intrinsically bears on *eudaimonia* is the quality of contemplative activity.[2]

Let me introduce a homely example. A combination corkscrew and bottle-opener has the function of removing corks and caps from bottles. This is a simple *ergon,* which allows us to evaluate the implement in terms of its capacity for successful performance. However, it does not seem simple enough to escape the question Aristotle has raised. It removes bottle caps, to be sure. But since it has that function in common with any mere bottle opener, *that* cannot be the special *ergon* (*to idion*) of our implement—the *ergon* by which its excellence is judged. So, by elimination, *to idion* must be removing corks. Unfortunately, that is a capacity it shares with mere corkscrews, so that can't be part of its special *ergon* either. Obviously this argument is no good. The thing must have a simple conjunctive *ergon,* and its excellence is a function of both conjuncts.

Why won't such a reduction work for the case of the human soul and *eudaimonia?* We have dispensed with digestion and procreation on the ground that clams do them too. Sensation and desire are common to dogs. So we are left with reason. But the gods have reason without having these other capacities, so *that* isn't the peculiar *ergon* of man, either. Therefore, we must abandon this method of arguing by elimination, and acknowledge that man has a conjunctive *ergon* that overlaps the *erga* of gods and dogs, as a combination corkscrew and bottle opener combines the functions of corkscrews and bottle openers. They just happen to find themselves in the same *ergon* box.

If this argument were correct, it would support not just a comprehensive position extending to nonintellectual areas of consciousness and activity, but the inclusion of all the lower life functions in the measure of

[2] This conclusion would require explanation even if a two-substance reading of the *Ethics* were correct. That is, even if the psychology of the *Nicomachean Ethics* included a soul composed of both a form or primary actuality of the body and a pure intellect that was distinct from this, we would still have to ask why the proper function of the hylomorphic section was not counted in the assessment of *eudaimonia*. And I suspect that any account that made sense of the restriction in light of the two-substance theory, could be applied with equal success to justify corresponding restrictions on what counts toward *eudaimonia* on a purely hylomorphic theory of persons, where *nous,* instead of being another soul, was just the highest type of first-order actuality in the complex— distinguishable only in thought from the other parts of the soul, and not really *distinct* from them. That Aristotle shares this view is shown by a parenthetical remark in *NE* Bk. 1, Ch. 13, where he is considering which part of the soul possesses the excellence that is to be identified with *eudaimonia*. "Whether these two parts are really distinct in the sense that the parts of the body or of any other divisible whole are distinct, or whether though distinguishable in thought as two they are inseparable in reality, like the convex and concave sides of a curve, is a question of no importance for the matter in hand" (1102 a 30–34).

human excellence. But in fact the conjunctive picture of the component capacities of the human soul is absurd, and if we can say why it is absurd, we may be able to understand why Aristotle accords to reason the title of *ergon idion* of man, despite the fact that it, like digestion, might be shared by other beings as well.

The operative idea is evidently that of a hierarchy of capacities. The life capacities of a complex organism are not all on a level: some serve to support others. This is not so easy to account for clearly. Take, for example, the prima facie subservience of nutrition to perception and locomotion. That might be a ground for denying that nutrition was part of the special *ergon* of a higher animal. But perception and locomotion, for example, in a giraffe, largely serve the ends of nutrition and reproduction, so the case is unclear. What is the point of being a giraffe? A giraffe leads a certain type of active life, supported by complex metabolic, digestive, and circulatory processes, and ordered in such a way as to permit those processes to proceed efficiently. One thing is clear: its walking and seeing and digesting are not simply three separate activities going on side by side in the same individual, like a doll that wets, cries, and closes its eyes. A giraffe is one organism, and its functions are coherently organized. Its proper excellence is not just the conjunction of the special excellences of its component functions, but the optimal functioning of the total system in the giraffe's *life*. And the highest level account of this will be concerned not with blood pressure and peristalsis but with activity—some of which, admittedly, helps to control blood pressure and provide material for peristalsis.

The main difference between a human being and a giraffe is that a human being has reason, and that his entire complex of organic functions supports rational as well as irrational activity. There is, of course, feedback as well: in humans, not only perception and locomotion, but also reason, are employed in the service of nutrition and reproduction. Reason is also involved in the control of perception, locomotion, and desire. Nevertheless, the highest level account of a human life puts all the other functions into a supportive position in relation to rational activity. And although reason helps us to get enough to eat and move around, it is not subservient to those lower functions. Occasionally, it may have to serve as the janitor or pimp of the passions, but that is not basically what it is *for*. On one plausible view, reason, despite its continual service to the lower functions, is what human life is all about. The lower functions serve it, provide it with a setting, and are to some extent under its control, but the dominant characterization of a human being must refer to his reason. This is why intellectualism tempts Aristotle, and why a conjunctive position, which lets various other aspects of life into the measure of good, is less plausible.

Neither a conjunctive nor a disjunctive view about *eudaimonia* is adequate to these facts. The supreme good for man must be measured in terms of that around which all other human functions are organized.

But at this point it is essential to recall that much of the practical employment of reason is in the service of lower functions. Is this a proper exercise of that faculty, or does it have a point beyond the uses of cleverness, prudence, and courage, beyond the rational calculation of the most sensible way to spend one's time and money, or to organize society? This question prompts Aristotle to pass from the vague characterization that human life, as opposed to other life, is rational, to a consideration of the *objects* best suited for the exercise of this capacity. This is a peculiar question, which did not arise about giraffes. The nonrational activity of giraffes and its feedback on the metabolic functions seems at first sight a perfectly satisfactory model, and we might be tempted to apply it to humans. Why can't we reach a parallel account of proper human functioning by just adding reason to the top of the class of capacities that cooperate in an organized fashion to further the life of the individual? Why should there be any doubt that the use of reason to earn a living or procure food should belong to the central function of man?

The answer is as follows: Human possibilities reveal that reason has a use beyond the ordering of practical life. The circle of mutual support between reason, activity, and nutrition is not completely closed. In fact, all of it, including the practical employment of reason, serves to support the individual for an activity that completely transcends these worldly concerns. The model of feedback does not work for the *ergon* of humans, because the best and purest employment of reason has nothing to do with daily life. Aristotle believes, in short, that human life is not important enough for humans to spend their lives on. A person should seek to transcend not only his individual practical concerns but also those of society or humanity as a whole.

In *Nicomachean Ethics*, Book 6, Chapter 7, while arguing that *sophia* is the highest type of knowledge, and knowledge of the highest objects, he says (1141 a 21–23): "For it is absurd to think that Political Science or Prudence is the loftiest kind of knowledge, inasmuch as man is not the highest thing in the universe." Theoretical and practical matters must compete for the attention of the rational faculty, and the capacity that enables humans to concentrate on subjects more elevated than themselves at the same time spoils them for lowlier concerns. The imperfection of applications of reason to practical matters is that these applications make human life the primary object of rational attention, whereas with reason man has become the only creature capable of concentrating on what is higher than himself and thereby sharing in it to some extent. His time is, so to speak, too valuable to waste on anything so insignificant as human life.

This does not mean that there is no distinction between excellence and depravity in the practical domain. It is certainly better to exercise reason well in providing for one's needs and in dealing with others, that is, to have moral virtue—than to exercise it badly. But this is essentially a caretaker function of reason, in which it is occupied with matters—that is, the sordid details of the life of a complex person—far below those it might be considering if it had more time and were less called upon merely to *manage*.

It is this point of view, I believe, that dominates chapters 7 and 8 of Book 10, where the intellectualist account of *eudaimonia* receives its strongest endorsement. Even there the possibility of doubt is acknowledged. Aristotle appears uncertain whether the result is to be described as a strictly human good. Having argued the claims of the contemplative life on a variety of grounds, he breaks in at 1177 b 27 with the remark that such a life would be higher than human. It is achieved not in virtue simply of being a man, but in virtue of something divine of which men partake. Nevertheless, this divine element, which gives us the capacity to think about things higher than ourselves, is the highest aspect of our souls, and we are not justified in forgoing its activities to concentrate on lowlier matters—our own lives—unless the demands in the latter area threaten to make contemplation impossible. As he says at 1177 b 33, we should not listen to those who urge that a human should think human thoughts and a mortal, mortal ones. Rather, we should cultivate that portion of our nature that promises to transcend the rest. If anyone insists that the rest belongs to a complete account of human life, then the view might be put, somewhat paradoxically, by saying that comprehensive human good isn't everything, and should not be the main human goal. We must identify with the highest part of ourselves rather than with the whole. The other functions, including the practical employment of reason itself, provide support for the highest form of activity, but do not enter into our proper excellence as primary component factors. This is because men are not simply the most complex species of animal, but possess as their essential nature a capacity to transcend themselves and become like gods. It is in virtue of this capacity that they are capable of *eudaimonia*, whereas animals are incapable of it, children have not achieved it, and certain adults, such as slaves, are prevented from reaching it.

Perhaps this is an unsatisfactory view of human nature and hence an unsatisfactory view of what it is for a human being to flourish. I believe it is a compelling position, however, and one that does not have to depend on a denial of the hylomorphic doctrine of the soul. It might be challenged in either of two ways. One might simply deny that the *ergon* of man is single, and allege that it is a collection of sub-*erga* without orderings of priority and support—like those of a many-bladed knife. This leaves us uncertain how to draw the line against good digestion as a component of *eudaimonia* (rather than just as a contribution to it). A second method would be to preserve the assumption that the *ergon* of man is one, but to offer a different account of its organization, according to which the highest level specification of human capacities was not just intellectual but involved both theoretical and practical concerns. While this seems to me the most promising line of attack, I shall not pursue it here.

12

Rawls on Justice

This was a review of John Rawls's A Theory of Justice *(Harvard University Press, 1971). Its most conspicuous criticism, that the argument for the two principles of justice must presuppose a liberal conception of the good rather than being based solely on an independent conception of the right, has been put forward by others and has been the subject of extensive discussion by Rawls's defenders and critics, as well as by Rawls himself. (See, for example, his recent book,* Political Liberalism *[Columbia University Press, 1993].) I myself have come around to the view that there is a defense of liberalism that does not depend on a liberal conception of human well-being and that can be accepted by those with other conceptions of the good. The idea is one of Rawls's most significant contributions, but this is clearly an ongoing argument. Rawls's position as the personification of philosophical liberalism ensures that he will continue to be a target of attack, for the political tolerance that is at the heart of liberalism earns the hostility of all those who want to use public coercive power in the service of their own deepest convictions about the ends of life and who therefore object to the restraint that liberalism requires.*

I am still skeptical about the cogency of the hypothetical contract method of justification—though it has undeniable appeal as an attempt to provide a distinctive model of impartiality that corresponds to the moral sentiment of fairness. The original position is supposed to get us to put ourselves fully in everyone's place, rather than merely imagining that we have an equal probability of being anyone. This thought experiment does seem to push us away

---

First published in *The Philosophical Review* 82 (1973).

from the sorts of interpersonal trade-offs that lead to utilitarianism and to encourage instead a method of pairwise comparisons based on a system of priorities among human needs—with first priority going to the most urgent, independently of the numbers of people involved. That result, whether or not it follows from the original position, seems to me to be a very important moral idea—clearly a conception of the right rather than of the good—that provides an attractive alternative to aggregative maximization as a method of settling interpersonal conflicts of interest.

The big thing I neglected in this essay was Rawls's conception of justice as fairness as a moral theory of interpersonal relations—specifically, a theory of the acceptable forms of interdependence among the lives and fates of persons engaged in a cooperative social enterprise. The moral nerve, I now think, of Rawls's conception of injustice is the idea of a benefit or loss resulting from certain unacceptable relations to others. It is an essentially causal rather than merely distributive idea. If someone gets a larger or smaller share of the goods of social cooperation, as an effect of the wrong kinds of causes—causes that are morally arbitrary and that confer no justification on their results—then he stands in a relation of unfair advantage or disadvantage to his fellow men, and he as well as the others should want things to be different for that reason. *If we have a sense of justice, we will, according to Rawls, want neither to gain nor to lose from certain kinds of relations with others, and a well-ordered society should cry to create a form of life that avoids such relations. I still find that idea more morally compelling in itself than the idea of its justification through the original position. But* A Theory of Justice *is a giant of a book; its many different lines of thought have different starting points, and if they don't all lead exactly in the same direction, that is not necessarily a defect.*

A Theory of Justice is a rich, complicated, and fundamental work. It offers an elaborate set of arguments and provides many issues for discussion. This review will focus on its contribution to the more abstract portions of ethical theory.

The book contains three elements. One is a vision of men and society as they should be. Another is a conception of moral theory. The third is a construction that attempts to derive principles expressive of the vision, in accordance with methods that reflect the conception of moral theory. In that construction Rawls has pursued the contractarian tradition in moral and political philosophy. His version of the social contract, a hypothetical choice situation called the original position, was first presented in 1958 and is here developed in great and explicit detail. The aim is to provide a way of treating the basic problems of social choice, for which no generally recognized methods of precise solution exist, through the proxy of a specially constructed parallel problem of individual choice, which can be solved by the more reliable intuitions and decision procedures of rational prudence.

If this enterprise is to succeed, and the solution to the clearer prudential problem is to be accepted as a solution to the more obscure moral one, then the alleged correspondence between the two problems must bear a great deal of weight. Critics of the theory have tended to take issue with Rawls over what principles would be chosen in the original position, but it is also neccessary to examine those features of the position that are thought to support the most controversial choices and to ask why the results of a decision taken under these highly specific and rather peculiar conditions should confirm the justice of the principles chosen. This doctrine of correspondence is both fundamental and obscure, and its defense is not easy to extract from the book. A proper treatment of the subject will have to cover considerable ground, and it is probably best to begin with Rawls's moral epistemology.

Rawls believes that it will be more profitable to investigate the foundations of ethics when there are more substantive ethical results to seek the foundations of. Nevertheless, in Section 9 he expounds a general position that helps to explain his method of proceeding. Ethics, he says, cannot be derived from self-evident axioms or from definitions, but must be developed, like any other scientific subject, through the constant interaction between theoretical construction and particular observation. In this case, the particular observations are not experiments but substantive moral judgments. It is a bit like linguistics: ethics explores our moral sense as grammar explores our linguistic competence.[1]

Intuitionism attempts to capture the moral sense by summarizing our particular moral intuitions in principles of maximum generality, relying on further intuitions to settle conflicts among those principles. This is not what Rawls means. He intends rather that the underlying principles should possess intuitive moral plausibility of their own and that the total theory should not merely summarize but illuminate and make plausible the particular judgments that it explains. Moreover, its intrinsic plausibility may persuade us to modify or extend our intuitions, thereby

---

[1] This seems to me a false analogy, because the intuitions of native speakers are decisive as regards grammar. Whatever native speakers agree on is English, but whatever ordinary men agree in condemning is not necessarily wrong. Therefore, the intrinsic plausibility of an ethical theory can impel a change in our moral intuitions. Nothing corresponds to this in linguistics (*pace* Rawls's suggestion on p. 49), where the final test of a theory is its ability to explain the data.

achieving greater theoretical coherence. Our knowledge of contingent facts about human nature and society will play a substantial part in the process.

When this interplay between general and particular has produced a relatively stable outcome, and no immediate improvements on either level suggest themselves, then our judgments are said to be in a state of *reflective equilibrium*. Its name implies that the state is always subject to change, and that our current best approximation to the truth will eventually be superseded. The indefinite article in Rawls's title is significant: he believes that all present moral theories "are primitive and have grave defects" (p. 52). His own results are provisional. "I doubt," he says (p. 581), "that the principles of justice (as I have defined them) will be the preferred conception on anything resembling a complete list."

If the principles and judgments of a theory are controversial and do not command immediate intuitive assent, then the support they receive from the underlying moral conception assumes special importance. To a certain extent that conception may reveal itself directly in the basic principles of the theory, but it is more clearly visible when the theory contains a model or construction that accounts for the principles and for their relation to one another. Alternative theories of justice are intuitively represented by different models (utilitarianism, for example, by the impartial sympathetic observer). Rawls's model is the original position, and the principles it is used to support are controversial. To enhance their appeal, the construction must express an intuitive idea that has independent plausibility. Before turning to the model itself, it will be useful to review briefly the substantive conclusions of the theory, identifying their controversial elements and thus the respects in which they are most in need of independent support.

Rawls's substantive doctrine is a rather pure form of egalitarian liberalism, whose controversial elements are its egalitarianism, its antiperfectionism and antimeritocracy, the primacy it gives to liberty, and the fact that it is more egalitarian about liberty than about other goods. The justice of social institutions is measured not by their tendency to maximize the sum or average of certain advantages, but by their tendency to counteract the natural inequalities deriving from birth, talent, and circumstance, pooling those resources in the service of the common good. The common good is measured in terms of a very restricted, basic set of benefits to individuals: personal and political liberty, economic and social advantages, and self-respect.

The justice of institutions depends on their conformity to two principles. The first requires the greatest equal liberty compatible with a like liberty for all. The second (the difference principle) permits only those inequalities in the distribution of primary economic and social advantages that benefit everyone, in particular the worst off. Liberty is prior in the sense that it cannot be sacrificed for economic and social advantages, unless they are so scarce or unequal as to prevent the meaningful exercise of equal liberty until material conditions have improved.

The view is firmly opposed to mere equality of opportunity, which allows too much influence to the morally irrelevant contingencies of birth and talent; it is also opposed to counting a society's advanced cultural or intellectual achievements among the gains that can make sacrifice of the more primary goods just. What matters is that everyone be provided with the basic conditions for the realization of his own aims, regardless of the absolute level of achievement that may represent.

When the social and political implications of this view are worked out in detail, as is done in Part Two of the book, it is extremely appealing, but far from self-evident. In considering its theoretical basis, one should therefore ask whether the contractarian approach, realized in terms of the original position, depends on assumptions any less controversial than the substantive conclusions it is adduced to support.

The notion that a contract is the appropriate model for a theory of social justice depends on the view that it is fair to require people to submit to procedures and institutions only if, given the opportunity, they could in some sense have agreed in advance on the principles to which they must submit. That is why Rawls calls the theory "justice as fairness." (Indeed, he believes that a similar contractual basis can be found for the principles of individual morality, yielding a theory of rightness as fairness.) The fundamental attitude toward persons on which justice as fairness depends is a respect for their autonomy or freedom.[2] Since social institutions are simply there and people are born into them, submission cannot be literally voluntary, but "a society satisfying the principles of justice as fairness comes as close as a society can to being a voluntary scheme, for it meets the

[2] Expanding on this point, Rawls submits that his view is susceptible to a Kantian interpretation, but the details of the analogy are not always convincing. See, for example, the claim on page 253 that the principles of justice are categorical imperatives because the argument for them does not assume that the parties to the agreement have particular ends, but only that they desire those primary goods that it is rational to want whatever else one wants. First of all, the desire for those primary goods is not itself the motive for obeying the principles of justice in real life, but only for choosing them in the original position. Second, imperatives deriving from such a desire would be hypothetical and assertoric in Kant's system, not categorical. But since our adherence to the two principles is supposed to be motivated by a sense of justice growing out of gratitude for the benefits received from just institutions, the imperatives of justice as fairness would in fact appear to be hypothetical and problematic (*Foundation of the Metaphysics of Morals,* pp.415–46 of the Prussian Academy Edition).

principles which free and equal persons would assent to under the circumstances that are fair" (p. 13).

Before considering whether the original position embodies these conditions, we must ask why respect for the freedom of others and the desire to make society as near to voluntary as possible should be taken as the mainspring of the sense of justice. That gives liberty a position of great importance from the very beginning, an importance that it retains in the resulting substantive theory. But we must ask how the respect for autonomy by itself can be expected to yield further results as well.

When one justifies a policy on the ground that the affected parties would have (or even have) agreed to it, much depends on the reasons for their agreement. If it is motivated by ignorance or fear or helplessness or a defective sense of what is reasonable, then actual or possible prior agreement does not sanction anything. In other cases, prior agreement for the right reasons can be obtained or presumed, but it is not the agreement that justifies what has been agreed to, but rather whatever justifies the agreement itself. If, for example, certain principles would be agreed to because they are just, that cannot be what makes them just. In many cases the appeal to hypothetical prior agreement is actually of this character. It is not a final justification, not a mark of respect for autonomy, but merely a way of recalling someone to the kind of *moral* judgment he would make in the absence of distorting influences derived from his special situation.

Actual or presumable consent can be the *source* of a justification only if it is already accepted that the affected parties are to be treated as certain reasons would incline each of them to want to be treated. The circumstances of consent are designed to bring those reasons into operation, supressing irrelevant considerations, and the fact that the choice would have been made becomes a further reason for adhering to the result.

When the interests of the parties do not naturally coincide, a version of consent may still be preserved if they are able to agree in advance on a procedure for settling conflicts. They may agree unanimously that the procedure treats them equally in relevant respects, though they would not be able to agree in advance to any of the particular distributions of advantages that it might yield. (An example would be a lottery to determine the recipient of some indivisible benefit.)

For the result of such a choice to be morally acceptable, two things must be true: (*a*) the choice must be unanimous; (*b*) the circumstances that make unanimity possible must not undermine the equality of the parties in other respects. Presumably they must be deprived of some knowledge (for example, of who will win the lottery) in order to reach agreement, but it is essential that they not be unequally deprived (as would be the case, for example, if they agreed to submit a dispute to an arbitrator who, unknown to any of them, was extremely biased).

The more disparate the conflicting interests to be balanced, however, the more information the parties must be deprived of to ensure unanimity, and doubts begin to arise whether any procedure can be relied on to treat everyone equally in respect of the relevant interests. There is then a real question whether hypothetical choice under conditions of ignorance, as a representation of consent, can by itself provide a moral justification for outcomes that could not be unanimously agreed to if they were known in advance.

Can such a procedure be used to justify principles for evaluating the basic structure of social insitutions? Clearly the preferences of individuals are so divergent that they would not voluntarily agree on a common set of principles if all were given an equal voice. According to the theory of the original position, the appeal to prior agreement can be utilized nevertheless, by requiring the hypothetical choice to be made on the basis of reasons that all men have in common, omitting those that would lead them to select different principles and institutions. By restricting the basis of the hypothetical agreement in this way, however, one may lose some of its justifying power. We must therefore look carefully at the conditions imposed on a choice in the original position. Since Rawls does not, in any case, offer an abstract argument for the contractarian approach, its defense must be found in its application.

The original position is supposed to be the most philosophically favored interpretation of a hypothetical initial status quo in which fundamental agreements would be fair. The agreements can then be appealed to in disputes over the justice of institutions. The parties have an equal voice and they choose freely; in fact, they can all arrive independently at the same conclusions. Each of us, moreover, can enter the original position at any time simply by observing its rather special restrictions on arguments and choosing principles from that point of view.

All this is possible because the grounds of choice are severely restricted as follows: The parties are mutually disinterested—that is, neither altruistic nor envious. About their own desires they know only what is true of everyone: that they have some life plan or conception of the good and a personal commitment to certain other individuals. Whatever the details, they know these interests can be advanced by the employment of very basic primary goods under conditions of liberty. They also possess general knowledge about economics, politics, and sociology, and they know that the circumstances of justice, conflicting interests and moderate scarcity obtain. Finally, they believe that they have a sense of justice that will help them to adhere to the principles selected, but they know enough about moral psychology to realize that their choices must take into account the strains of commitment that will be felt when the principles are actually adopted, and the importance of choosing principles that will, when put into application, evoke their own support and thereby acquire psychological stability. Everything else—their talents, their social position, even the general nature or stage of development of their particular society—is covered over with a thick veil of ignorance on the ground that it is morally irrelevant. The choice should not be influenced by social and natural contingencies that would lead some parties to press for special advantages or give some of them special bargaining power.

Rawls contends that these restrictions "collect together into one conception a number of conditions on principles that we are ready upon due consideration to recognize as reasonable" (p. 21). "One argues," he says, "from widely accepted but weak premises to more specific conclusions. Each of the presumptions should by itself be natural and plausible; some of them may seem innocuous or even trivial. The aim of the contract approach is to establish that taken together they impose significant bounds on acceptable principles of justice" (p. 18).

I do not believe that the assumptions of the original position are weak or innocuous or uncontroversial. In fact, the situation thus constructed may not be fair. Rawls says that the aim of the veil of ignorance is "to rule out those principles that it would be rational to propose for acceptance, however little the chance of success, only if one knew certain things that are irrelevant from the standpoint of justice" (p. 18). Let us grant that the parties should be equal and should not be in possession of information that would lead them to seek advantages on morally irrelevant grounds like race, sex, parentage, or natural endowments. But they are deprived also of knowledge of their particular conception of the good. It seems odd to regard that as morally irrelevant from the standpoint of justice. If someone favors certain principles because of his conception of the good, he will not be seeking special advantages for himself so long as he does not know who in the society he is. Rather, he will be opting for principles that advance the good for everyone, as defined by that conception. (I assume a conception of the good is just that, and not simply a system of tastes or preferences.) Yet Rawls appears to believe that it would be as unfair to permit people to press for the realization of their conceptions of the good as to permit them to press for the advantage of their social class.

It is true that men's different conceptions of the good divide them and produce conflict, so allowing this knowledge to the parties in the original position would prevent unanimity. Rawls concludes that the information must be suppressed and a common idea substituted that will permit agreement without selecting any particular conception of the good. This is achieved by means of the class of primary goods that it is supposedly rational to want whatever else one wants. Another possible conclusion, however, is that the model of the original position will not work because in order to secure spontaneous unanimity and avoid the necessity of bargaining one must suppress information that is morally relevant, and moreover suppress it in a way that does not treat the parties equally.

What Rawls wishes to do, by using the notion of primary goods, is to provide an Archimedean point, as he calls it, from which choice is possible without unfairness to any of the fuller conceptions of the good that lead people to differ. A *theory* of the good is presupposed, but it is ostensibly neutral between divergent particular conceptions and supplies a least common denominator on which a choice in the original position can be based without unfairness to any of the parties. Only later, when the principles of justice have been reached on this basis, will it be possible to rule out certain particular interests or aims as illegitimate because they are unjust. It is a fundamental feature of Rawls's conception of the fairness of the original position that it should not permit the choice of principles of justice to depend on a particular conception of the good over which the parties may differ.

The construction does not, I think, accomplish this, and there are reasons to believe that it cannot be successfully carried out. Any hypothetical choice situation that requires agreement among the parties will have to impose strong restrictions on the grounds of choice, and these restrictions can be justified only in terms of a conception of the good. It is one of those cases in which there is no neutrality to be had, because neutrality needs as much justification as any other position.

Rawls's minimal conception of the good does not amount to a weak assumption: it depends on a strong assumption of the sufficiency of that reduced conception for the purposes of justice. The refusal to rank particular conceptions of the good implies a very marked tolerance for individual inclinations. Rawls is opposed not only to teleological conceptions according to which justice requires adherence to the principles that will maximize the good. He is also opposed to the natural position that even in a nonteleological theory what is just must depend on what is good, at least to the extent that a correct conception of the good must be used in determining what counts as an advantage and what as a disadvantage, and how much, for purposes of distribution and compensation. I interpret him as saying that the principles of justice are objective and interpersonally recognizable in a way that conceptions of the good are not. The refusal to rank individual conceptions and the reliance on primary goods are intended to ensure this objectivity.

Objectivity may not be so easily achieved.[3] The suppression of knowledge required to achieve unanimity is not equally fair to all the parties because the primary goods are not equally valuable in pursuit of all conceptions of the good. They will serve to advance many individual life plans (some more efficiently than others), but they are less useful in implementing views that hold a good life to be readily achievable only in certain well-defined types of social structure, or only in a society that works concertedly for the realization of certain higher human capacities and the suppression of baser ones, or only given certain types of economic relations among men. The model contains a strong individualistic bias, which is further strengthened by the motivational assumptions of mutual disinterest and absence of envy. These assumptions have the effect of discounting the claims of conceptions of the good that depend heavily on the relation between one's own position and that of others (though Rawls is prepared to allow such considerations to enter insofar as they affect self-esteem). The original position seems to presuppose not just a neutral theory of the good, but a liberal, individualistic conception, according to which the best that can be wished for someone is the unimpeded pursuit of his own path, provided it does not interfere with the rights of others. The view is persuasively developed in the later portions of the book, but without a sense of its controversial character.

Among different life plans of this general type the construction is neutral. But given that many conceptions of the good do not fit into the individualistic pattern, how can this be described as a fair choice situation for principles of justice? Why should parties in the original position be prepared to commit themselves to principles that may frustrate or contravene their deepest convictions, just because they are deprived of the knowledge of those convictions?

There does not seem to be any way of redesigning the original position to do away with a restrictive assumption of this kind. One might think it would be an improvement to allow the parties full information about everyone's preferences and conception of the good, merely depriving them of the knowledge of who they were. But this, as Rawls points out (pp. 173–74), would yield no result at all. For either the parties would retain their conceptions of the good and, choosing from different points of view, would not reach unanimity, or else they would possess no aims of their own and would be asked to choose in terms of the aims of all the people they might be—an unintelligible request which provides no basis for a unified choice, in the absence of a dominant conception. The reduction to a common ground of choice is therefore essential for the model to

[3] For the ideas in this paragraph I am indebted to Mary Gibson.

operate at all, and the selection of that ground inevitably represents a strong assumption.

Let us now turn to the argument leading to the choice of the two principles in the original position as constructed. The core of this argument appears in Sections 26–29, intertwined with an argument against the choice of the principle of average utility. Rawls has gone to some lengths to defend his controversial claim that in the original position it is rational to adopt the maximin rule, which leads one to choose principles that favor the bottom of the social hierarchy, instead of accepting a greater risk at the bottom in return for the possibility of greater benefits at the top (as might be prudentially rational if one had an equal chance of being anyone in the society).

Rawls states (p. 154) that three conditions which make maximin plausible hold in the original position to a high degree. (1) "There must be some reason for sharply discounting estimates of . . . probabilities." (2) "The person choosing has a conception of the good such that he cares very little, if anything, for what he might gain above the minimum stipend that he can, in fact, be sure of by following the maximin rule." (3) "The rejected alternatives have outcomes that one can hardly accept." Let us consider these in turn.

The first condition is very important, and the claim that it holds in the original position is not based simply on a general rejection of the principle of insufficient reason (that is, the principle that where probabilities are unknown they should be regarded as equal). For one could characterize the original position in such a way that the parties would be prudentially rational to choose as if they had an equal chance of being anyone in the society, and the problem is to see why this would be an inappropriate representation of the grounds for a choice of principles.

One factor mentioned by Rawls is that the subject matter of the choice is extremely serious, since it involves institutions that will determine the total life prospects for the parties and those close to them. It is not just a choice of alternatives for a single occasion. Now this would be a reason for a conservative choice even if one knew the relative probabilities of different outcomes. It would be irresponsible to accept even a small risk of dreadful life prospects for oneself and one's descendants in exchange for a good chance of wealth or power. But what is needed is an account of why probabilities should be totally discounted, and not just with regard to the most unacceptable outcomes. The difference principle, for example, is supposed to apply at all levels of social development, so it is not justified merely by the desire to avoid grave risks. The fact that total life prospects are involved does not seem an adequate explanation. There must be some reason against allowing probabilities (proportional, for instance, to the number of persons in each social position) to enter into the choice of distributions above an acceptable minimum. Let me stress that I am posing a question not about decision theory but about the design of the original position and the comprehensiveness of the veil of ignorance. Why should it be thought that a just solution will be reached only if these considerations are suppressed?

Their suppression is justified, I think, only on the assumption that the proportions of people in various social positions are regarded as morally irrelevant, and this must be because it is not thought acceptable to sum advantages and disadvantages over persons, so that a loss for some is compensated by a gain for others. This aspect of the design of the original position appears, therefore, to be motivated by the wish to avoid extending to society as a whole the principle of rational choice for one man. Now this is supposed to be one of the *conclusions* of the contract approach, not one of its presuppositions. Yet the constraints on choice in Rawls's version of the original position are designed to rule out the possibility of such an extension,[4] by requiring that probabilities be discounted. I can see no way to avoid presupposing some definite view on this matter in the design of a contract situation. If that is true, then a contract approach cannot give any particular view very much support.

Consider next the second condition. Keeping in mind that the parties in the original position do not know the stage of development of their society, and therefore do not know what minimum will be guaranteed by a maximin strategy, it is difficult to understand how an individual can know that he "cares very little, if anything, for what he might gain above the minimum." The explanation Rawls offers (p. 156) seems weak. Even if parties in the original position accept the priority of liberty, and even if the veil of ignorance leaves them with a skeletal conception of the good, it seems impossible that they should care very little for increases in primary economic and social goods above what the difference principle guarantees at any given stage of social development.

Finally, the third condition, that one should rule out certain possibilities as unacceptable, is certainly a ground for requiring a social minimum and the priority of basic personal liberties, but it is not a ground for adopting the maximin rule in that general form needed to justify the choice of the difference principle. That must rely on stronger egalitarian premises.[5]

[4] That is, they do not just refuse to assume that the extension is acceptable: they assume that it is unacceptable.

[5] A factor not considered in Rawls's argument, which suggests that the difference principle may be too weak, is the following: If differential social and economic benefits are allowed to provide incentives, then the people at the top will tend to be those with certain talents and abilities, and the people at the bottom, even though they are better

Some of these premises reveal themselves in other parts of the argument. For example, the strongly egalitarian idea that sacrifice at the bottom is always worse than sacrifice at the top plays a central role in the appeal to strains of commitment and psychological stability. It is urged against the utilitarian alternative to the difference principle, for example, that the sacrifices utilitarianism might require would be psychologically unacceptable.

> The principles of justice apply to the basic structure of the social system and to the determination of life prospects. What the principle of utility asks is precisely a sacrifice of these prospects. We are to accept the greater advantages of others as a sufficient reason for lower expectations over the whole course of our life. This is surely an extreme demand. In fact, when society is conceived as a system of cooperation designed to advance the good of its members, it seems quite incredible that some citizens should be expected, on the basis of political principles, to accept lower prospects of life for the sake of others. (p. 178)

Notice that if we substitute the words "difference principle" for "principle of utility," we get an argument that might be offered against the difference principle by someone concentrating on the sacrifices it requires of those at the top of the social order. They must live under institutions that limit their life prospects unless an advantage to them also benefits those beneath them. The only difference between the two arguments is in the relative position of the parties and of their sacrifices.[6] It is, of course, a vital difference, but that depends on a moral judgment—namely, that sacrifices that lessen social inequality are acceptable while sacrifices that increase inequality are not.

This appeal to psychological stability and the strains of commitment therefore adds to the grounds of choice in the original position a moral

---

off than they would be otherwise, will tend to lack those qualities. Such a consistent schedule of rewards inevitably affects people's sense of their intrinsic worth, and any society operating on the difference principle will have a meritocratic flavor. This is very different from the case where an unequal distribution that benefits the worst off is not visibly correlated with any independent qualities. Rawls does suggest (p. 546) that "excusable envy" may be given its due in the operation of the difference principle by including self-esteem among the primary goods. But he does not stress the *bases* of income inequality. The phenomenon I have described is not *envy*. Rawls is too willing to rely on equal liberty as the support of self-esteem; this leads him to underrate the effect of differential rewards on people's conception of themselves. A reward that is consistently attached to a certain quality stops being perceived as mere good luck.

6 Exactly the same sacrifice could, after all, be either at the bottom or at the top, depending on the stage of advancement of the society.

view that belongs to the substantive theory. The argument may receive some support from Rawls's idea about the natural development of moral sentiments, but they in turn are not independent of his ethical theory. If a hypothetical choice in the original position must be based on what one can expect to find morally acceptable in real life, then that choice is not the true ground of acceptability.[7]

Another strong conclusion of the theory is the priority of equal liberty, expressed in the lexical ordering of the two principles. The argument for *equal* liberty as a natural goal is straightforward. No analogue of the difference principle can apply permanently to liberty because it cannot be indefinitely increased. There will come a point at which increases in the liberty of the worst off can be achieved not by further increasing the liberty of the best off, but only by closing the gap. If one tries to maximize for everyone what really has a maximum, the result is equality.

The priority of liberty over other goods, however, is chosen in the original position on the basis of a judgment that the fundamental interest in determining one's plan of life assumes priority once the most basic material needs have been met, and that further increases in other goods depend for their value primarily on the ability to employ them under conditions of maximum liberty. "Thus the desire for liberty is the chief regulative interest that the parties must suppose they all will have in common in due course. The veil of ignorance forces them to abstract from the particulars of their plans of life thereby leading to this conclusion. The serial ordering of the two principles then follows" (p. 543). The parties also reflect that equal liberty guarantees them all a basic self-esteem against the background of which some differences in social position and wealth will be acceptable. Here again an explicitly liberal conception of individual good is used to defend a choice in the original position.

I have attempted to argue that the presumptions of the contract method

---

[7] A similar objection could be made to Rawls's claim that the difference principle provides a condition of reciprocal advantage that allows everyone to co-operate willingly in the social order. Obviously, those at the bottom could not prefer any other arrangement, but what about those at the top? Rawls says the following: "To begin with, it is clear that the well-being of each depends on a scheme of social cooperation without which no one could have a satisfactory life. Secondly, we can ask for the willing cooperation of everyone only if the terms of the scheme are reasonable. The difference principle, then, seems to be a fair basis on which those better endowed, or more fortunate in their social circumstances, could expect others to collaborate with them when some workable arrangement is a necessary condition of the good of all" (p. 103). But if some scheme of social cooperation is necessary for *anyone* to have a satisfactory life, everyone will benefit from a wide range of schemes. To assume that the worst off need further benefits to co-operate willingly while the best off do not is simply to repeat the egalitarian principle.

Rawls employs are rather strong, and that the original position therefore offers less independent support to his conclusions than at first appears. The egalitarian liberalism he develops and the conception of the good on which it depends are extremely persuasive, but the original position serves to model rather than to justify them. The contract approach allied with a nonliberal conception of the good would yield different results, and some conceptions of the good are incompatible with a contract approach to justice altogether. I believe that Rawls's conclusions can be more persuasively defended by direct moral arguments for liberty and equality, some of which he provides and some of which are indirectly represented in his present account through the grounds and conditions of choice in the original position. He remarks that it is worth

> noting from the outset that justice as fairness, like other contract views, consists of two parts: (1) an interpretation of the initial situation and of the problem of choice posed there, and (2) a set of principles which, it is argued, would be agreed to. One may accept the first part of the theory (or some variant thereof), but not the other, and conversely. (p. 15)

He suggests that the principles are more likely to be rejected than their contractual basis, but I suspect the reverse. It seems to me likely that over the long term this book will achieve its permanent place in the literature of political theory because of the substantive doctrine that it develops so eloquently and persuasively. The plausibility of the results will no doubt be taken to confirm the validity of the method, but such inferences are not always correct. It is possible that the solution to the combinatorial problems of social choice can be reached by means of a self-interested individual choice under carefully specified conditions of uncertainty, but the basis of such a solution has yet to be discovered.

This is already a famous and influential book, and inevitably for a certain time it will engage the attention of students of philosophy, politics, law, and economics. The longer life of a work and its broader impact on the habits of thought of reflective persons can never be predicted with certainty, but it is an interesting question. Although A Theory of Justice is for the most part very readable, it does not possess the literary distinction that has helped to make other important political works—those of Hobbes or Mill, for example,—part of the common intellectual property of mankind. It does, however, possess another feature of great importance. Reading it is a powerful experience, because one is in direct contact at every point with a striking temperament and cast of mind. It is in that sense a very personal work, and the perceptions and attitudes one finds in it are vivid, intelligent, and appealing. The outlook expressed by this book is not characteristic of its age, for it is neither pessimistic nor alienated nor angry nor sentimental nor utopian. Instead, it conveys something that today may seem incredible: a hopeful affirmation of human possibilities. Yet the hope has a basis, for Rawls possesses a deep sense of the multiple connections between social institutions and individual psychology. Without illusion he describes a pluralistic social order that will call forth the support of free men and evoke what is best in them. To have made such a vision precise, alive, and convincing is a memorable achievement.

13

Nozick: Libertarianism without Foundations

This was a review of Robert Nozick's Anarchy, State, and Utopia *(Basic Books, 1974). This fairly relentless attack was an attempt to deny the support that Nozick's brilliance might be thought to provide for a political position that I found, and still find, highly objectionable. Nozick has since modified his views (see* The Examined Life *[Simon and Schuster, 1989], pp. 286–92; and* The Nature of Rationality *[Princeton University Press, 1993], p. 32), but the book remains the canonical statement of philosophical libertarianism, and while radical libertarianism is not itself a political danger, some of its moral ideas form an important element of modern right-wing antiegalitarianism. Nozick's work always displays great intelligence and charm, but in this case what was intuitively plausible to him—some of the unargued premises on which the whole structure is based, as well as its specific consequences—seemed to me completely unbelievable.*

I don't think my reaction was unusual, but although the book may have persuaded very few people, that hasn't prevented it from becoming a classic—which is in itself a remarkable fact about political philosophy.

Liberalism is the conjunction of two ideals. The first is that of individual liberty: liberty of thought, speech, religion, and political action; freedom from government interference with privacy, personal life, and the exercise of individual inclination. The second ideal is that of a democratic so-

---

Reprinted with permission from *The Yale Law Journal* 85 (1975).

ciety controlled by its citizens and serving their needs, in which inequalities of political and economic power and social position are not excessive. Means of promoting the second ideal include progressive taxation, public provision of a social minimum, and insulation of political affairs from the excessive influence of private wealth. To approach either of these ideals is very difficult. To pursue both of them inevitably results in serious dilemmas. In such cases liberalism tends to give priority to the respect for certain personal rights, even at substantial cost in the realization of other goods such as efficiency, equality, and social stability.

The most formidable challenge to liberalism, both intellectually and politically, is from the left. It is argued that strong safeguards of individual liberty are too great a hindrance to the achievement of economic and social equality, rapid economic progress from underdevelopment, and political stability. A majority of the people in the world are governed on this assumption. Perhaps the most difficult issue is posed by economic power and the political inequality it can create. The criticism from the left is that harmful concentrations of economic power cannot be attacked—or prevented from forming—unless individual actions are more closely restricted than is permitted by the liberal ideal of personal freedom. Radical redistribution is unlikely in a liberal democracy where private wealth controls the political process. A defense against this criticism must either challenge the factual claim or argue that the importance of freedom outweighs these disadvantages.

Liberalism is also under attack from the right. The most conspicuous attacks are not theoretical: the right in its more prominent political manifestations is not particularly attached to individual liberty when that liberty threatens the unequal distribution of wealth and power. But there is also a theoretical challenge from the right, called libertarianism, and while it does not present as serious a moral issue for liberals as does the attack from the left, the two are in some ways symmetrical. Libertarianism, like leftism, fastens on one of the two elements of the liberal ideal and asks why its realization should be inhibited by the demands of the other. Instead of embracing the ideal of equality and the general welfare, libertarianism exalts the claim of individual freedom of action and asks why state power should be permitted even the interference represented by progressive taxation and public provision of health care, education, and a minimum standard of living.

In *Anarchy, State, and Utopia*, Robert Nozick attempts to set forth the libertarian position in a way that will persuade some of those who do not already accept it. Despite its ingenuity of detail, the effort is entirely unsuccessful as an attempt to convince, and far less successful than it might be as an attempt to explain to someone who does not hold the position why anyone else does hold it. The book may come to occupy the position of an official text of libertarian political theory, but it is unlikely to add to the ranks of believers in that view unless it converts a few unwary philosophical anarchists by persuading them that the minimal state need not after all violate their austere moral requirements.

To present a serious challenge to other views, a discussion of libertarianism would have to explore the foundations of individual rights and the reasons for and against different conceptions of the relation between those rights and other values that the state may be in a position to promote. But Nozick's book is theoretically insubstantial: it does not take up the main problems and therefore fails to make the kind of contribution to political theory that might have been hoped for from someone of his philosophical attainments.[1] In the preface he announces that he was converted to libertarianism by the decisive force of the arguments (p. ix), but no such arguments appear in the book. He has left the establishment of the moral foundations to another occasion, and his brief indication of how the basic views might be defended is disappointing. I shall explain below why it is unlikely to survive further development.

Nozick starts from the unargued premise that individuals have certain inviolable rights that may not be intentionally transgressed by other individuals or the state for any purpose. They are the rights not to be killed or assaulted if one is doing no harm, not to be coerced or imprisoned, not to have one's property taken or destroyed, and not to be limited in the use of one's property so long as one does not violate the rights of others. He concludes that the only morally permissible state would be the minimal nightwatchman state, a state limited to protecting people against murder, assault, theft, fraud, and breach of contract. The argument is not one which derives a surprising conclusion from plausible premises. No one (except perhaps an anarchist) who did not already accept the conclusion would accept the premise, and the implausibility of each can only serve to reinforce a conviction of the implausibility of the other.

Naturally, any opposition to the power of governments will meet with a

---

[1] Nozick is the author of three important articles: "Coercion" in *Philosophy, Science, and Method* (S. Morgenbesser, P. Suppes and M. White, eds., 1969); "Newcomb's Problem and Two Principles of Choice," in *Essays in Honor of Carl G. Hempel* (N. Rescher, ed., Reidel, 1969); "Moral Complications and Moral Structures," *Natural Law Forum* 1 (1968). The book reaches their level of trenchancy only in Chapter 4, "Prohibition, Compensation, and Risk" (pp. 54–88), a brilliant discussion of the choice among various methods of dealing with injurious or dangerous behavior: when to prohibit, when to punish, when to require compensation, when to compensate someone who is inconvenienced by a prohibition. It is also the chapter with the greatest importance for legal theory.

certain sympathy from observers of the contemporary scene, and Nozick emphasizes the connection between his view and the fight against legal regulation of sexual behavior, drug use, and individual life-styles. It is easy to develop an aversion to state power by looking at how actual states wield it. Their activities often include murder, torture, political imprisonment, censorship, conscription for aggressive war, and overthrowing the governments of other countries—not to mention tapping the phones, reading the mail, and regulating the sexual behavior of their own citizens.

The objection to these abuses, however, is not that state power exists, but that it is used to do evil rather than good. Opposition to these evils cannot be translated into an objection to welfare, public education, or the graduated income tax. A reasonably persuasive practical argument for reducing the power of governments can perhaps be based on the unhappy results of that power. But it is doubtful that a government limited to the functions of police, courts, prisons, and national defense would be conspicuously benign, or that it would be especially protective of individual rights.[2] In practice, it would probably include the worst parts of what we have now, without much of the best. That is why those concerned with individual liberty are usually not opposed to strong government with power to promote desirable ends, so long as the exercise of that power is limited by strong safeguards. Governments should promote what is good and prevent evils, as well as protecting rights. How could anyone disagree?

If there is an answer to this question, it must come from the ethical foundation of political theory. Nozick states:

> Moral philosophy sets the background for, and the boundaries of, political philosophy. What persons may and may not do to one another limits what they may do through the apparatus of a state, or do to establish such an

---

[2] This helps to account for the romantic appeal of anarchism. Nozick's attempt to refute the anarchist view that even a minimal state will violate individual rights is not, I think, successful. He argues at length that a minimal state could arise by an invisible hand process from a state of nature without the process violating anyone's rights: people could voluntarily join private protective associations, one of which would naturally achieve dominance over a territory even if not everyone had agreed to join. It could then exercise limited control without violating anyone's rights. This is supposed to show that a minimal state is morally permissible. But why should the mere conceivability of such a process persuade an anarchist of that conclusion? He would already have been prepared to admit that a minimal state established by *unanimous* agreement of the participants would be allowable. He just believes no actual state will be of this sort. Similarly, he may credit Nozick with having imagined another way in which a minimal state "could" arise that violated no one's rights, even though based on less than unanimous agreement. But the likelihood of any actual state meeting these moral conditions will be almost as low. The rejection of anarchism requires the rejection of its moral premises.

apparatus. The moral prohibitions it is permissible to enforce are the source of whatever legitimacy the state's fundamental coercive power has. (p. 6)

I believe that this principle is correct and important. The exercise of state power is not the action of a separate entity with moral rights greater than those of individual persons, rights to use force against persons for reasons that would not justify the use of force by individuals or groups of individuals per se. If governments have the right to coerce, it must be a right possessed by the people who establish and sustain governmental institutions, and those who act through them.

There is a problem about stating this position in a way that avoids triviality. For someone who believes that governments have much larger rights than individuals could always add that the existence of such rights implies a corresponding individual right to combine with others to institute a government and act through it to exercise those larger rights of coercion and control. But in such a view, these individual rights would be derivative from the rights of the state, and not the other way around. Nozick's position, which seems correct, is that individual rights and duties are the basis of what governments may and should do.

But he appears to infer from this ethical principle a strong epistemological consequence that it does not have: that it is possible to determine what governments may and should do by first asking what individuals, taken a few at a time in isolation from large-scale society, may do, and then applying the resultant principles to all possible circumstances, including those which involve billions of people, complicated political and economic institutions, and thousands of years of history. What is more surprising, he discovers in himself intuitions about the moral requirements on men in a state of nature which he is willing to endorse as universal principles unmodified in their cumulative effects when applied in any circumstances whatever.

Abstractly described, this procedure sounds hopelessly misguided.[3] It is hard to see how anyone could seriously arrive at firm moral opinions about the universal principles of human conduct without considering what it would be like if they were universally applied, in iterations that might

---

[3] Nozick defends the procedure in a section entitled "Macro and Micro." He says: [C]omplex wholes are not easily scanned; we cannot easily keep track of everything that is relevant. The justice of a whole society may depend on its satisfying a number of distinct principles. These principles, though individually compelling (witness their application to a wide range of particular microcases), may yield surprising results when combined together. . . . [O]ne should not depend upon judgments about the whole as providing the only or even the major body of data against which to check one's principles. One major path to changing one's intutive judgments about some complex whole is through seeing the larger and often surprising implications of principles solidly founded at the micro level (pp. 205–6). Obviously, but another way to change

create complex effects of scale. When we pass from an abstract to a more substantive description, the implausibility of the view increases. For the intuition that Nozick discovers in himself is that everyone has an absolute right to be free from coercion, and an absolute right to acquire and dispose of his property—so long as he is not violating the same rights of others and so long as his acquisition of property does not, for example, give him sole title to the formerly public water supply of a desert community.[4]

Nozick's intuition is that each person is entitled to his talents and abilities and to whatever he can make, get, or buy with his own efforts, with the help of others, or with plain luck. He is entitled to keep it or do anything he wants with it, and whomever he gives it to is thereby equally entitled to it. Moreover, anyone is entitled to whatever he ends up with as a result of the indefinite repetition of this process, over however many generations. I assume that most readers of Nozick's book will find no echo of this intuition in themselves and will feel instead that they can develop no opinion on the universal principles of entitlement, acquisition, and transfer of property, or indeed whether there are any such universal principles, without considering the significance of such principles in their universal application. One might even agree in part with Nozick's views about what people should do in the limited circumstances that define interpersonal relations in the state of nature, but not agree that the proper generalizations of those judgments is their unmodified application to all cases no matter how complex or extended. They might be based instead on principles that give these results for small-scale individual transactions but rather different results for the specification of general conditions of entitlement to be applied on an indefinitely large scale.[5]

---

intuitive judgments about the scope or truth of principles at the micro level is by seeing their larger implications. The fact that the rights of governments derive from the rights of individuals does not imply that we can come to know the rights of individuals without thinking about governments, just as the fact that the properties of molecules derive from the properties of atoms does not imply that we can come to know the properties of atoms without investigating molecules. The logical and the epistemological connections need not go in the same direction: even if political philosophy is logically dependent on ethics, our knowledge of some aspects of ethics may derive from an investigation of political philosophy.

[4] The latter is the familiar proviso in Locke's theory of property acquisition, but according to Nozick it will not operate as a serious restriction in a free market system; see page 182.

[5] The example of entitlement that he offers (p. 206) as a decisive retort to such skepticism—a natural right not to be deprived of one's vital organs for the benefit of others—is plausible partly because of the extreme character of such an assault and partly because there is no possibility that protection of this right will lead to the accumulation of vast hereditary wealth or inequalities of social and political power.

The fact is, however, that Nozick's moral intutions seem wrong even on a small scale. He denies that any of the rights he detects may be overridden merely to do good or prevent evil. But even if it is not permissible to murder or maim an innocent person to promote some highly desirable result, the protected rights do not all have the same degree of importance. The things one is supposed to be protected against are, in order of gravity: killing, injury, pain, physical force, deprivation of liberty of many different kinds (movement, association, and activity), destruction of one's property, taking of one's property, or the threat of any of the above (with all *their* variations in gravity). It is far less plausible to maintain that taking some of an innocent man's property is an impermissible means for the prevention of a serious evil, than it is to maintain that killing him is impermissible. These rights vary in importance, and some are not absolute even in the state of nature.

The sources of morality are not simple but multiple; therefore, its development in political theory will reflect that multiplicity. Rights limit the pursuit of worthwhile ends, but they can also sometimes be overridden if the ends are sufficiently important. The only way to make progress in understanding the nature of individual rights is to investigate their sources and their relations to each other and to the values on whose pursuit they set limits. Nozick says little about the basis of the inviolability of persons, but the following remark indicates where he would be inclined to look:

[W]hy may not one violate persons for the greater social good? Individually, we each sometimes choose to undergo some pain or sacrifice for a greater benefit or to avoid a greater harm: we go to the dentist to avoid worse suffering later; we do some unpleasant work for its results; some persons diet to improve their health or looks; some save money to support themselves when they are older. In each case, some cost is borne for the sake of the greater overall good. Why not, *similarly,* hold that some persons have to bear some costs that benefit other persons more, for the sake of the overall social good? But there is no *social entity* with a good that undergoes some sacrifice for its own good. There are only individual people, different individual people, with their own individual lives. Using one of these people for the benefit of others, uses him and benefits the others. Nothing more. What happens is that something is done to him for the sake of others. Talk of an overall social good covers this up. (Intentionally?) To use a person in this way does not sufficiently respect and take account of the fact that he is a separate person, that his is the only life he has. *He* does not get some overbalancing good from his sacrifice, and no one is entitled to force this upon him—least of all a state or government that claims his allegiance (as other individuals do not) and that therefore scrupulously must be *neutral* between its citizens (pp. 32–33; emphasis in original; footnote omitted)

It is not clear how Nozick thinks individual rights derive from the fact that each person's life is the only one he has. He appears to draw the implication that a benefit to one or more persons can never outweigh a cost borne by someone else. This, however, is far too broad a claim for Nozick's purposes. It is both obviously false and unsuitable as a basis for constraints on the treatment of individuals.

To make sense of interpersonal compensation, it is not necessary to invoke the silly idea of a social entity, thus establishing an analogy with intrapersonal compensation. All one needs is the belief, shared by most people, that it is better for each of ten people to receive a benefit than for one person to receive it, worse for ten people to be harmed than for one person to be similarly harmed, better for one person to benefit greatly than for another to benefit slightly, and so forth. The fact that each person's life is the only one he has does not render us incapable of making these judgments, and if a choice among such alternatives does *not* involve the violation of any rights or entitlements, but only the allocation of limited time or resources, then we regard those comparisons as excellent reasons for picking one alternative rather than the other. If we can help either ten people or one person, not included in the ten, and we help the ten, then we can say that rescue of the ten outweighs the loss of the one, despite the fact that *he* does not get some overbalancing good from his sacrifice, and his is the only life he has.

So for the purpose of comparing possible outcomes of action, where the violation of rights is not in question, it is clear that the distinctness of individuals does not prevent balancing of benefits and harms across persons. If special constraints enter in when a sacrifice is to be imposed on someone as a *means* to the achievement of a desirable outcome, their source must lie elsewhere. Such constraints should not derive from a principle that also has the consequence that practically nothing can be said about the relative desirability of situations involving numbers of different people.

Furthermore, the source of rights of the general kind Nozick advocates cannot be discovered by concentrating, as he suggests we should, on the meaning of individual human lives and the value of shaping one's own life and forming a general conception of it. Vague as his suggestions are (see pp. 49–50), they all suffer from an error of focus, for they concentrate solely on features of persons that make it bad for certain things to *happen* to them, and good for them to have the opportunity to do certain things. But rights of the kind that interest Nozick are not rights that certain things not *happen* to you, or rights to be provided with certain opportunities. Rather, they are rights not to be deliberately treated or used in certain ways, and not to be deliberately interfered with in certain activities. They give rise to claims not against the world at large, but only against someone who contemplates deliberately violating them. The *relation* between the possessor of the right and the actor, rather than just the intrinsic nature of the possessor and of his life, must enter into the analysis of the right and the explication of its basis.

Any theory of rights must explain this structural feature, even if it does not follow Nozick in elevating the unimpeded exercise of the will into the supreme principle of morality. It is of the first importance that your right not to be assaulted is *not* a right that everyone do what is required to ensure that you are not assaulted. It is merely a right not to be assaulted, and it is correlated with other people's duty not to *assault* you. This cannot be explained simply by the fact that it is bad to be assaulted, which is merely an item in the catalogue of values by which the desirability or undesirability of occurrences or sets of occurrences is to be weighed. That assault is disagreeable or bad does not explain why the prohibition of it should serve as a constraint on the pursuit of other values or the avoidance of other harms, even if those other values outweigh the badness of assault in a pure calculation of the relative desirability of possible outcomes. Sometimes one is required to choose the less desirable alternative because to achieve the more desirable one would have to violate a right.

As Nozick points out (p.29), the constraints on action represented by rights cannot be equivalent to an assignment of large disvalue to their violation, for that would make it permissible to violate such a right if by doing so one could prevent more numerous or more serious violations of the same right by others. This is not in general true. It is not permissible in Nozick's view (or mine) to kill an innocent person even to prevent the deliberate killing of three other innocent persons. A general feature of anything worthy of being called a right is that it is not translatable into a mere assignment of disvalue to its violation.

An explanation of the basis of rights would therefore have to concentrate on the actor and his relation to the person he is constrained not to treat in certain ways, even to achieve very desirable ends. And it would have to explore the interaction between those constraints and the goals whose pursuit they constrain. There is no reason to think that either in personal life or in society the force of every right will be absolute or nearly absolute, that is, never capable of being overridden by consequential considerations. Rights not to be deliberately killed, injured, tormented, or imprisoned are very powerful and limit the pursuit of any goal. More limited restrictions of liberty of action, restrictions on the use of property, and restrictions on contracts are simply less serious and therefore provide less powerful constraints.[6]

Moreover, there is a big difference between suddenly expropriating half of someone's savings and attaching monetary conditions in advance to activities, expenditures, and earnings—the usual form of taxation. The latter is a much less brutal assault upon the person.[7] Whether this kind of limitation of individual liberty should be permitted, to acquire resources for the promotion of desirable ends, is a function of the gravity of the violation and the desirability of the ends. (And as I have observed, this does not mean that it is justified whenever the result is a maximal social balance of benefits and costs.)

Nozick would reply that such ends can be achieved by voluntary donations rather than by compulsion and that people who are well-off and who deplore the existence of poverty should donate significant portions of their assets to help those who are unfortunate (pp. 265–68). But this is no more plausible coming from Nozick than it was coming from Barry Goldwater. Most people are not generous when asked to give voluntarily, and it is unreasonable to ask that they should be. Admittedly, there are cases in which a person should do something, although it would not be right to force him to do it. But here I believe the reverse is true. Sometimes it is proper to force people to do something even though it is not true that they should do it without being forced. It is acceptable to compel people to contribute to the support of the indigent by automatic taxation, but unreasonable to insist that in the absence of such a system they ought to contribute voluntarily. The latter is an excessively demanding moral position because it requires voluntary decisions that are quite difficult to make. Most people will tolerate a universal system of compulsory taxation without feeling entitled to complain, whereas they would feel justified in

---

[6] The fact that a right can be overridden to avoid sufficiently serious consequences does not mean that its violation can be assigned a disvalue comparable to the disvalue of those consequences. For that would give the occurrence of such a violation greater weight in a calculation of outcomes (e.g., when the question is what may be done to prevent such violations by others) than it in fact has. Therefore, although rights may on occasion be overridden, the violation of some people's rights cannot automatically be justified because it leads to a reduction in the more serious violation of other people's rights. This issue arises in connection with preventive detention, wiretapping, and search and seizure, all of which might be useful in the prevention of robbery, murder, assault, and rape.

[7] It may be objected that taxation must be backed up by the threat of stronger force and even violence. But this arises only if there is resistance at the first level. If the original, nonviolent demand is legitimate, escalation may occur if the subject resists it and uses stronger methods to resist each succeeding method for enforcing the previous one.

refusing an appeal that they contribute the same amount voluntarily. This is partly due to lack of assurance that others would do likewise and fear of relative disadvantage, but it is also a sensible rejection of excessive demands on the will, which can be more irksome than automatic demands on the purse.

A political theory that reflected these moral complexities would assign society the function of promoting certain goods and preventing certain evils, within limits set by the differing constraints of different individual rights. It would not judge processes and procedures solely by their tendency to produce certain outcomes, nor would it judge outcomes solely by the processes that had produced them. Social institutions and the procedures defining them would be assessed by reference both to their respect for individual rights and liberty and to their tendency to promote desirable ends like the general welfare.

Nozick offers a classification of principles of distributive justice into which such a theory does not fit.[8] After defining a *historical* principle as one that asserts that the justice of a distribution depends on how it came about (p. 153) and an *end-result* principle as one that denies this (p. 155), he defines a *patterned* principle as one that specifies "that a distribution is to vary along with some natural dimension, weighted sum of natural dimensions, or lexicographic ordering of natural dimensions (p. 156).[9] His own theory, the entitlement theory, is easy to describe in these terms. It is a nonpatterned historical principle, for it specifies that any distribution is just if it was arrived at by a series of individual transactions among people entitled, by natural rights of acquisition and transfer, to make them.

But suppose a theory says that a distribution is just if it results from a process governed by rules that reflect (*a*) the suitability of certain patterns, (*b*) the desirability of increasing certain good results and decreasing certain evils independently of any pattern, and (*c*) a respect for individual rights of differing importance. Such a theory will be at bottom neither purely historical nor purely patterned. It will be formally historical, but the "historical" or process criterion will be partially determined by considerations of pattern and considerations of total outcome. Therefore, Nozick's concentrated attack on patterned principles and nonhistorical principles provides no reason to think that his alternative is correct.[10]

[8] Of course, distribution is only one of the things covered in any political theory, but we may leave others aside for the moment.

[9] "To each according to his need" would be an example.

[10] More specifically, his arguments against Rawls are seriously weakened by a procrustean attempt to portray Rawls's principle of distributive justice as a nonhistorical or end-result principle. Rawls does not maintain that the justice of a distribution can be determined independently of how it was produced. He believes that its justice depends

Apart from this defect, the attack is still unsuccessful. Nozick asks us to imagine some patterned principle realized and then argues that its preservation would require interference with individual liberty: people would have to be prevented from using their allocations under the pattern as they wish. For example, preservation of a reasonably equal distribution would require that individuals not be permitted to pay Wilt Chamberlain 25 cents for each basketball game they see him play with the understanding that he can keep it all, even if it amounts to $250,000 a year. This is perfectly obvious, and it is part of what would be *meant* by a patterned principle of distribution: the adoption of a general system of acquisition, taxation, and exchange that tends to preserve a certain pattern.

It only seems a problem to Nozick, and a further violation of liberty, because he erroneously interprets the notion of a patterned principle as specifying a distribution of *absolute entitlements* (like those he believes in) to the wealth or property distributed. But absolute entitlement to property is not what would be allocated to people under a partially egalitarian distribution. Possession would confer the kind of qualified entitlement that exists in a system under which taxes and other conditions are arranged to preserve certain features of the distribution, while permitting choice, use, and exchange of property compatible with it. What someone holds under such a system will not be *his property* in the unqualified sense of Nozick's system of entitlement. To suppose otherwise is to beg the question, and that is exactly what Nozick does when he says:

> There is *no* question about whether each of the people was entitled to the control over the resources they held in D_1 [the original patterned distribution]; because that was the distribution (your favorite) that (for the purposes of argument) we assumed was acceptable. . . . If the people were entitled to dispose of the resources to which they were entitled (under D_1), didn't this include their being entitled to give it to, or exchange it with, Wilt Chamberlain? (p. 161; emphasis in original)

This mistake drains the argument of its force.

Let me turn briefly to the difficult subject of equality. While the elimination of misery, poverty, and disease are probably more important social goals than the achievement of economic equality, the latter is one of the ends some people regard as legitimate. Nozick's view is predictable. If

---

on the justice of the institutions, including legal institutions defining entitlement, which were involved in its production. These are assessed only partly on the basis of their tendency to promote a certain distributive end state. Rawls, for example, gives priority to the preservation of individual liberty, and while he does not mean by this what Nozick means, it certainly restricts the procedures by which a distribution can be justly arrived at. See generally, J. Rawls, *A Theory of Justice* (Harvard University Press, 1971).

inequality arises as a result of the free exercise of entitlements, it cannot be objected to on grounds of injustice, and liberty may not be in any way infringed to reduce it. Since people are entitled not only to the wealth they inherit but to their natural assets (p. 225), further inequalities resulting from the employment of these assets are just.

But there is no reason to believe in an absolute natural right to profit from one's natural assets, even if a less than absolute right to their free exercise is acknowledged as a limitation on the pursuit of equality or other social goals. Someone who regards equality as a good will assume that its achievement does not take absolute precedence over efficiency, liberty, and other values. Nevertheless, more than this is required to answer Nozick, for it is not clear what makes equality of distribution a good thing *at all*. Nozick does not acknowledge the right of the state to limit liberty to produce any merely desirable outcome. But why should someone with a more standard view about individual rights be in favor of a goal of social and economic equality? Perhaps he can argue that the average level of well-being—both in material terms and in terms of contentment and self-esteem—is likely to be higher in a relatively equal society than in an unequal one of comparable total wealth. Perhaps he will argue that the political effects of economic inequality are harmful to individual liberty and general welfare. But these considerations, though very important, are not reasons for regarding equality as a good in itself, yet that is a common moral view.

It cannot be defended by claiming that inequalities are arbitrary unless based on morally relevant differences among people. Arbitrariness is a moral defect only if it can be contrasted with an alternative that is selected on the basis of morally relevant factors. Unless there is independent justification for equality, an equal distribution is just as arbitrary from a moral point of view as any other. To defend equality as a good in itself, one would have to argue that improvements in the lot of people lower on the scale of well-being took priority over greater improvements to those higher on the scale, even if the latter improvements also affected more people. While I am sympathetic to such a view, I do not believe it has ever been successfully defended.

I have dwelt on the book's theoretical shortcomings; there is much in it that I have not discussed, including a final chapter that describes a pluralistic libertarian utopia (pp. 297–333), and interesting analyses of such diverse topics as Marx's labor theory of value (pp. 252–62) and the treatment of animals (pp. 35–41). Unlike most works of philosophy, it is funny, fast-paced, and a pleasure to read. Nozick's writing has great energy, and it meets a high standard of clarity and definiteness. One is rarely in doubt about what Nozick is claiming or about what one denies in rejecting his views.

14

Hare: Moral Thinking

This was a review of R. M. Hare's Moral Thinking: Its Levels, Method, and Point *(Oxford University Press, 1981). Hare's lifelong commitment to finding the foundations of morality through the analysis of language is a particularly striking example of the error of trying to understand a basic subject from too far outside—a tendency encouraged by the once prevalent view that language is the key to everything in philosophy.*

According to Professor Hare, most contemporary moral philosophers are benighted. They cannot get through their thick skulls the clear principles of moral reasoning that he has set out and developed in two previous book-length studies of ethical theory, *The Language of Morals*[1] and *Freedom and Reason*,[2] and that he spells out again and develops further in this one. Like a teacher of dim-witted children, he can't always conceal his impatience at having to repeat himself, but the importance of the issues keeps him at it.

He finds the subject infested with "intuitionists." These are philosophers who limit their moral thinking to one level—that of the rough, general, prima facie principles that they have been brought up to follow in everyday life, when they must act without having too much time to think and without perfect knowledge of the facts. Intuitionists take these principles, and the moral feelings associated with them, as the basis of moral

---

Reprinted with permission from *The London Review of Books*, July 1–14, 1982.

[1] Oxford University Press, 1952.
[2] Oxford University Press, 1963.

thought, when actually they are derived from something else and can be justified or criticised only by moving to a different level, where moral intuitions are not relied upon.

This is the level of what Hare calls "critical thinking," and its rules are determined entirely by the logic of the moral concepts—a logic that is discovered by investigating ordinary linguistic usage and not by the exercise of any form of moral intuition or judgment. It is only by getting outside morality in this way, he believes, that we can hope to provide morality with a firm foundation instead of going around in circles. Once we do so, we shall discover that the unique moral position that it is possible to justify on the basis of the logic of the moral concepts is utilitarianism. It also turns out that utilitarianism, properly interpreted, is what underlies those common moral intuitions that intuitionists erroneously take to be basic and that they use to try to refute utilitarianism.

Hare has come to this view gradually. He did not formerly believe that one could derive a single substantive moral position from the logic of the moral concepts—and for good reason. What is so implausible about this claim is its implication that all fundamental moral disagreements are in a sense illusory. Provided the parties to a disagreement are really making moral claims at all, they can reach different conclusions only because they disagree about the nonmoral facts or because at least one of them has made a logical error in applying the moral concepts. There are no disagreements that are moral all the way down. A libertarian who believes in the inviolability of individual property rights and a socialist who believes in promoting equality by progressive taxation will discover, if they consider carefully what they both mean by the words "right" and "wrong," "ought" and "must," that they are both committed to a single method of deciding which of their positions is correct—an empirical method that depends on which social system will most effectively satisfy the preferences of all the people affected by it.

How does Hare manage to extract this large moral rabbit from what looks at first like a rather small and empty linguistic hat? His theory about logic of the moral concepts—universal prescriptivism—seems innocent enough. It says that a judgment about what ought to be done on a particular occasion commits one to prescribing that the same thing be done in any situation that is similar in all its universal characteristics—in particular, any situation in which the individual persons involved are different or in which they occupy different roles.

This looks like something that the libertarian and the socialist could agree on. The libertarian who believes that he should not be taxed to provide subsistence for indigent single mothers also believes that if he were an indigent mother or one of her children, it would be wrong to tax others to feed him. And the socialist who favors taxing the rich favors it whoever the rich happen to be. The two of them can use the same moral vocabulary to disagree about what ought to be done because they differ over the importance to be assigned, universally, to liberty, equality, property, and the satisfaction of individual preferences.

But Hare has come to believe that universal prescriptivism is much less hospitable to different moral convictions than this because he interprets it in a way that permits each person to prescibe universally only one thing, given the facts of a particular situation, and it is the same thing that anyone else must prescribe. The only rational basis for a universal prescription, he believes, is to put yourself in the position of all the people affected by a given act and ask whether you would want it to be done or not if you had their preferences. The preferences that you recognize you *would* have, were you in a given situation, lead immediately and unavoidably to equally strong preferences that you *now* have, regarding what *should* happen if you were in that situation. You then add up all these hypothetical preferences, pro and con, allowing for their different weights, and the choice that has the greater weight of preferences on its side determines whether the act ought to be done or not, by determining whether you can prescribe universally that it should be done.

All this is supposed to be contained in the logic of the moral words used by all speakers of English and other languages translatable into English. But it clearly isn't. Not only would many people regard criticism of their moral views by this method as invalid, but even most of those who agree with Hare's moral position would not regard those who reach moral judgments by a different method as misusing the language. Instead, they would hold that if someone believes, say, that each person may favor himself over others whether or not that will work out to everyone's advantage in the long run, then he is in substantive moral disagreement with utilitarianism at a fundamental level. This is a disagreement not over logic or the facts, but over the method of determining what is to be universally prescribed.

The unsurprising truth is that Hare has smuggled a moral intuition into his analysis of moral language, and that is what gives him his method. It is a perfectly respectable intuition, the same one that Sidgwick saw to be the basis of utilitarianism: "I ought not to prefer my own lesser good to the greater good of another." But there are those who do not share it. The move from what one would want to happen to oneself in each possible circumstance to what one wants to happen universally is not a logical one, for there is more than one way of combining such preferences: simple maximization of expected satisfaction, counting all the possibilities as equally probable, may not be the right choice even for an individual. But more important, the move from what one wants to happen universally to what one is prepared to prescribe should happen universally is not a logical one. An alternative method for arriving at universal prescriptions is to ask what any person would have reason to *do* in the given situation. One answer to this is the utilitarian answer, but there are others, including those that permit a person to give extra weight to his own concerns, and those that distinguish only some of the interests of others as those he should be concerned with.

Hare cannot get his moral theory out of the logic of the moral concepts, and the illusion that he is doing so condemns the work to one kind of superficiality, for it prevents him from seeing his most important assumptions and therefore from defending them. This is a defect in the book even if his substantive moral position is correct.

But his defense of utilitarianism is partly independent of these claims about moral language. He presents a version of the view that emphasizes the distinction between the ordinary rules that must be followed in the confusing and often emotionally fraught circumstances of everyday life, and the method of critical thinking that can be used in a cool moment, without constraints of time and information, to devise, evaluate, or criticize those prima facie rules and settle conflicts between them. Only an omniscient being whose mind worked like lightning and who suffered from no emotional weaknesses could use the full method of utilitarian critical thinking for every action he had to perform. Real humans have to approximate conformity to utilitarianism by following rules that are simple, clear, and learnable and that do not permit much scope for self-deception. Hare also thinks they shouldn't make excessively heavy demands on our motives—a curious point to which I shall return.

Hare says that many of the most popular arguments against utilitarianism—those that claim it would require some obviously wicked action, like murder or torture or the punishment of an innocent scapegoat, in sufficiently bizarre circumstances—depend on ignoring this pervasive distinction between the critical and intuitive levels of moral thought. I think he is right. A reasonable form of utilitarianism will require not only the creation of stable institutions that promote the general welfare but also the inculcation of consistent virtues, habits of conduct, instinctive reactions, and feelings that will lead people to act on the whole for the best under ordinary circumstances of ignorance and temptation. We do not know the total outcomes of many of our acts in sufficient detail to permit utilitarian calculation to proceed act by act. It is much better that there should be an overwhelming revulsion against torture for any reason than that people should feel prepared to consider the possibility case by case. The utilitarian justification for training people to have such moral inhibitions depends on the real facts of human life, so it is no argument against utilitarianism that sound intuitions would prevent someone from doing the best thing on the basis of perfect knowledge in a bizarre situation of a kind that rarely or never actually occurs. I think it is very unlikely that Hare's form of utilitarianism would in practice justify obvious moral atrocities (even though moral atrocities have often been defended by spurious utilitarian reasoning). The difficult theoretical question is whether Hare's two-level account gives an adequate explanation of the rights, duties, and prohibitions of common morality, or whether they have independent sources, not wholly derivable from the single intuition of moral impartiality that yields utilitarianism.

I have two doubts: first, whether Hare's view gives the right explanation of common moral intuitions where it does endorse them; second, whether utilitarianism really coincides with common morality as much as he believes it does. In considering such requirements as veracity, loyalty, or fidelity to commitments we have made to others—requirements that demand that we ignore apparent general utility in particular cases—Hare asks us to believe that they have no sources of their own, no reasons coming from the particular circumstances and relations to which they apply. In other words, if, without regard to utility, I refrain from lying to someone or betraying someone who has trusted me, the ultimate justification lies in the general utility of a fairly inflexible disposition not to do such things. But even if such a disposition does have general utility, something else is going on. It is very implausible to claim that intuitive repugnance at personal betrayal is just an artifact of upbringing on principles warranted by utility. Hare's view requires us to regard the sense of immediacy that these claims have as a kind of illusion, and all moral conflicts that seem to arise from them as soluble by rising to the level of utilitarian critical thinking. But without the support of his axiom that the sole method of moral justification is the appeal to pure impartiality, the diagnosis of illusion is unconvincing, and the operation of other, more personal reasons of a basic kind in ordinary morality seems likely.

In fact, personal reasons seem to cause ordinary morality to deviate substantially from even a two-level utilitarianism. This is my second doubt about Hare's position. He softens the demanding character of utilitarian impartiality by an illegitimate device that makes it easier to explain the other aspects of common morality in terms of his theory. The device is to tailor the prima facie principles that people are asked to follow in everyday life to the natural partiality of ordinary people, toward themselves and those near them. A utilitarian will praise individuals of supererogatory virtue for doing more, but he will see no point in demanding of others, or of himself, a level of beneficence that would simply be rejected as too onerous. As Hare puts it, "If I were very saintly like Albert Schweitzer or Mother Teresa, I might have much more exacting principles than in fact I have."

I would put it another way: if Hare were very saintly, he might be more of a utilitarian. As it is, he is committed to prima facie principles for the conduct of life that often permit him to do what is wrong by utilitarian standards, simply because, like the rest of us nonsaints, he is unwilling to swallow the more stringently impartial principles whose acceptance-utility, if they *were* accepted, would be higher. If he doesn't think he's doing anything wrong in behaving less selflessly than Albert Schweitzer, then he is giving his natural partiality a veto over the excessive demands of impartiality, and this is to fall away from a full utilitarianism—even allowing for differences of level.

I find Hare's actual position more plausible than unadulterated utilitarianism, but to begin to settle the issue requires work in the foundations of ethics. These are not to be found in the analysis of moral concepts alone, though I agree with Hare that they are not to be found in the systematization of our moral sentiments either. My own view is that the methods of moral thinking now available to us are fairly primitive—that while we have a grasp on what the basic kinds of moral reason are, including those on which utilitarianism is exclusively based, we don't have a sound method for combining them to give a result when they conflict, as they do constantly in real life, when a variety of disparate claims can bear on a decision. I don't know how to make the choice among different available interpretations of moral equality, nor do I think that ethical theory to date has exhausted the possibilities. Hare offers a single method, and this book presents it with the lucidity, economy, and bite that make all his work so readable. But though it is worth careful study, it tends to confirm the view that in ethics theoretical simplicity is not a virtue.

15

Hare: The Foundations of Impartiality

This rather dry piece pursues in greater detail some of the points raised in the previous essay. The volume in which it appeared includes replies by Hare to each of the critics.

I

Can an ethical theory be too successful? If it proposes a foundation for moral argument that lies beyond the reach of moral disagreement, it may leave the existence and intractability of actual moral disagreements unexplained. If it tries to appeal only to facts outside morality that all parties must admit, then the most fundamental disagreements are likely to resurface, either in the interpretation of what has been proved or in dispute over moral assumptions hidden in the premises.

I believe that Hare's attempt to ground morality in the logic of the moral concepts runs into this problem. It is true that when people disagree about what is right and wrong, and how they should live, they must mean the same thing by the terms they use to express their differences. But this common ground does not by itself provide the materials needed to settle their disagreements, and the attempt to show that it does inevitably intro-

---

Reprinted with permission from *Hare and Critics,* Douglas Seanor and N. Fotion, editors (Oxford University Press, 1988).

duces morally controversial elements into the interpretation of the alleged common ground. This happens elsewhere in philosophy, when one or another view is criticized for violating the logic of the terms in which it is stated. The mistake, if there is one, is usually located in another place.

It may happen sometimes, in the case of specialized, quasilegalistic disputes among members of the same moral sect, that the method of settling a moral disagreement can be extracted from the meanings of the terms that parties to the disagreement must use in common. But I believe this is not possible with respect to those large-scale moral issues that are of greatest philosophical interest. There we must look beyond the terminology, and we may find that no shared method is available at all that is not itself the subject of moral controversy. The best we can hope for is to discover arguments and counterarguments that display the basis of disagreement more clearly within the confines of morality and perhaps to identify some contributing nonmoral differences. This puts us in a better position to continue the search for a method on which wider agreement can be secured, as we gradually emerge from the moral Bronze Age.

The theory developed in *Moral Thinking*[1] holds that the possible content of a morality is more narrowly restricted by the logic of moral language than Hare had thought it was at the time of *The Language of Morals*.[2] That is because he includes in his later account of what moral judgments mean an interpretation of their universality that amounts to a strong substantive requirement of impartiality among all persons. It is this interpretation that I want to discuss, concentrating mostly on its relation to the logic of moral language, rather than on its independent plausibility as a moral assumption.

Hare believes that actual moral disagreements, if they are not based on confusion, can best be accounted for as differences over what follows from such a requirement, in conjunction with the facts—differences due partly to variation in the accuracy of reasoning and partly to variation in belief about the relevant nonmoral facts. But I believe that some disagreements are at the level of the principle itself—disagreements within morality about the stringency and proper interpretation of moral impartiality.

II

What gets us from bare universality to Hare's strong form of impartiality? The bare universality of moral claims is relatively uncontroversial and

[1] Oxford University Press, 1981.
[2] Oxford University Press, 1952.

might well be called part of their meaning. If I make a judgment about what I or someone else ought to do, I am committed to the view that anyone else in the same circumstances (construed in as finely grained a way as you like) ought to do the same. The particular judgment is a consequence of more general principles, perhaps highly general ones. But this by itself yields nothing like impartiality in the content of moral judgments; indeed, it tells us very little about their content at all. Ethical egoism, for example, meets the condition of bare universality perfectly. And Hare in his earlier discussion of the "fanatic"[3] recognized that some appalling positions could be embraced as universal prescriptions, in some sense.

We get impartiality only if we give a particular answer to the question, What is the attitude I take toward the acts covered by such a universal principle when I judge that they ought (or ought not) to be done? That is, we need an account of what it is to *prescribe* that they be done—that everyone act in a certain way. Hare's view is that a prescription that something be done is the expression of a desire or preference that it be done. And a universal prescription expresses a desire that the thing be done in all similar cases in the actual world and also in all similar hypothetical cases that differ from the actual ones only in the identities of the participants.

If we permute the identities of all the people in the world through each position in all the actual cases covered by a given universal prescription, this yields a vast number of cases. But Hare assumes that my preference with regard to this universalization can be taken to depend on what I want to happen to myself, in those cases in which I occupy one of the positions. He argues further that what I want to happen to myself in each of those cases will depend directly on what the person actually occupying the position would want, given his preferences and full information. And he claims finally that what I want to be done universally, in all of these cases, will be determined by a balancing out of the preferences I have about each of them, so that total preference-satisfaction is maximized.

With this we have arrived at preference-utilitarianism: the right thing to do is what will maximize the total satisfaction of the preferences of all the parties affected. (I omit complications arising from the distinction between critical and intuitive levels of moral thinking. My discussion has to do entirely with what Hare calls the critical level.)

This amounts to a strong substantive moral position, involving a number of morally controversial elements that cannot plausibly be assigned to the logic of moral language. Specifically, it embodies a view about how moral judgments should give equal consideration to everyone, how everyone's interests should be understood for moral purposes, and how the

[3] *Freedom and Reason* (Oxford University Press, 1963), Chapter 9.

conflicting interests of different individuals should be combined to reach moral conclusions.

We can set out the path from universal prescriptivism to utilitarianism in a series of propositions:

1. To say that something ought morally to be done is to prescribe that it be done in all similar hypothetical cases with the personnel switched.
2. To prescribe that something be done is to express the desire that it be done.
3. What we desire to be done in a set of hypothetical cases with the personnel switched depends only on what we desire to be done in those cases in which we occupy one of the positions.
4. What we desire to be done in a hypothetical case in which we are in someone else's shoes, with his desires and preferences, depends on what we believe he would desire in those circumstances.
5. What we desire to be done universally in a set of hypothetical cases is a simple additive function of what we desire to be done in each of them.

Propositions (2), (4), and (5) are controversial and in the context morally substantive. I find Hare's claim[4] that something like (4) is a conceptual truth particularly unconvincing. But I want to concentrate on (2) and, to a lesser extent, on (5). While (4) ensures that the resulting moral theory will take preference-satisfaction as the basic measure of value, (2) and (5) ensure that it will be a form of agent-neutral, maximizing consequentialism. The rightness of actions will depend on their tendency to increase the quantity of a value that is the same for all agents and is defined independently of the perspective of the agent. If Hare were right that all this is part of the meaning of the moral terms, then the most prominent alternatives to utilitarianism could not even be consistently stated in moral language.

III

We can begin to discuss assumption (2) by asking what alternative interpretations of what it is to prescribe an act are being ruled out. Hare's answer to the question what we are to prescribe universally derives from his definition of what it is to prescribe universally. To call the answer into question, it is necessary to propose an alternative definition—not necessarily one incompatible with Hare's substantive moral view, but one that

---

[4] *Moral Thinking*, pp. 95–96.

does not entail it. I believe the place to start is with the idea of what everyone has a reason to do.

Assumption (2) has a peculiar consequence. When I prescribe universally in the sense defined by that assumption, this does not imply that I believe everyone has a reason to act in accordance with my prescription: at best, it implies that I acknowledge a reason to obey it myself—(though even that follows only if we assume that in using moral language I acknowledge a reason to care about universalizability). But a moral judgment ought to have a connection with practical reason not only for the person who produces it but also for the persons to whom it is addressed. If it is supposed to be correct, it ought to claim that others have a reason to obey it, even if they do not yet happen to recognize that reason.

This claim can be expressed by a moral judgment even if it does not also express the utterer's *desire* that those others act as it says they should. It is only when the judgment is about his own conduct that any such desire need be implied.

This is not meant as a complete account of moral judgment. More would have to be said to differentiate moral prescriptions from the class of judgments of practical rationality in general—moral reasons must have some degree of independence from the particular interests and desires of the agent, for example. But whatever may have to be added, the condition that it must imply the existence of reasons for the person to whom it is addressed ensures the connection with motivation that should be preserved by any account of moral prescription. It follows that if I apply a moral prescription to myself, I must recognize a reason to act; this connection with motivation is an essential condition of a judgment's being prescriptive at all. But it is not essential in addition that any motivation or desire on my part be expressed by a prescription about what someone else ought to do—even if particular moral views make this connection.

Hare's position to the contrary is due to his interpreting moral judgments as imperatives in a fairly literal sense, and not in the sense in which Kant thought they were imperatives. In the literal sense, I would not ordinarily tell someone to do something unless I wanted him to do it. But in the Kantian sense, the utterance of either a hypothetical or a categorical imperative has a closer connection with the utterer's conception of the reasons that might motivate the addressee than with the utterer's own desires. This conception would count as prescriptive a judgment I made about someone else, even if I had no desire that he conform to it, so long as *he* could not sincerely assent without accepting a reason to conform.[5] In

---

[5] I am not referring here to Kant's view of the content of the categorical imperative, which of course does include a reference to what we can will that everyone do. I am referring to the *concept* of a categorical imperative.

his interpretation of the universal prescriptions of morality, Hare does not allow for this reading. But it seems to me natural and perfectly intelligible to think of a universal prescription simply as a claim about how everyone ought to act, such that if anyone sincerely assents to it, he must acknowledge a reason to act that way.

This interpretation is quite weak, for it says nothing about what type of reason it might be. It could be the type recognized by utilitarianism, but it might not be. The question is how the interests of all parties affected by the act, including the agent, enter into the generation of the universal reasons implied by a moral judgment.

One answer to this question is that the interests of all affected parties generate reasons on an equal basis, in proportion to the strengths of their individual preferences. This is equivalent to Hare's view of the content of morality, for it corresponds to what you would want, taking up the point of view of each of the parties in turn, and somehow combining all those vicarious viewpoints into a collective preference. But other universal systems of reasons are imaginable that also give consideration to everyone, in some sense.

Specifically, some moral views can be formulated only in terms of agent-relative reasons. One fairly common view, right or wrong, is that an individual may count his own interests and the interests of those to whom he is personally attached more heavily than the interests of strangers: there is not a single, neutral measure of the good that everyone is morally required exclusively to try to promote (though such a neutral value may form *part* of the basis of morality). Other agent-relative principles are involved in the belief in selective obligations to those to whom we are related in certain ways, and also in the belief in deontological restrictions of the kind that limit what we may intentionally do, as opposed to what we may bring about. To avoid the complications of discussing a moral permission, which is the denial of a moral requirement, let me use the example of an agent-relative requirement to favor the interests of one's children over the interests of strangers—a requirement that many people would accept. I am concerned for the moment not with its truth but with its formal character.

Unless such a moral view is covertly derivative from something more fundamental, it clearly cannot express a universal prescription interpreted in accordance with assumption (2). If someone believes that he ought to favor his own children, he believes that anyone ought to do this, and that this is true of all similar actual and hypothetical cases, including those in which he occupies a different position. But that does not mean that he *desires* that everyone should act that way in all those cases. If he puts himself in each relevant position successively and considers what he would want to be done and how strongly, he might get a very different result.

For example, an affluent American or European might refer to his obligation to his children to explain why he should not (even if he were inclined) contribute over half of his income to famine relief—because although this would save many African children from starvation, it would seriously lower the standard of living of his own children. But if he puts himself in the position of even one of the starving African children who would be saved from death by his sacrifice, or in the position of one of their parents, his desire for the donation will greatly outweigh the desire he has not to give it as things actually are. He may, in fact, think that if he were in their position he would be justified in taking the needed resources by force, if he could. So this agent-relative obligation claims that each person has a reason for concern about his own children that can, in cases of conflict, lead him to wish that others would pursue their children's interests as wholeheartedly as they would if they gave that reason its full weight. And the result may be that what one universally prescribes is not what one desires should universally be done.

Hare's response would be that such a special obligation appears only at the level of intuitive moral thinking: perhaps it can be justified at the critical level on account of the general utility of people's having a deeply ingrained disposition to take special care of their children—but if it cannot be justified in that way, no such special obligation exists.[6]

Perhaps Hare is right. But if someone else disagrees and claims there are special obligations and permissions far in excess of what utilitarianism would allow, he cannot be refuted by an appeal to the logic of the moral concepts that they both share, because Hare's crucial logical claim, that to prescribe universally is to express a universal desire of a particular kind, embodies the central moral view that is in dispute.

It is hard to know how these disputes can be settled if they cannot be settled by logic. Their real subject matter is human motivation, specifically practical reason. We are not in possession of a general method of discovering what people have reason to do, and therefore of discovering those universal principles of practical reason, concerning the ways in which we must consider each other, that form the basis of morality.

Derek Parfit has argued that some agent-relative principles like the one I have discussed may be criticized on the ground that they are collectively self-defeating. For example, it might be the case that if we each give priority to our own children, the results will be worse for all our children

---

[6]Cf. *Moral Thinking*, p. 199.

than if none of us does. It might even be the case that each of us will be able personally to benefit his own children less than if none of us follows this policy.[7] But in the actual world, it is clear that if no one gave priority to his own children, or if everyone radically reduced the degree of this priority, some children would gain and some would lose; the policy would not be collectively self-defeating in this strong sense.

So the criticism of such principles cannot be merely an internal one. It must be a defense of radical impartiality among persons as the motivational foundation of morality. The question is, Do I have a reason to regulate my conduct by principles designed to give equal weight to everyone's preferences?

For Hare, that is not a question within morality, since he believes it follows from the logic of the moral concepts that these are the only kinds of principles that can be correct. Moral argument stops at this point, and if there are any arguments to be given, they must be of another kind. To some extent he believes it is possible to appeal to prudential reasons in addressing the motivational question.[8] But to the extent that such reasons recommend utilitarianism, they are likely to work even better, for most of us, in defense of a less demanding morality with agent-relative permissions to favor yourself and those close to you.

In the end, we are left with a confrontation between someone who is willing to do only what he can universally prescribe in the strong sense implied by assumption (2), and someone Hare calls the amoralist—who does not prescribe anything in this sense and therefore has to refrain from using the moral vocabulary. Since I believe this to be a dispute within morality, I would describe as an amoralist only someone still farther out, who refuses to produce universal prescriptions even of a much weaker kind: he has no views about how everyone should behave, or what reasons for action everyone should recognize. Someone who does not think he ought to do what he wants done in all similar cases may not be an amoralist at all, but just someone with a different moral position.

The question whether agent-relative principles have a place in morality at the fundamental level is a complex one with many aspects. It includes the analysis of rights and permissions as well as of special obligations. Hare's position on all these apparent exceptions to agent-neutral morality is that they can be explained, insofar as they are valid, as consequences at the intuitive level of utilitarian thinking at the critical level. But the main theoretical question is whether the utilitarian method is correct at the

[7] See Derek Parfit, *Reasons and Persons* (Oxford University Press, 1984), pp. 100–108.
[8] *Moral Thinking*, Chapter 11.

critical level, and this, I believe, depends on whether an impartial consequentialism has overriding weight as the governing principle of practical
reason. This is probably the first question of ethical theory. It requires that
we consider further the alternative degrees of subordination of our conduct to the review of a detached, external standpoint that abstracts from
who we are. I do not think we have ready to hand a general method for
thinking about these sorts of questions.

IV

Let me move briefly to another issue. I shall pass over assumption (4),
except to mention that the question of whether the concern we owe to
others should be determined by their preferences or by something else—a
restricted subset of their preferences, or their interest measured by some
objective standard—has received extensive discussion recently.[9] Here
again, what Hare assumes is certainly not a moral tautology. But what I
want to discuss next is how conflicting interests are to be combined in
moral deliberation, once they have been recognized, in whatever form.

The question is answered for Hare by assumption (5). The right thing to
do is determined by balancing the strengths of the preferences I would
have for different courses of action if I were in the position of each of the
affected parties, including the agent. The course of action with the greatest quantitative balance of favorable over unfavorable preferences for all
these possibilities taken together is the right one. It is the one I would
prescribe, if I had to prescribe universally.

My question is not whether this is what I *would* want, given such a choice,
but whether this form of balancing is the right way to accord equal moral
consideration to everyone. Obviously it is *a* way of according equal consideration: everyone's preferences (or interests, if some other measure of
individual benefit and harm is used) are counted the same way in the total.
But even if we assume that morality requires us to be impartial, or that at
least a component of morality does, is this the way to do it?

The problem about a maximizing principle is familiar. Can the relatively weak preferences or minor interests of a large number of people
legitimately outweigh the much stronger preferences or interests of a
small number? This kind of aggregation is particularly uncomfortable
when the majority is significantly better off than the minority in other
respects. It seems possible that the straight maximizing answer is wrong in

[9] For example, by Rawls in his theory of primary goods, and by T. M. Scanlon in
"Preference and Urgency," *Journal of Philosophy* 19 (1975).

some cases—that a marginal advantage to the majority or the better-off should not always win.

Hare, like Rawls, finds the model for moral reasoning in a specially constrained situation of rational individual choice. Instead of ignorance of who one is and a great deal else, Hare uses the device of imaginative identification with each person to guarantee that each person's point of view will be fully considered. But the question is whether we can combine our concern for the well-being of distinct persons by the same principles that are appropriate for settling conflicts among the different interests of a single person. Hare's position is clear: "I can see no reason for not adopting the same solution here as we do in cases where our own preferences conflict with one another."[10]

This question has been discussed at length and with inconclusive results in recent years. I myself think there is something in the view that compensation across lives cannot take the same form as compensation within lives, and that the same principles should not govern the two kinds of conflict. If we take an equal interest in everyone's interests, our concern for all those people will be as divided as its target, and it just is not obvious how the components can be combined.

I incline to think that we should give priority to those individuals who are most in need of help because they are objects of a concern that has priority over our concerns for those better-off, even if the latter are far more numerous. Where there is no interpersonal compensation for benefits and harms, some kind of priority ranking seems a reasonable device, at least as part of the solution. But no doubt there are other, better alternatives that I have not imagined. Moral theory suffers here from an impoverishment of possibilities. None of the familiar options seems clearly right. Again the situation requires us to search for a method of thinking that we do not yet have, rather than to extract one from the rules that already govern our moral language.

V

My limited aim has been to show that the elements of Hare's logic of the moral concepts that do the crucial work in his argument for utilitarianism are best understood not as part of the logic of those concepts at all, but as moral claims, whose foundation remains to be discovered and that can be denied without violating the logic of moral language. The foundations of morality have not yet been discovered anywhere else, either. But by mak-

---

[10] *Moral Thinking*, pp. 109–10.

ing his main moral claims part of the definition of morality, Hare excludes the search for their basis from moral theory, which is where it belongs.

There is another drawback to this method, having to do with moral motivation. Hare sometimes compares his view to that of Kant. But on Hare's reading, the imperatives of morality are hypothetical imperatives. Someone has a reason to obey them only if he cares about acting in ways that he could prescribe universally. We may be able to show him that he has reasons of self-interest to care about this—to be the type of person who will be governed by moral principles. But unless some external motive like that is present, he will have no reason to be moral at all. He will have no reason to ask himself whether he could prescribe universally the sort of conduct he is about to engage in, and no reason to be influenced by the answer to the question if he does ask it. (If he concludes that he could not prescribe his form of conduct universally, he can just say "So what?") If someone does not have the motives that according to Hare are presupposed by the use of moral language, then Hare's theory implies that moral argument cannot reveal any reasons for action that he does not already recognize.

It is only if we begin with a conception of morality as a set of claims about how everyone has a reason to behave that we will not discover, at the end of our account, that the question of motivation has been left outside ethical theory—to be answered perhaps by a doubtful appeal to self-interest. The search for the foundations of morality ought to be part of a general theory of reasons for action. Whatever arguments are offered in this context to support a moral position would show that we have reasons to live in accordance with it. A theory that packs a strong motivational assumption into the conditions for using moral language, and then derives the content of morality from the logic of this language, has not provided a secure foundation for the morality it defends. The hard old questions have merely been excluded from the field of moral argument.

16

Williams: One Thought Too Many

This was a review of Bernard Williams's Moral Luck: Philosophical Papers 1973–1980 *(Cambridge University Press, 1981). Williams's wonderful expression "moral luck" is one of those linguistic inventions that noticeably expands our understanding. It was the title of a paper he gave at the Aristotelian Society meetings in 1976, to which I was the respondent. I stole the title for my reply, and later republished it in* Mortal Questions, *which appeared in 1979. Though the origin of the phrase was specified in a footnote, I am distressed to learn that some people think I invented it myself—an error that probably bothers me more than it does Williams, whose lack of vanity always makes it easy to review his books.*

Over the past decade Bernard Williams has attacked the objectivity of ethics with mounting intensity. He denies that ethics can tell us the truth about what to do and how to live by discovering principles that are revealed when we regard our lives and our societies not from a subjective or individual standpoint but from a detached, impartial one. Such a standpoint would be the analogue in the domain of choice and action of the objectivity pursued in science by detachment from each individual's perception of the world. Scientific detachment enables us to form a conception of how the world is in itself, rather than how it looks from here—or even how it generally appears to creatures like us.

The strongest analogue would be the position that ethical judgments are about an external moral reality, as astronomy is about an external physical

---

Reprinted with permission from *The Times Literary Supplement*, May 7, 1982.

reality, but Williams denies much more than this. He denies that there can be any universal principles of conduct that must recommend themselves even internally to all rational human beings, however different their personal feelings, ambitions, and attachments. He denies it because ethics, if it is to have a real bearing on action, must engage the will, and he believes that motivation starts from and is limited by a set of desires and sentiments that varies greatly from person to person, and even within one person over time. This theoretical issue about the objectivity of ethics is intimately connected with the more immediate question of how complete a submission morality can demand of us. Williams is prepared to offer stiff resistance. He rejects both the utilitarian position that we are required to live in a way that will promote the welfare of everyone impartially and the Kantian position that we are required to live in accordance with principles that could be endorsed impartially as standards that everyone must follow. And he has serious doubts about how viable or important morality is in any form.

Scorn for the view *sub specie aeternitatis* was already marked in his contribution to *Utilitarianism: For and Against,* published in 1973 (his fellow author, J. J. C. Smart, was *for*). The thirteen essays collected in *Moral Luck* have appeared since then, and they form an extremely interesting book, the product of fine philosophical intelligence and irreverent temperament concentrated on difficult and unavoidable problems. Williams writes vividly and with force and manages to treat abstract questions together with problems of actual life in a way that makes their connections stand out. A few of the pieces are slight or too quickly written, but altogether it is an important collection. Though its central thesis is in my opinion false, anyone interested in the current state of moral philosophy must pay attention to this book.

While most of the essays are about ethics, two of the strongest are about objectivity and realism outside ethics, a topic that also receives penetrating treatment in his *Descartes: The Project of Pure Enquiry* (1978). Williams has thus been concerned generally with the question of how far outside ourselves we can and should try to get, in thought and action. But his treatment of morality is not the consequence of a broader skepticism: he is not among that incomprehensibly large number of philosophers who currently deny the objectivity of factual and scientific knowledge. His attack on what he regards as excessive pretensions in ethics are specific to it and depend on its claim to a role in individual life.

The transcendent impulse in ethical theory comes out both in claims about the universal content of morality and in claims about its supreme authority over our lives. Williams challenges both these claims (whether in their utilitarian or in their Kantian forms), but he is unsure how to divide his opposition between the two. A challenge with respect to content would say that any morality must be grounded in the dominant attitudes and feelings of the person whose morality it is and therefore cannot be impersonal. A challenge with respect to authority would say that because morality is grounded in only some of our motives, it should sometimes be overridden by others that are more important to us: not just motives of self-interest, but altruistic concern for particular persons or the commitment to achieve or pursue some special project or aim. (The "should" here doesn't express a moral judgment, obviously.)

The ambivalence appears, for instance, in the title essay, which deals with the question whether actions can be assessed retroactively in virtue of outcomes that were not and could not have been foreseen with certainty in advance. Can luck determine whether what we have done is justified or not, and if so, is that a truth internal to morality or a limitation on it? Williams argues that it is not possible always to act in such a way that one will have no reason to reproach oneself, whatever happens: "The perspective of deliberative choice on one's life is constitutively *from here*. Correspondingly the perspective of assessment with greater knowledge is necessarily *from there*, and not only can I not guarantee how factually it will then be, but I cannot ultimately guarantee from what standpoint of assessment my major and most fundamental regrets will be." If there is no timelessly valid external standpoint of evaluation, I cannot even claim that my present choice is objectively right relative to my current *beliefs* about the likelihood of various outcomes.

Williams discusses the example of Gauguin, or someone like him, who abandons his family to pursue his art, and who will be able to regard the choice retroactively as justified if, and only if, he turns out to be a great artist. "The project in the interests of which the decision is made is one with which the agent is identified in such a way that if it succeeds, his stand-point of assessment will be from a life which then derives an important part of its significance for him from that very fact; if he fails, it can, necessarily, have no such significance in his life."

This seems to imply relativity to point of view in the *content* of moral judgments. But are such assessments moral at all? Williams says that the fact that Gauguin can't use them to justify himself to his family doesn't show that they are not. In general, he believes, the moral justification of one person's action need not silence the complaints of others to have been wronged by it. (This is also taken up in the essay "Politics and Moral Character," which is about the problem of dirty hands.) But here he is drawn to the different view that though Gauguin is not morally justified by success, his moral luck consists nevertheless in the relation of his life to morality: he would for moral reasons have had to regret what he did if he had failed, but those moral reasons are swamped, for him and also for us if not for his family, by all those paintings. And that depends on the luck of turning out to be a great artist. Williams concludes that if for such reasons we reject the authority of any morality that claims to tell us what would be right however things turn out, we will be left with a morality less important than ours is usually taken to be. I myself should prefer to say that Gauguin was justified by his success, but that this justification, though probably not moral, was not simply a product of his later standpoint either, but was something more objective.

The dominance of impersonal principles is also attacked in the well-known essay "Persons, Character, and Morality," from which I shall mention two points. Williams argues against Charles Fried that it is a mistake to want a *justification* for saving one's wife rather than a stranger from drowning—instead of flipping a coin, in an either/or situation. He objects that if the rescuer thinks it is *permissible* to save his wife, that gives him "one thought too many." In the same essay, Williams claims that there may be certain ground projects in a person's life that are a condition of his wanting to go on living at all, and that it cannot be reasonable to demand that he give up such projects in the name of an impartial morality, whether utilitarian or Kantian—presumably because if he leaves the scene, the morality can have no hold on him.

This is an audacious and rather original form of motivational blackmail: "If I have to serve the greatest good of the greatest number or the categorical imperative, I might as well be dead!" It's a claim few people could make without bluffing. While the demands of some forms of impersonal morality on individual motivation do seem excessive, it is much harder than Williams makes out simply to deny jurisdiction to the impersonal standpoint with regard to our most fundamental feelings and commitments.

The man who plunges into the waves to save his wife will not have Kantian or rule-utilitarian arguments running through his head, but that need not prevent him from having something to say in retrospect, if only to himself, that justifies not having done anything to inhibit the natural impulse of extreme partiality. (Suppose he had a somewhat better chance of rescuing the stranger.) It is the same thought that he would need to deal with a case in which the tables were turned and his wife drowned because the only available rescuer was not he but another man who rescued his own wife instead. Perhaps Williams would say that in that case anything but pure grief would be indecent, but I believe most of us are impelled to try to lead our personal lives and form our basic aims in a way that can be reconciled with an impersonal standpoint from which everyone is judged alike.

It is one of our standpoints, after all: an important part of what makes us human. And if partiality is to have any limits, they must be set from outside. The difficulty is to achieve some kind of integrity in human life without either overwhelming its personal core with a pervasive impartiality or bulldozing the impersonal standpoint in the name of what one personally must do. Both these reactions to the problems Williams so vividly poses have the flavor of reactions to oneself: on the one hand, guilt about the personal and selfish; on the other hand, rebellion against the impersonal admonitions of conscience. The discovery of an alternative that we can live by I take to be the task of ethical theory.

Williams believes there cannot be such a thing as ethical theory, for nothing so purportedly universal could explain by what right it legislates to the moral sentiments. In "Internal and External Reasons," he sets forth the position that all reasons a person can have for doing or wanting anything must derive by deliberative reasoning from his subjective motivational set, which is simply a given for any person at a time, though it may change. If there were such things as external reasons, which held for all rational persons independently of the details of their motivational sets, they would have to be reachable, to the point of becoming motivationally effective, by some rational process other than the ordinary deliberative one of drawing practical conclusions from existing motives. "I see no reason to suppose," says Williams, "that these conditions could possibly be met."

I see no reason to suppose that they couldn't. Williams himself is prepared to allow that "there is essential indeterminacy in what can be counted a rational deliberative process." And he thinks reasoning can sometimes lead to changes in the motivational set. Why can't there be, as different defenders of impartial morality have thought, a form of insight about our nonunique place in the world that leads us to acknowledge that we should live in a way we can endorse from outside, and for everyone similarly situated, as well as from within? What form that result would take and how dominant it would be are further questions. But why isn't putting oneself in other people's shoes a genuine form of reasoning?

Allowing such regulative authority to the impartial view need not imply the neglect or suppression of those personal feelings, attachments, projects, and individualities of character that Williams so rightly emphasizes. In "Utilitarianism and Moral Self-Indulgence," he says that even if the aim of objective knowledge is to dissociate thought about the world from what is distinctively oneself and perhaps from anything that is distinctively human, "that cannot be the aim of moral thought and experience, which must primarily involve grasping the world in such a way that one can, as a particular human being, live in it." This is absolutely right, but it seems to me to set the main task for ethical theory rather than to provide a reason to give it up.

The same essay deals subtly and convincingly with the charge that those who reject certain means to the achievement of the best overall consequences must be guilty of moral self-indulgence. Williams acknowledges that such self-indulgence can exist, but locates it in a reflexive concern with one's own virtue, of which a utilitarian may be as guilty as anyone else. He has no sympathy for this, but a great deal of respect for the less self-conscious phenomenon of moral *character,* which makes it impossible or difficult or necessary for a person to do certain things, even though he may be unable to supply reasons that provide universal justification. This is important for the moral virtues, and it is one of the reasons that conflicts of value cannot always be smoothed out by reducing them to a common rational basis and adding up the components.

In "Conflicts of Values" Williams makes the related point that, in a context of shared moral sentiment, the fact that a further reason is not needed to support a moral distinction (between, say, abortion and infanticide) does not mean that the distinction is irrational. "'You can't kill that, it's a child' is more convincing as a reason than any reason which might be advanced for its being a reason." This seems right, but it also seems compatible with the possibility of later criticism or justification.

"The Truth in Relativism" claims that we cannot morally appraise as right or wrong systems of moral belief that stand in purely "notional" as opposed to "real" confrontation with our own: that is, systems that, while inconsistent with our own, are not real options for us. Williams gives as examples the life and outlook of a Greek Bronze Age chief or a medieval samurai, asserting that they "lack the relation to our concerns which alone gives any point and substance to appraisal." This is a severely restricted relativism, but the reference to "point and substance" provides no independent argument for it. If there were, contrary to Williams's conviction, such a thing as moral objectivity, then there might not be much point but there would certainly be substance in the moral appraisal of Pharaonic slavery, even though it is not a real option for us.

I cannot do justice here to the final essays, "Wittgenstein and Idealism" and "Another Time, Another Place, Another Person." The former is the best treatment I know of the question to what extent Wittgenstein's later writing expresses a transcendental idealism of the first-person plural, using a *we* that is the plural descendant of the idealist *I*. The world then is not *my* world but *our* world. Williams finds such a view in the later Wittgenstein, together with a problem present also in the *Tractatus,* of how to express it without talking nonsense (by saying, for example, that the truths of mathematics depend on our decisions).

The latter essay demonstrates brilliantly the incoherence in positivism and its heirs that comes from trying to wed verificationist empiricism, with its emphasis on the human perspective, to a scientific worldview that seeks a representation of the world not from here or from any other particular perspective. Note, this is a mirror image of the attack on the Kantian fusion of impersonal detachment with the basic moral aim of guiding individual life inside the world.

Moral Luck is an arresting book. Williams is a provocative and stimulating writer, and the leading contemporary disparager of transcendent ambitions in moral philosophy. In attacking those ambitions, and in doubting the preeminent importance of morality, Williams is at the beating heart of the subject. It matters whether he is right.

17

Williams: Resisting Ethical Theory

This was a review of Bernard Williams's Ethics and the Limits of Philosophy *(Harvard University Press, 1985). Williams's skeptical attacks on impersonal morality have had an extraordinary impact on the field—mostly by
provoking people who disagree with him to produce reams of counterin-
surgent ethical theory of the kind he thinks is impossible. Life would be much
less interesting for us Kantians without him.*

This highly absorbing book is an attack on the possibility of ethical theory
as a philosophical discipline. Its central thesis is that the view *sub specie
aeternitatis*, though an appropriate vantage point from which to seek an
understanding of the natural world, is entirely inappropriate as the standpoint from which to construct our world, the world in which we must live.
Since the question of how we should live in relation to one another is the
defining question of ethics, it follows that the characteristic ambition of
ethical theory—to discover universal, objective moral principles—cannot
be realized. That is not because there are no ethical truths but because
truth in this realm is neither universal, nor objective, nor based on reason.
It is only another philosophers' delusion that without a philosophical
foundation ethical thought is impossible.

   Some of the arguments for this conclusion are frankly philosophical,
particularly the negative ones having to do with the nature and limits of
objectivity—among recent representatives of the new romanticism, this
book stands out for its level of argument. But also evident is a current of

---

Reprinted with permission from *The Journal of Philosophy* 83 (1986).

exasperation with modern ethical theory, judged to be of little use in dealing with the practical issues of contemporary life, and even further removed from anything concrete than the religion it replaced. About the hope of achieving practical results by a philosophical justification of morality, Williams says rather chillingly, "What will the professor's justification do, when they break down the door, smash his spectacles, take him away?" (p. 23).

Williams attacks the leading candidates for a general theory and offers the hope of an alternative form of ethical thought more skeptical and less ambitious, but also more socially and psychologically realistic than its rivals: he thinks we can retain many of the Enlightenment's ideals without an Enlightenment moral epistemology. The positive conception is no more than a hope and is not very fully developed, and I think it would be a mistake for ethical theorists to abandon their efforts in the face of the negative arguments. But this is a superior book, glittering with intelligence and style, and, as with any work of strong philosophical interest, one can learn a great deal from it without becoming convinced.

Williams draws a contrast between scientific objectivity and practical reason. He takes the unfashionably sane view that science tells us about the world that is already there independent of our theories, and elaborates this in terms of the idea (taken from his earlier book on Descartes) of an "absolute" conception of reality, a conception that is to a maximum degree independent of our human or personal perspectives and their peculiarities, but at the same time places those perspectives within the world and explains both why the world appears to them as it does and how it is possible for us to form the absolute conception itself. The way the world really is explains how we can form a correct conception of it by transcending the appearances, even if we start from distinct subjective points of view.

But ethical thought is concerned with the question of how we should live, not how things are. Even if this question were to admit of convergence on a single answer from different perspectives, the explanation could not be anything like the one science offers for convergence in our beliefs about what the world is like. Ethical convictions and disagreements are not like perceptions caused by the action on our senses of a single external world.

So the defense of objective principles in ethics requires an alternative account of how convergence on the truth is possible, as well as a theory of error to explain the evident and frequent failures of convergence. But Williams argues that there is no such alternative. Mathematics provides no better a model for ethical truth and knowledge than science does: any account must be specifically suited to the subject matter. The question is whether any of the leading candidates has a chance of being right.

Not every ethical theory tries to provide ethics with a universal and inescapable foundation. Williams also criticizes certain forms of utilitarianism and contractualism, represented by R. M. Hare, John Rawls, and Thomas Scanlon, which start from the motivational assumption of some form of impartiality without claiming that such impartiality is itself universally required. He argues that they are in different ways motivationally unrealistic. (About the peculiar state of moral consciousness required by indirect or two-level utilitarianism, for example, he says: "One cannot separate, except by an imposed and illusory dissociation, the theorist in oneself from the self whose dispositions are being theorized" [p. 110].) But I want to concentrate on his objections to the two traditions of strictly foundational theory he thinks it most important to rule out: the Kantian and the Aristotelian.

One tries to ground ethics in our rationality, and the other, in our humanity. This means the first has somewhat more universal pretensions than the second, but both attempt to prove the authority of ethics inescapable by basing it on something essential about us. And both purport to offer an objective solution, in the form of an endorsement of certain principles and dispositions from a standpoint outside the cultural and personal contingencies of our lives—a standpoint that could be shared by beings very different, historically and personally, from ourselves.

On the Kantian view, as Williams interprets it, ethical requirements arise from the idea of rational freedom—an idea that applies both to the justification of beliefs and to the formation of desires and intentions. In both cases we are supposed to be able to stand back from our initial impressions or inclinations and decide whether from this external standpoint they should be admitted as rational considerations. Just as I must ask, if I am to be freely rational, what, on the evidence, this person who I am should believe—so I must ask what, in the light of available considerations, this person who I am should do. In both cases the answer will depend not just on my personal situation and inclinations, but on principles that would apply to anyone similarly situated—and ultimately perhaps on principles of thought or practical reason that are completely general.

We can set aside here the substantive results that are supposed to follow when we take this step. Williams objects to the step itself. His argument against it is brief. He believes that the analogy between factual and practical reflection is a poor one, because factual deliberation is not essentially first-personal. In trying to decide what to believe, I am simply trying to decide what is true, and the objective relations of evidence to conclusion should govern the result, whether the evidence is found in my experience or in someone else's. But:

> It is very different with deliberation for action. Practical deliberation is in every case first-personal, and the first person is not derivative or naturally replaced by *anyone*. . . . The *I* that stands back in rational reflection from my desires is still the *I* that has those desires and will, empirically and concretely, act; and it is not, simply by standing back in reflection, converted into a being whose fundamental interest lies in the harmony of all interests. (pp. 68–69)

If this were an effective argument, it would work against all versions of the idea of practical reasoning from a detached standpoint, whether or not they give authority to the harmony of all interests. The claim is that by standing back from my desires I don't bring into play an impersonal motivational standpoint that supersedes their authority. My perceptual beliefs naturally defer to such an authority, because they aim at the truth about the world outside me, but my prereflective desires aim only at something much more personal: what I am to do. Reflection, if it is to have practical effect, cannot leave this *I* and its particular motives behind, cannot convert it into a mere *object* of consideration.

The Aristotelian alternative—for which Williams has much more sympathy because of its emphasis on the virtues and the whole character of life—would ground a universal answer to the question of how we should live in a theory of human nature and human well-being. If there were a universal human nature and if, contemplating it from outside, we could see that there was a single form of individual and social life and a set of emotional and practical dispositions that was best for any being with that nature, this would provide an objective basis for the endorsement (for humans) of that life and those dispositions. It would harmonize the internal and the external view and derive ethics from a true conception of our place in the universe.

Williams's objection to this is not that it is unintelligible, but simply that it is no longer plausible to believe that such a controlling teleology of human nature exists. Apart from the biological basics, human good is underdetermined by human nature. Moreover, we have learned to expect that the dispositions that define any more particular form of life will lose rather than gain in conviction when looked at from outside:

> The outside point of view of his dispositions is available to the agent himself. But if he tries in his reflection to abstract himself totally from those dispositions, and to think about himself and the world as though he did not have them, then he should not be surprised if he cannot get an adequate picture of the value of anything, including his own dispositions. He cannot do so, pre-

cisely because those dispositions are part of the content of his actual self. (p. 51)

From outside it is evident that many incompatible perspectives are compatible with human nature; the ultimate support of an ethical point of view can lie only in the agent's actual dispositions, unsanctified by a universal teleology.

What does this leave us with? Williams believes that there are truths about how we should live and that they can be known, but he holds that this makes sense only if we take a nonobjectivist view of the matter. If we try to ascend to an objective standpoint, we will lose the perspectives from which alone ethical knowledge is possible. If we insist on being moved only by what is a rational *consideration* for us, we will paint ourselves into an empty corner from which nothing seems to matter. We must start from what we are—not merely what we are as human or rational beings, but rather what we are as particular creatures of a particular culture.

One of the marks of such particularity is the capacity to apply substantive or "thick" ethical concepts, like *coward, lie, brutality, gratitude,* and so forth. These terms can be properly employed only from within a certain ethical perspective, by those with the appropriate dispositions to feel and act; nevertheless, they can be used to make true statements and to express ethical knowledge, knowledge that may not be available to someone who cannot occupy the perspective or who abandons it. (Williams here refers to recent work of John McDowell.) This implies a qualified form of relativism, according to which our moral judgments can clash only with other judgments tied to forms of life actually or imaginatively accessible to us (perhaps through a historical connection with our own)—so that they represent competing answers to the question, How should *we* live? It also implies that reflection may actually destroy ethical knowledge, since an external view may undermine the prereflective dispositions on which traditional judgments depend, without replacing them by anything more objective.

This seems to imply a kind of ethical conservatism. But although Williams distrusts the impulse to start over from first principles and set everything on a new foundation, he also believes we can't go back to a prereflective, traditional social state, if there ever was such a thing. His positive conception of ethical thought is obscure to me, however. Here is a characteristic passage:

> Reflective criticism should basically go in a direction opposite to that encouraged by ethical theory. Theory looks characteristically for considerations that are very general and have as little distinctive content as possible, because it is

trying to systematize and because it wants to represent as many reasons as possible as applications of other reasons. But critical reflection should seek for as much shared understanding as it can find on any issue, and use any ethical material that, in the context of the reflective discussion, makes some sense and commands some loyalty. (pp. 116–17)

The state of mind toward the ethical that we are supposed to hope for is not knowledge or that frequently suggested alternative, decision, but rather something else that Williams calls *confidence*. He describes it as "basically a social phenomenon," but doesn't tell us much more. I assume he means it to capture those convictions that survive reflection, discussion, and experience, even though they are not provided with an objective ground.

Admittedly, when reasonable persons try to decide what to do, this is often all they rely on, and it is certainly better than trying to settle everything by appeal to philosophically produced universal principles. But that has no tendency to show that nothing more is possible, and in fact when confidence begins to fail or when it encounters equal confidence going in the opposite direction, we find it natural to move to a more objective standpoint instead of simply relying on "what we are." This is not a philosophically imposed tendency, but a natural movement of human thought, and we attempt it even if it often cannot be expected to solve our problems.

Williams would repress the impulse: he argues that it is a delusion fostered by the current dominance of administrative rationality (in our culture every dispute is supposed to have a rationally and publicly defensible resolution). He is particularly impatient with the kind of search for universal foundations that underlies Michael Tooley's denial of the moral relevance of the distinction between abortion and infanticide, or the increasingly common charge of "speciesism" with respect to our preferential treatment of humans as against animals. "It is more revealingly called 'humanism,'" says Williams, "and it is not a prejudice" (p. 118).

There is an undeniable appeal to this effort to block philosophy's insatiable appetite for justifications; by pushing the demand too far, one may lose everything. But if we follow Williams, we may err on the side of complacency instead. To me, his negative arguments seem inadequate to his radical conclusions.

To begin with, the search for objective ethical principles could be represented more charitably: it need not be so comprehensive or reductive as Williams assumes. He defines an *ethical theory* as "a theoretical account of what ethical thought and practice are, which account either implies a general test for the correctness of basic ethical beliefs and principles or else implies that there cannot be such a test" (p. 72). But theoretical principles may be universal without being totalitarian; they may handle some conflicts of values without handling them all. They can be regulative, allowing room for a great deal of pluralism and culturally determined ethical variation within the framework that they define. The idea that ethical theory is always after the single best form of life for all humans or all rational beings is just a bogeyman. At one point Williams suggests that a contractualist theory might legitimately play the more limited moral role needed to justify liberalism, but he thinks that the desire for reasonable agreement on which it depends will be strong enough to withstand the strain of divergent particular values only in rather special circumstances, so that it can't serve as a general theory. Still, pessimism about the claims of ethical theory seems less warranted if its ambitions of external dominance are less than total.

How far outside of ourselves can we legitimately go in practical reasoning, even in search of limited results? Williams believes that the external standpoint is fundamentally a standpoint of observation, that it is not the source of independent practical or evaluative judgments. He attributes the smoothness of the transition from perception to science to the fact that ordinary perceptual judgments, despite their subjectivity, purport to be about the external world and lend themselves naturally to criticism and replacement or supplementation from progressively more objective vantage points toward that same world. His claim is that to attempt this in the practical domain is to leap into the void.

He finds this intuitively obvious, but the arguments he offers seem uncompelling to someone who doesn't. Admittedly, objectivity here would have to be *sui generis* and nothing like scientific objectivity, but that doesn't prevent us from telling a story about practical reason that is at least structurally analogous. Our initial judgments about what to do and how to live are, on this interpretation, not merely subjective but implicitly, perhaps inchoately, objective in intention. That would be so if an external view of ourselves, which is after all one of the essential features of rational humanity, were involved in practical judgments from the start—so that a judgment about what I should do was also, at least implicitly, a judgment about what the person who I am should do. This is entirely compatible with the recognition that the *I* who reflects is also the *I* who desires and acts. Practical deliberation can be simultaneously first and third personal.

The external view need not be very clearly or consciously formulated in order to provide an entry for more sophisticated objective criticism and justification. After all, the fledgling objectivity that makes perceptual judgments continuous with the results of particle physics does not anticipate the remarkable forms of objectivity by which it will be replaced. But this structural analogy is useless unless the notion of practical objectivity can be given some content. What general method of objective advance corresponds in the practical domain to the scientific method of explaining the appearances as perspectives on an independent reality?

The Aristotelian option is implausible not just factually but morally. Even if we could recognize from outside a universal human nature and a correlative human good, that wouldn't prove that each person should pursue that good for himself or even for humanity as a whole to the exclusion of everything else. Aristotelian teleology, if it were available, would be no more irresistible than sociobiology: we may have reason to transcend human nature in certain respects.

That brings us to the other option: Kantian objectivity. What corresponds here to the scientific effort to place our perceptual perspectives in the context of an absolute conception of reality constructed on explanatory principles is the ethical effort to place our pretheoretical personal judgments of what to do in the context of a general conception of what people should do. These pretheoretical judgments are regarded not as the results of our causal interaction with ethical reality, but simply as primitive examples of evaluative or practical reasoning, and we hope that the progressively more objective versions generated by ethical theory will be more advanced examples, manifesting our capacity to take up a universal standpoint distinct from that of any particular person.

The belief in objectivity clearly implies a commitment to some kind of realism—not realism about a world of values with which we causally interact, but realism about the existence of reasons or values that we can discover by certain processes of thought. The example of mathematics is marginally relevant in this connection, not because mathematics is anything like ethics—parts of it govern the physical world, after all—but because it is an example of the exploration of a domain of objective truth that does not proceed through causal interaction with the world and construction of a causal theory of the pretheoretical appearances. Mathematical knowledge is explained by our capacity to follow mathematical arguments, and we do that in our heads.

In ethics also, if realism is correct, the truth of certain principles and the existence of certain reasons will explain our capacity to know them through our capacity to follow the forms of thought and argument that reveal their correctness. We begin with limited access to the truth, from a limited, personal point of view, and in the course of our explorations we may go astray or get lost. But we can also make discoveries, and those discoveries will alter our motives and expand our perspective as agents. The capacity to appreciate and give weight to the lives of other persons, whoever they are, is a form of understanding. To say that it is in the end still I who must act does nothing to discredit the claim of such objective motives to moral authority.

No abstract philosophical argument can rule this out: that is my own conviction about ethics and the limits of philosophy. The test of skepticism must come from ethical arguments themselves. If they produce convincing examples of an extended knowledge about how we should live and deal with one another, knowledge acquired in part by transcending our personal and societal starting points, then the reality of the results will not be discredited by their dissimilarity from other types of knowledge or truth or by the fact that individuals must in the end be motivated by them.

The best reasons for skepticism about ethical theory are the meagerness and controversiality of its results and the lack of agreement over methods. There is, of course, disagreement and uncertainty in science and mathematics, but there is also an enormous body of incontestable discoveries, which make the rejection of realism in those domains nothing but a philosophical fantasy. Ethics is different, and the attempt to give it premature definition can result in disengaged moralizing. However, nothing in the primitive current state of ethical theory requires us to give up hope for the possibility of eventual progress and for the retrospective validation of the modest apparent progress that some of us believe has already been made. This optimism is best combined with the view that ethical theory, if there is such a thing, is in its infancy.

For that reason unrepentant theorists can agree with Williams in one respect about the practice of ethical thought. We should not despise ethical convictions for which we can provide no theoretical foundation; they may be insights into the truth, or part of it; in any case, they may be all we have. He is right that all-embracing theories are by themselves no substitute in the present state of things for a method of thinking that employs all the insights and forms of criticism we can muster—even if the result is somewhat anarchic. But this doesn't mean that theory is impossible—even if it won't help much when they break down the door.

18

Schelling: The Price of Life

This was a review of Thomas Schelling's Choice and Consequence *(Harvard University Press, 1984). Though it's rather slight, I include it for the interest of Schelling's views on criminal monopolies, the value of life, and intrapersonal strategies of conflict.*

A central subject of economics is human motivation in the aggregate: how the decisions, rational or irrational, of millions of people combine to produce large-scale results. It relies on an understanding of the way in which each individual's decisions are affected by the perception of the motivations of others whose interests may conflict or overlap with his. Game theory studies the rational principles of such interaction.

Thomas Schelling, a subtle and imaginative economist, is distinguished for having extended the economic style of systematic and relatively precise thinking about human interaction into new domains. His famous earlier book, *The Strategy of Conflict,* published in 1960, dealt mostly with war, deterrence, and international relations. While four of the fifteen chapters in this new collection of essays deal with the bomb and related matters, most of it is about other things: the value of life and death, organized crime, strategies for conflict of a person with himself, and, somewhat bashfully, ethics.

What makes Schelling such a pleasure to read, apart from his lean, clear, wry, conversational style, is the shrewdness and human insight with which he breaks down complex problems and phenomena into their parts, per-

---

Reprinted with permission from *The New Republic,* August 27, 1984.

mitting systematic understanding to develop. Some of his observations have the charm one associates with the work of Erving Goffman. For example, have you ever wondered what on earth organized crime was doing in the laundry business, as reported in recent years? Schelling proposes an explanation: it's a particularly efficient avenue for extortion, somewhat more refined and better for both criminal and victim than the traditional crude "protection" racket. Typical victims are restaurants, which are easily disrupted and often individually owned. Forcing them to subscribe to an overpriced monopoly laundry service is better than simply demanding cash because (a) the victim can put the transaction on his books without revealing to creditors or revenue agents that he pays tribute, (b) his embarrassment and loss of self-respect is reduced because he can tell himself, his wife, and his employees that he's merely a victim of excessive laundry prices, and (c) the payment is a tax-deductible business expense, so more can be demanded by the extortionist at less cost to the victim.

Most of the direct victims of organized crime, however, are small illegal businesspersons—bookies, prostitutes—who pass the cost of payoffs on to their customers. They can't complain to the police, and sometimes the police are employed directly by the syndicate to enforce payment, through selective application of the laws. Schelling suggests that the real money that sustains a large criminal organization and makes it look for other opportunities probably has to come from a black-market monopoly, created by the legal prohibition of something for which there is an unquenchable demand. Outlawing novocaine would probably do it, but in fact alcohol seems to have propelled organized crime into economic takeoff in this country during prohibition, and now narcotics provide the infrastructure. Schelling asks "whether the goal of somewhat reducing the consumption of narcotics, gambling, prostitution, . . . or anything else that is forced by law into the black market, is or is not outweighed by the costs to society of creating a criminal industry." My impression is that he thinks it's not worth it, but here as elsewhere he prefers to analyze the facts that bear on the question rather than to answer it directly. If, as he suggests, most of the harm done by narcotics results from their being illegal and vastly overpriced, they should probably be legalized.

One particularly fascinating question to which he is prepared to offer a tentative answer is this: How much should we require people to spend, or spend on their behalf out of tax revenues, on measures that reduce the risk of death? This bears upon the current controversy over requiring air bags in automobiles, but it applies also to medical care, airport safety, lifeboats, smoke alarms, and other lifesaving measures whose costs must be borne by someone, either as consumer or as taxpayer. Schelling proposes that we look at these expenditures from the point of view of their value to the parties whose risk is being reduced, and then ask if from that point of view there would be some better way to spend the money.

This requires an answer to the question of how much a human life is worth to its possessor, which is discussed in the important essay, "The Life You Save May Be Your Own." The first thing to notice is that poor people's lives are worth less to them in monetary terms than rich people's lives are—as measured by what they would spend to reduce the risk of death by a given amount. This is not, of course, because poor people value life less—everybody has only one—but because they value money more, having less of it to meet their most urgent needs.

On the basis of an informal survey of what well-paid professionals would pay for small incremental reductions in the probability of death. Schelling concludes that they value their lives at anywhere from ten to one hundred times a year's income. "In crude numbers this could mean that a Boeing 707 full of professional business people might value their own lives in a way that would make prevention of the fatal crash of a (yet unidentified) full airplane worth about $250 million." (Note that by parallel reasoning, a planeload of migrant farm workers would probably turn out to be worth less than $10 million.)

Schelling believes the state generally shouldn't force people to spend more on safety than it is worth to them: if they'd rather spend that sum on food or rent, let them. But what if the safety measures are paid for out of public funds, or can be provided at affordable cost only if everyone is required to have them? Schelling still wants to ask whether an alternative use of those funds would be worth more to the beneficiaries, so the problem of variation between rich and poor in the monetary value of life becomes acute. Is an amount that is well spent on the safety of flying business executives wasted if spent on the safety or health of garment workers or farm laborers? In determining the value of life for the purpose of assessing a mandatory or public safety measure, whose evaluation should be used? Should we calculate some kind of average, or should the state spend more on safety for the rich than for the poor?

This is not simply a question of distributive justice, because it can be posed even if we are committed to taxing the rich heavily for the benefit of the poor. The question is whether the money should be spent instead on something the poor value more than a given increment of safety. Schelling's instinct, if we can't turn over the money to them and let them decide how to spend it—is to try to simulate the results of such a process in public expenditure. But if this is done, and if we continue to live in an unequal society in which the well-off are taxed not only for the benefit of the poor but also for their own benefit, we may find ourselves with a double standard for public safety.

Schelling recognizes that this may be politically distasteful, but his sympathy for the imposition of equality in specific goods seems limited. After alluding to the fate of different classes in the sinking of the *Titanic* he makes this startling statement:

> We do not tolerate that any more. Those who want to risk their lives at sea and cannot afford a safe ship should perhaps not be denied the opportunity to entrust themselves to a cheaper ship without lifeboats; but if some people cannot afford the price of passage with lifeboats, and some people can, they should not travel on the same ship.

The question of whether there are goods that, even in a very unequal society like ours, should be provided in equal measure to everyone—even at considerable cost in efficiency and in preference to benefits that the poor might value more—is an important moral question. Schelling's examples pose it vividly, but his uneasiness about moral thinking prevents him from addressing it. He seems to think that for these purposes, we're all in the same boat only if we're all literally in the same boat. But some may feel that the limited concession to equality for its own sake that he admits in the case of the *Titanic* could be extended in certain respects to society as a whole—in regard to the provision of basic medical care, for example.

Two of the essays are about situations in which an individual can be seen as containing more than one self, simultaneously or in sequence, whose relations to each other may mimic interpersonal strategies: the alcoholic who wants to give up drinking, the smoker who wants to quit, the long-distance runner who wants to keep going despite exhaustion, the chronic procrastinator, the desperate dieter. Schelling's descriptions of the ways we can trick, coerce, and manipulate ourselves as if we were someone else are often perceptive and diverting. Yet his suggestions about how the law might be used to help us control ourselves are not very plausible.

He speculates that we might come to recognize legally binding promises not to smoke, for example, from which a person could not later release himself. But in ordinary interpersonal contracts at a later stage, one of the parties can release the other from the agreement they both made earlier. If at any time we are the sole representatives of our earlier selves for these purposes, how could we be denied the authority to overrule our past selves in the intrapersonal case? Either I'm the same person or I'm not; if I am, the decision is up to me at each point; if I'm not, my past self shouldn't be able to call in the law to help force me now to do what he wanted but I never agreed to.

Schelling's discussion here is uncharacteristically weak and lacking in realism. I think the reason is that he hasn't thought hard enough about the concept of personal identity and the fundamental role it plays in morality. In most moral reasoning the basic unit, for purposes of benefit or responsibility, is the temporally extended person, represented at each point in his life by its current stage, with some exceptions for madness and immaturity. The primacy of this unit has been attacked, notably by Derek Parfit in his remarkable book *Reasons and Persons*,[1] but it requires a deeper approach than Schelling can offer. These aren't empirical questions of the kind he likes.

The essays on strategy and nuclear weapons are preceded by a short introduction to game theory, which is then used in the discussion of such matters as the hazards of building weapons as "bargaining chips" and the various ways in which deadly conflict need not be a zero-sum game: there are plenty of choices from which both parties lose or both parties win, and Schelling tries to provide analytic guidance for distinguishing the latter from the former. There's an informative and optimistic chapter on whether small terrorist groups will get the bomb, though Schelling notes that the envisaged uses of nuclear weapons by governments are terrorist in any case. Lest this be taken to have moral implications, he adds: "I imply nothing derogatory or demeaning about strategic nuclear forces by emphasizing the traditional expectation that their primary use is to deter or to intimidate, and thereby to influence behavior, through the threat of enormous civilian damage."

But one shouldn't look a gift horse in the mouth. Schelling's analytical power, his shrewdness, his lucidity, and his uneasiness with ethics give his work a unique flavor. In this book he says illuminating things about rent control, gasoline rationing, tax deductions, euthanasia, nuclear proliferation, whether parents should fly in separate planes, and many other topics. Wherever one's political sympathies may lie, it is an invaluable resource for posing and thinking about difficult social questions.

[1] Oxford University Press, 1984.

19

Schelling: Personal Identity and Self-Command

This is a response, previously unpublished, to Thomas Schelling's Tanner Lecture delivered at the University of Michigan in March 1982. The lecture was published as "Ethics, Law, and the Exercise of Self-Command" in Sterling M. McMurrin, editor, The Tanner Lectures on Human Values IV *(University of Utah Press, 1983) and reprinted in his* Choice and Consequence *(Harvard University Press, 1984). These comments go into more detail about one of the issues touched on in my review.*

The enormous importance accorded to personal identity in law and in ethics can seem puzzling and perhaps unjustified when we observe how complex and fragmented human beings and their lives can be. Professor Schelling presents some very interesting grounds for doubt, by stating the case for a view that intrapersonal motivational conflict is like a contest between different selves, which may give scope for considerations of distributive justice between or among them and may also make it appropriate for other parties, including the state, to take sides in their disputes or help them to enforce their claims against one another. But I think it will be even more difficult than he suggests to reduce significantly the importance of the personal identity of the single individual who comprises these separate "selves." Even if some legal or even moral fiction is at work in the idea of the sovereignty of the whole person, there are strong reasons for it.

There are various ways in which personal identity—whatever it is that makes all the aspects and stages of a person's life *his*—is accorded moral importance, but I believe they can be summed up in the principle that, with certain fairly well-defined exceptions, any part may be taken as representative of the whole. By parts I mean either temporal stages or distinct aspects of the personality or motivational system, though in this discussion I shall concentrate on temporal stages.

Representation of this kind can be either active or passive. Active representation requires that a stage of a person should be able to speak for the whole, make promises that commit future stages to action, take risks, commit crimes, or behave nobly in ways that incur penalties or rewards for future selves. The conditions for active representation are moderately strict. We do not allow children, the insane, or the temporarily deranged to commit stages over the indefinite future course of life even if they want to, and we don't penalize later stages for their offenses to the same extent.

Passive representation means that anything good or bad that happens to one stage of a person is deemed to have happened to the whole. This means that compensation and trade-offs are allowable within lives that are morally dubious when they are imposed across lives. We much more readily cauterize Ahab's stump to save Ahab's life than to save someone else's life.[1]

I won't discuss this topic. The relation between distribution of benefits and compensation within and across lives, and the bearing this relation shows personal identity to have on problems of distributive justice, have received much discussion lately, since Derek Parfit opened up the subject. Let me say only this: if whole persons continue to be regarded, as I suspect they will be, as the fundamental moral units, there will be scope for standards of distributive justice across lives that do not apply within lives—such as egalitarian principles. But if personal identity is downgraded in importance, it is unclear whether this should result in less compensation within lives or more compensation across lives, that is, whether the trade-off restrictions now thought appropriate for the group should be applied to different stages of one person or whether the trade-offs now thought permissible within one life should be applied to the group.

I want to concentrate on active representation, because there we encounter the fascinating problems about contract and promise that Schelling has posed. He asks us to consider how remarkable it is that one may not make a legally binding promise to oneself and speculates about ways in which this might be changed, to enlarge the possibilities of self-command. I would like to begin by considering how remarkable it is that we can make binding promises at all, to anyone. As Schelling says, it is not self-evident

---

[1] This refers to an example of Schelling's, taken from the movie *Moby Dick:* Ahab has to be forcibly restrained while the stump of his amputated leg is cauterized (*Choice and Consequence,* p. 83).

that the right to enter a contract is one that should be widely recognized. He says this is an empirical question, but if we take seriously his suggested image of the person as a multiplicity of selves that succeed and alternate with one another, it is morally problematic even apart from empirical considerations.

If I enter into a contract or make a promise, I bind future selves to perform. Suppose I take out a large loan, which I must pay back over the next two years, thus lowering the standard of living of those future stages. It doesn't matter whether I want the money for a pleasure-filled vacation or for my favorite charity. If I worked and saved the money for two years and spent it or gave it away at the end, there would be no problem: it would be voluntary altruism toward my later self or the charity. But with the time reversed, it becomes more like involuntary servitude, if we think in terms of successive selves. Of course, the later self who has to do with less money may do so gladly because he is grateful for the memory of the vacation or because he still believes the charity is a worthy cause. But it doesn't matter whether this is so. Even if I hated the vacation or have become completely disenchanted with the charity, my later self can be forced to pay off the loan that the earlier self received.

We wouldn't tolerate a system that allowed one person to make an enforceable promise that was binding on another: that would be a form of slavery. Why do we tolerate it here? We tolerate it because the important unit is the whole person, and we take the promising self and also the later performing self to be legitimate representatives of the whole. So if the later self complains about the burden of his debt payments, the reply (given certain conditions of competence already mentioned) is that *he* got himself into it, *he* received the money earlier, *he* took the vacation, and if he didn't enjoy it, that was a risk *he* undertook. *He* here is not the later stage or the earlier stage, but the whole person of whom both are representatives.

There is something artificial about this, and perhaps there should be more limits to the right of contract than are now generally imposed. Liberalized divorce laws are a move in this direction; it is now impossible in most principalities to enter a marriage that is irrevocable for the life of the partners. This may reflect a conviction that life is too complicated to permit men and women in their twenties such absolute authority over the personal form of their lives for the next fifty years, even if they want to exercise it. But in less personal matters I would expect contract to survive doubts about personal identity, mainly because the later self, even if it feels exploited by the earlier one whose debts it has to pay, can impose similar burdens on *its* successors and can maintain its credit rating only by making good on the promises of the past, like a new government honoring the commitments of a despised prior regime.

Why is a promise to myself different? If I can commit my future self to make payments to a bank, why can't I make a legally enforceable promise not to smoke, or drink, or eat grilled pigs' feet? Why can the later self always release me from any such promise I make to myself?

The simple answer is that there is no second party involved. But if we take the idea of multiple selves seriously, it is not so clear how this answer works. Why shouldn't one of the selves, the one to whom the promise is made, play the role of the party whose interests are served by its enforcement?

To see why, we must return to the case of promise to another, seen in terms of multiple selves. Such a promise involves three parties: the promiser, the promissee, and the performer. Promiser and performer are stages of the same person, and the first is allowed to commit the second. Only the promissee (the third party) can release him.

What would be the corresponding structure of a promise to oneself? It would also involve three parties—promiser, promissee, and performer—but they would all be stages of one person: the promiser and promissee simultaneous or perhaps identical, and the performer later.

If this were going to work like a promise to someone else, then only the promissee could release the performer from his obligation. If we identify the promissee with an earlier stage, then he is no longer around at the time of performance, especially if the performer has no wish to stick to the agreement. However, this by itself is no obstacle to the enforcement of the promise, for in general the death of a promissee does not cancel the obligation to perform, as we know from the strict conditions, extending beyond the life of the donor, that can be put on bequests to museums. The interests of a dead promissee can be safeguarded by trustees.

Why can't the same thing be done if I promise myself never to take another drink? The one who wanted me never to drink may no longer exist, but why can't a board of trustees, or the state, see that I carry out my commitment to him? The answer is that no one else can be as appropriate a trustee for the interests of my past self as my present self. If my past self has the authority, by virtue of some personal connection, to commit my present self to perform onerous tasks, then my present self, by virtue of the same personal connection, should have the authority to oversee commitments made to my past self, and to release the performer from his obligation should it seem desirable, whether the performer is myself or someone else. The two temporal directions of authority must stand or fall together: anything else would be grossly unfair.

Later selves are at a disadvantage with respect to earlier ones because they can be committed by the earlier but can't commit them in return. On the other hand they are compensated somewhat by being able to release other parties from commitments made to earlier selves, whereas earlier selves can't forgive promises made to later selves, however much they might have wanted to. Nor can an adolescent raise the allowance that his subsequent middle-aged self gives to his children.

But to describe all this in terms of the relations among component selves is misleading because it obscures the importance of personal identity in the matter. The only reason an earlier self can commit a later, or a later can forgive an earlier, is that both are taken as representatives of the whole person, of all of his interests over time. They may not be fully competent or unbiased representatives, but apart from certain conditions of gross incompetence, temporary or permanent, that justify someone else in taking over as trustee, these successive states of the person himself are reasonably regarded as the rightful custodians of *his life*. It is *I,* and not my past self, who is the beneficiary of a promise made to me in the past, and it is I, acting in the present, who can release someone from that promise. Likewise it is I, and not my present self, who can make a promise to perform in the future, and it is I acting in the future who must keep the promise. Without a strong element of personal identity, problematic as it may be, none of this makes sense.

After childhood, no time has any more claim than another to represent the whole self, and, derangement apart, we follow a crude principle of the right of possession. Because sooner or later every time gets to be now, this provides a rough equity, especially since we don't let people sell themselves into slavery.

The only plausible alternative to this sort of autonomy would be an increase in paternalism by the law or society, the intrusion on more occasions of objective judgments as to whether someone was adequately representing the interests of his life as a whole. I don't think a credible way to accomplish this is to give the present more authority to enlist the law in enforcing its will on the future. Schelling points out that the "wrong self" might get legal control. I think the only way around this problem would be to impose external standards, and I am not optimistic about the possibility of formulating any that would not destroy more liberty than they would create.

The right to make legally binding self-commitments of certain socially accepted kinds—to exercise, to diet, not to smoke, not to drink—would be a weakened form of paternalism. But I'm not sure that the arguments for it are much stronger than the arguments for outright paternalistic requirements in these areas. These are choices that not only are best left to the individual but also are best left open for revision or renewal as life goes on.

Perhaps I am only revealing my doubt that dieting is really worth it, since I don't object to the paternalism of social security or motorcycle crash helmets. But I think those who would be most likely to avail themselves of institutions of optional commitment are those who are probably most in need of protection from the severe ambitions of the parental self.

20

Dworkin: Interpretation and the Law

This was a review of Ronald Dworkin's Law's Empire *(Harvard University Press, 1986).*

This important theoretical work appears in a definite political context. In the United States, theories of jurisprudence are politically controversial. The public is vividly aware that the way in which the law is interpreted, especially by federal courts of appeal and the Supreme Court, has had and will continue to have large consequences for their lives and liberties. Controversy arises not just over specific issues like prayer in the schools, censorship, abortion, reverse discrimination, and the rights of accused criminals, but over the sorts of grounds on which cases involving these issues are to be decided. Much of the name-calling that breaks out anew with every major Court decision or right-wing nomination to the federal bench has a distinctly philosophical character: liberals accuse conservatives of refusing to recognize individual rights; conservatives accuse liberals of inventing law rather than discovering it.

Growing out of the same legal culture, American philosophical jurisprudence is also enmeshed with political controversy, and at the theoretical level with moral and political philosophy. The most distinguished and original American philosopher of law, Ronald Dworkin, has been professor of jurisprudence at Oxford for many years, but his heart, and much of his influence, are to be found in the United States. Though he often uses examples from British law, the large questions that most engage him

---

Reprinted with permission from *The London Review of Books*, September 18, 1986.

are those concerning equality and the rights of individuals before the power of the state, which are especially conspicuous on the American legal scene.

Dworkin is a liberal, in the American sense—one of the most prominent intellectual representatives of that position. He is just the sort of person American conservatives have in mind when they accuse liberals of asking judges to ignore what the law is and to substitute their personal views of what it ought to be—an abuse of power and a circumvention of the democratic process. Conservative judges, it is implied, will not allow their political views to influence their judicial practice, but will sternly uphold what the law plainly says.

This is a familiar sort of humbug: invoking the authority of a higher-order, ostensibly neutral position of principle in support of one's substantive, partisan convictions. But it is an important and difficult question, about all parties to these jurisprudential debates, what the relation is between their general theories of law and their specific views on controversial cases. Dworkin is identified, for example, with strong liberal positions on the permissibility of reverse discrimination and the impermissibility of suppressing pornography. He is also identified with the position that moral reasoning plays a crucial role in legal interpretation. Those who disagree with him on the substantive issues may be tempted to charge that his theory of adjudication is just an excuse for reading his own moral and political preferences into the law.

One of the many virtures of his new book is that it enables one thoroughly to examine and to dispose of that charge. *Law's Empire* is a rich and multilayered work: it brings out the distinctions among the many strands of Dworkin's thought about law, politics, and morality, and the ways in which they are and are not independent of one another. Up to now he has written essays, many of them collected in two previous books, *Taking Rights Seriously*[1] and *A Matter of Principle*.[2] But this is the first sustained, full-length treatment of his general theory of law, and the first book he has written from scratch. It is an ambitious book, and it does not disappoint the expectations appropriate to a major work by an important thinker. Dworkin has developed a complex and powerful system of ideas, and they are expounded here with the clarity and elegance to which his readers are by now accustomed.

Judges inevitably exercise great power in any society where important disputes are settled by appeal to the law—all the greater where laws may be struck down by appeal to a written constitution. This is because the law

[1] Harvard University Press, 1977.
[2] Harvard University Press, 1985.

must be applied to actual cases whose range of variation over many dimensions is open-ended, and no significant statute or constitutional provision or earlier decision, however carefully drawn, can say on its face how it should be applied in every possible case that could be brought under it. Often the application will be clear, but sometimes, and often in very important cases, the law must be interpreted to be applied, and the correct interpretation will not be obvious. To be a judge, it is not enough to be able to read.

Dworkin's first point is that when judges disagree over the correct decision in a difficult case, they are disagreeing over the correct interpretation of the law—over what the law is. There is not in such cases a plain fact as to what the law is, which anyone with enough information can discover. But that does not mean that there is no law at all, so that judges can make it up. Law, as Dworkin puts it, is an interpretive concept. To decide what the law requires in a given case, it is necessary to consider, not only the facts of the case, the "plain language" of the statute, and the examples of its previous application, but also the point of the law and of the larger institutions and practices in which it is embedded. All this is built into the practice of adjudication.

In justifying a decision in a controversial case, it is impossible to avoid reliance on some conception of the role of courts in the political order, their relation to the legislature and the executive, and the principles that warrant the use of state power to constrain or protect individual liberty. Legal argument always presupposes a jurisprudential foundation, even if it is concealed. And since the role of the judiciary can be justified only in terms of a broader conception of the legal-political order, it presupposes a political morality as well. Dworkin sums up the fundamental point of legal practice in this way: "Law insists that force not be used or withheld, no matter how useful that would be to ends in view, no matter how beneficial or noble these ends, except as licensed or required by individual rights and responsibilities flowing from past political decisions about when collective force is justified."

Jurisprudence, however, is not identical with political theory, which can be utopian in a way that jurisprudence cannot be. A political theory can attempt to describe an ideal legal and political order, but one of the most important tasks of jurisprudence is to explain why judges must apply and enforce laws of which they do not approve, that they would not have voted for, and that they think should be repealed. A legal system with legislative supremacy and a doctrine of respect for precedent faces judges with that responsibility all the time. Moreover, it arises not only where the meaning of the law is uncontroversial but also in cases where interpretation is required. And since interpretation inevitably involves judgment about the best way to realize the purpose or point of the law and of the system to which it belongs, it is a particularly delicate task to define the way in which the judge's point of view can combine with other factors to yield a conclusion about what the law is that may not correspond to what he thinks it ought to be.

Dworkin's answer to this question, and the theoretical core of his book, is a conception he calls Law as Integrity. I thought at first that this title was designed merely to give the theory a coating of sanctity. (Opposing views get names like Conventionalism and Pragmatism.) But the term makes a significant point. Consider what an ambiguous virtue integrity is. It can be ascribed with grudging respect even to someone whose principles you reject and whose purposes you oppose. A person of integrity is someone whose conduct follows from his principles in spite of public opinion, official pressure, or personal temptation, whose conduct forms a certain kind of morally intelligible whole, even if his values are wrong.

This is not a bad model for judicial interpretation: construal of the law and its purposes in a manner that makes decisions flow from a coherent set of principles, even if those principles are not your own. The imaginative aim is to personify the legal system, so that each judgment can be seen as one manifestation of a coherent and pervasive, though complex, point of view. A judge is obviously constrained in such decisions by the requirement of fit with the language of the law and with earlier decisions, and he may have to accept some inconsistency among these antecedents. But the difficult problem is to say what it means to continue to adhere to principle when fit alone does not determine a clear result—when more than one possible decision could be thought to fit, some perhaps better than others. What kinds of argument can be used to identify the correct one?

According to Dworkin, judicial interpretation should aim to discover that reading of the law that makes its enforcement most justifiable in the light of the best justification that can be given of the total system of law and precedent to which it belongs—where this includes the best justification of the role of the judge in that system. This is not only a self-referential but a normative task: the best sense of the law is the sense, relative to the constraints of fit with what is already given, that makes the system the best it could be—best in both fit and substance, balanced against one another in a way that is itself a matter of evaluative interpretation. The arguments about such a question will inevitably call upon the judge's basic moral and political convictions—not because those convictions can be assumed to be correct, but because moral and political issues form an important part of what he has to think about in carrying out the task of interpretation. (In this respect it is no different from a juror's having to rely on his empirical convictions in evaluating evidence.)

For example, after several divided Supreme Court decisions, it is a continuing issue in American law whether compensatory reverse discrimination—preferential hiring or admission of blacks by public institutions—is unconstitutional by the same standard of "equal protection of the laws" that was used to rule old-style state discrimination against blacks unconstitutional. A crucial question is whether the equal protection clause of the Fourteenth Amendment requires (*a*) that the *category* of race not be used in allocating differential treatment or (*b*) that differential treatment not be based on a certain kind of *reason*, namely, racial prejudice. Traditional racial discrimination would be ruled out by either of these principles: neither the language of the Constitution nor the requirement of fit with past precedent decides between them. The issue, then, is which interpretation of the equal protection clause, as an obstacle to racial discrimination, makes better sense of it in the context of the American legal system. This is partly a moral judgment, but it has a legal point: principle (*a*) would rule reverse discrimination unconstitutional; principle (*b*) would not. Dworkin holds that (*b*) is the correct reading—that we must look through the category to the reason to account for what is wrong with discrimination.

Such a method may seem to give the judge complete freedom to inject his politics into the law in controversial cases—to read the law as being whatever he would have voted for as a legislator. But this is not so, for the role of the courts is itself a matter of judicial interpretation, and the best sense that can be made of their role in the overall political system will not grant them full discretion in controversial cases. That is, given the constraints of fit with actual written law and precedent to date, the best interpretation of the system, the one that makes the best moral and political sense of it, requires of the courts much more respect for coherence with pre-existing and surrounding law than is required of the legislature.

Dworkin's general framework leaves room for a range of views on the subject of judicial restraint. We should note a useful distinction he draws between two very different senses of the "liberal-conservative" contrast that are often confused in public discussion. A judge may be conservative in the sense that his convictions about fit are strict, leaving as little room as possible for substantive values to influence the choice between interpretations, but a judge who is conservative in this sense may be liberal in his political and moral convictions—about justice and individual freedom, for example—and this will influence his interpretations within the bounds permitted by his strict convictions about fit. Similarly, a judge who is politically conservative may be liberal or even radical about fit, in which case he will be a judicial activist who permits himself wide latitude to decide cases in a conservative direction and to overturn precedent when the letter of the law does not clearly rule this out. (This is true of Justice

Rehnquist, for example, soon to be elevated to Chief Justice, whose Supreme Court opinions are strongly "result-oriented": easily predictable on the basis of his personal political views.)

Dworkin's substantive political convictions are liberal: economically and socially egalitarian, and committed to strong individual rights against the will of the majority in the conduct of personal life. With regard to strictness of fit he is moderately liberal, allowing significant though not dominant weight to such factors. But within the general conception of law as integrity, as he recognizes, his particular position could be attacked as being either too liberal or too conservative with respect to fit, and either not conservative enough or not radical enough with respect to moral substance.

Let me describe one area of controversy by way of illustration. Someone less sympathetic than Dworkin to the greatly expanded protection of individual rights against legislative and executive power in American constitutional intepretation over the past few decades might argue as follows, combining several points. He might say first that insufficient respect was being shown to the intention of the framers of the Constitution. Clearly they did not have in mind a right of privacy of the kind that has been used to strike down laws prohibiting abortion. Nor did the framers of the First Amendment have in mind that the publication of pornography would be protected under freedom of the press. He might say also that even if the framers' intention and past precedent did not rule out such interpretations, it is in such cases contrary to fundamental principles of democracy to go against the will of the majority, as expressed by the legislature, on the basis of controversial interpretations arrived at by the moral and philosophical reasoning of unelected judges. The power to strike down democratically passed laws should therefore be exercised sparingly and only on the strongest of textual grounds. Finally, he might say that many of the "rights" that have been recognized in recent decisions are morally spurious and that a system that protects them is worse than one that does not, even apart from questions of constitutional history.

Dworkin has several replies to the point about intention, but the most important is this. Even if we leave aside the question of whose intentions we are to consider, how we are to discover them, what to do if they conflict with one another, and what to do where the framers never gave any thought to the question we are now trying to decide, there remains the problem that any author of a constitutional provision or statute may have both abstract and concrete intentions that in our own opinion are in conflict, and we must decide which of these to take as dominant.

For example, to return to the equal protection clause: when it was adopted, it was thought not to rule out racially segregated public schools.

The Congress that proposed the Fourteenth Amendment in 1866 continued to maintain segregated schools in Washington D.C. (for whose government it was directly responsible), and they remained segregated until segregation was ruled unconstitutional on the basis of that same amendment in the case of *Brown v. Board of Education,* eighty-eight years later.

The *Brown* decision can be explained as a finding that the abstract intention of the framers, to guarantee equal protection of the laws, was inconsistent, contrary to their own belief, with their concrete intention to permit segregated public schools—and a decision to take the abstract intention as dominant. (This is also an example of the distinction between concept and conception: the concept of equality of treatment can be filled out by various different particular conceptions of how it is to be realized.)

The judgment of inconsistency is not a logical but an ethical-political one, which employs ideas about race and society that have become widely accepted over time. Dworkin believes that it is right to take the abstract rather than the concrete intention as dominant in this and other cases of conflict, being guided by what makes best moral sense of the system as a whole. Indeed, he claims that this license to correct their concrete intentions by reference to their abstract ones is in accordance with the intentions of the framers themselves (who didn't assume they were infallible about such things as what constitutes equal treatment) as well as being authorized by a long tradition of judicial practice. If this is right, courts of appeal have considerable freedom to use moral reasoning in the interpretation of abstract expressions like "cruel and unusual punishment," "freedom of the press," "establishment of religion," and "due process of law."

But that brings us to the question of whether allowing unelected judges so much power to thwart the will of the majority is undemocratic, in a way that makes it not the best interpretation of the role of the judiciary in the American legal system—either from the point of view of fit with American traditions and practices or from the point of view of political morality. This involves a very difficult issue of political theory—the part played by restrictions on majority rule in guaranteeing the legitimacy of democratic government—and it inevitably brings up the third point in the argument: skepticism about the strength or reality of certain individual rights.

Dworkin's position on these issues and his understanding of integrity in law follow from a general view about political legitimacy: about what it takes for a community to be able to claim the special allegiance of its members and their obedience to its collective decisions as a matter of obligation and not bare power. In an interesting discussion of the ethics of association, he argues that a true community of principle must be more than a framework for political compromise among opposing interests and that legitimacy requires that it realize both the virtue of justice—treating the members of the community as equals—and what he somewhat idiosyncratically calls fairness: giving citizens more or less equal influence in the decisions that govern them. Obviously these can conflict, as when by democratic vote a majority seeks to suppress a minority religion: the minority are not being treated as equals even though they have a vote like everyone else. The balance between these two elements in a legitimate system, often taking the form of the balance between majority rule and individual rights, can be drawn in various ways. But responsibility for maintaining the integrity of the system can legitimately be assumed, Dworkin believes, by the courts.

Some would argue that equality of political influence is, relatively, far more important for legitimacy than Dworkin thinks it is, and that many of the rights protected by the U.S. Constitution are actually designed to keep vulnerable minorities from being deprived of it. They would hold that controversial decisions about the requirements of justice should in any case be left more in the hands of elected legislators, as is true in Britain, rather than of judges. This does not mean that legislation should ignore moral argument about which individual rights need protection against the claims of general welfare or popular will—only that the authority to afford such rights the protection of the law should be more broadly based than it is when vested in an unelected court of appeal. (This claim has less plausibility with regard to the protection of discrete minorities.)

Dworkin would reply, plausibly enough, that the popular will or even the legislature is not to be relied on to determine the limits of its own authority. But one might think that the Supreme Court is no more to be relied on to determine the limits of *its* authority: which is precisely what it does under the present system. This results, on Dworkin's interpretation, in the legitimate assumption by the Court of very great power to overturn legislation on grounds that are partly historical but largely moral. Though the character of the moral ground is restricted, this claim of legitimacy remains a radical one, and readers may feel that the basis for skepticism about this particular division of labor between the courts and the legislature has not been seriously reduced by Dworkin's arguments.

Dworkin is careful to say that he is not engaged in utopian political theory and that perhaps a system very different from the best interpretation of the one we have would be better. Nevertheless, it is clear that his philosophical convictions about individual rights and the role of moral philosophy in their discovery play an important part in convincing him of what the best interpretation of Anglo-American law is—as they should on the theory of law as integrity. Others, with different convictions about morality and political legitimacy, can defend different interpretations within the same framework. This helps to make the character of real jurisprudential debates more intelligible and locates the sources of disagreement accurately.

One thing keeps cropping up in the book that it really would be better without, like crabgrass in a smooth lawn. Dworkin has a mysterious weakness for analogies between judicial and literary interpretation; going further, he seriously compares adjudication to writing the next chapter in a chain novel, which hardly strengthens his position that there is a right answer in hard cases. Since his general claims about interpretation are much less credible than his specific claims about law, it is fortunate that his case doesn't rest on parallels like this: "Interpretation of works of art and social practices, I shall argue, is indeed essentially concerned with purpose not cause. But the purposes in play are not (fundamentally) those of some author but of the interpreter. Roughly, constructive interpretation is a matter of imposing purpose on an object or practice in order to make of it the best possible example of the form or genre to which it is taken to belong." This suggests that we have custody over the works of art produced by others, as over our social practices and institutions. Those who find this as implausible as I do can safely subtract it from the main argument of the book.

Dworkin also argues unpersuasively that the best interpretation of the common law of economic compensation for damages involves an ideal of equality in the allocation of resources, rather than efficiency or some mixture of efficiency and freedom. Here he really seems to be straining to find his own views in the law and to dismiss alternatives too easily. The argument is in any case highly compressed and too dependent on references to his long and complex discussion of equality in *Philosophy and Public Affairs* (1981). Dworkin's very interesting views on distributive justice, still in the process of development, do not receive adequate representation here. But for the most part the book is self-contained and unusually accessible for a work dealing with abstract questions at such a high level. It is full of substance and admirably suited for the prominent and influential role it will undoubtedly achieve.

21

MacIntyre versus the Enlightenment

This was a review of Alasdair MacIntyre's Whose Justice? Which Rationality? *(Duckworth/University of Notre Dame Press, 1988). I'm never sure
whether MacIntyre is expressing real beliefs or just being provocative, but
the aggressiveness of this review is due partly to my own conviction that he
has the intelligence to see what is wrong with his own arguments and that he
simply doesn't give himself a hard time because it would slow him down.*

Every human endeavor has a history, and those engaged in it are faced
with the question of how to relate their present engagement to that history, including its eventual comprehension of the present. Excessive historical self-consciousness can be crippling, but some measure of it is unavoidable, and its problems are especially acute in the field of ethics. In
thinking about questions of right and wrong, any reflective person knows
perfectly well that his conception of the issues, of the relevant arguments,
of the place of the burden of proof, is strongly influenced by the moral
climate that surrounds him. Yet he cannot simply accept this without
qualm, in the way he can accept the influence of a linguistic culture on the
sense of grammar, usage, and style that guides the choice of his words. We
want to write and speak well within the language of our place and time,
but there is no *right* language. By contrast, merely to act well by the
standards of some morality is not enough: one would have to be very
morally lazy to be unconcerned with the possibility that the prevailing
morality of one's culture had something fundamentally wrong with it.

Reprinted with permission from *The Times Literary Supplement*, July 8–14, 1988.

But how are we are to understand the nonrelativistic idea of truth as applied to moral beliefs? The same question arises about truth in other disciplines, such as the natural sciences and mathematics, whose members, if they have not been corrupted by bad philosophy, think of themselves both as working within an intellectual tradition that changes over time and as trying to discover how things really are. But even if there were a generally accepted answer to the question in these other areas, which there is not, it wouldn't transfer. We must ask about morality itself what kind of objectivity we can aspire to—what standard independent of what we are used to is implied in the thought that what we are used to may be seriously wrong, whether it has to do with private property, war, the relations between the sexes, the punishment of criminals, or whatever.

Alasdair MacIntyre believes that in modern culture the attempt to find ethical and political standards independent of specific, historically contingent moral outlooks has been a disaster, and in this sequel to *After Virtue* (1981) he continues his Enlightenment-bashing. "Of what," he asks,

> did the Enlightenment deprive us? What the Enlightenment made us for the most part blind to and what we now need to recover is, so I shall argue, a conception of rational enquiry as embodied in a tradition; a conception according to which the standards of rational justification themselves emerge from and are part of a history in which they are vindicated by the way in which they transcend the limitations of and provide remedies for the defects of their predecessors within the history of that same tradition.

This is offered early on, with an air of challenge, but it is not immediately clear what it means. The problem is to find an interpretation of the conception we are said to have lost, such that the post-Enlightenment liberals MacIntyre is attacking really are blind to it.

There is one perfectly natural reading of the statement about rational inquiry as being embodied in a tradition, and of other things he says about how a tradition works, which is compatible with the strongest claims to be pursuing universal principles by the exercise of reason: namely, that one cannot think about any complex subject except in language and by methods of justification, criticism, and argument that develop gradually over time, and one cannot understand either the questions or the answers without having internalized that background. MacIntyre's formulation applies in this sense to every mathematical discovery that builds on what came before it, and it would certainly apply to the results of any modern ethical theory, however rationalistic and universal its ambitions. In this sense, there is no systematic form of thought that would *not* count as a tradition.

So even if it lends MacIntyre's position a spurious plausibility, that banal reading cannot be right. But neither can another obvious candidate: the relativistic reading according to which standards not only emerge from a historical tradition but are so internal to it that rational choice among rival traditions is meaningless. This reading is ruled out because MacIntyre firmly rejects relativism. So even if modern liberals reject it too, that cannot be what they have lost.

What MacIntyre means by the claim that rationality must be rooted in a tradition has to be something else, something that depends on a special, restricted sense of the term, according to which no form of moral or political thought will count as a tradition if it claims that everyone can be given a reason to accept it. In MacIntyre's view there are no universal reasons, only reasons for this or that group. While a tradition makes claims to truth and may have to admit defeat in face of the greater success of a rival tradition in dealing with the same problems, it does not even attempt to defend itself by arguments that any rational individual should be able to accept: it is essentially particular. "Progress in rationality is achieved only from a point of view." Thus the lengthy intellectual tradition of modern secular ethical theory is not a tradition in MacIntyre's sense, and liberalism can be regarded as a tradition only in its guise as the official public morality of affluent late-twentieth-century societies. Ancient and medieval moral theories, by contrast, do spring from traditions and thus have at least some chance of being true.

MacIntyre describes himself as an Augustinian Christian, and this has shaped his idea of what any morality worth its salt should be like—an idea that he applies to secular moralities as well. What appeals to him about traditions in his sense is that they give their members something more basic than arguments and justifications to ground their moral convictions in: they actually create persons whose nature is such that certain things count without question as reasons, justifications, and criticisms of conduct for them. They generate the dispositions of thought and character on which reasoning of that kind depends and thus provide a confidence in the results that reason alone is powerless to bestow.

By contrast, the successors of the Enlightenment have engaged in a fruitless search for principles "which would be found undeniable by all rational persons. . . . Within that kind of academic philosophy which is the heir to the philosophies of the Enlightenment enquiry into the nature of rational justification has continued with ever-increasing refinement and undiminishing disagreement." In other words, all this talk is getting us nowhere, and it would be better to have confident agreement in principle among the members of a narrower group with a common formation than endless disagreement among everybody.

This type of view is not necessarily religious, for someone could take it up in a spirit of secular romanticism, with an emphasis on the priority of shared feeling and instinct. But MacIntyre is not a romantic in that sense: he believes in the truth, but thinks it will be reached only through a particular local path, as one of the many rival traditions proves itself superior to the others in dealing with the problems of life, and the others are forced to concede that it has succeeded while by their own standards they have failed—something that can become internally evident through what he calls an "epistemological crisis."

I see the appeal of this position: why not forget about universal principles and concentrate on developing a particular form of collective life from the inside? That is the only way anything valuable is ever created. But speaking from the other side of the fence, I believe it is much easier for an Augustinian Christian to offer this advice than it is for a nonbeliever to take it. For why should we be confident that one historically contingent path with its internal standards is leading us to the truth, unless it is because God is guiding our feet? If we do not believe that, and if we nevertheless do not wish to succumb to relativism or hopeless skepticism, the best we can do is to try to develop a capacity to criticize and evaluate particular traditions, including the one that has formed us, in ways that do not simply presuppose their validity. That is not the same thing as sweeping the boards and starting over with a few moral axioms "which would be found undeniable by all rational persons," as in MacIntyre's travesty. There are no axioms, only questions that aim to be as widely comprehensible as possible, and answers of increasing sophistication that attract a wide range of agreement and disagreement, followed by further questions. The aim is to construct gradually a point of view that all reasonable persons can be asked to share.

This, too, is a tradition, though not in MacIntyre's sense, and it evolves its methods, principles, and forms of reasoning over time—even if some modern philosophers have aimed for more finality than it was ever reasonable to expect. It will not jettison what more local traditions of morality have to offer without some reason, such as the elimination of arbitrary discrepancies in the treatment of different groups of people—one of the more powerful tools of post-Enlightenment moral thought. The persistence of disagreement among the participants in such an enterprise is only to be expected; the growth in our understanding of the issues and agreement on partial solutions to the problems of a decent society seem to me far more impressive, in spite of the anti-Enlightenment horrors with which the world is filled. But to see this requires an attention to the actual content of modern ethical theories for which MacIntyre has no patience.

I have been talking about his general thesis, but most of the book is taken up with the examination of four historical examples, which are intended to support the thesis by showing how moral reasoning always depends on a tradition and cannot be understood or evaluated except within its historical context. The examples are Aristotelianism culminating in Aquinas, the Augustinian tradition, the Scottish Enlightenment eventually subverted by Hume, and modern liberalism (shorn of its universal pretensions and reinterpreted as the tribal code of American constitutional lawyers and their ilk).

A long story takes us from the Homeric heroes, through tragic drama, Pericles, Thucydides, the Sophists, and the aftermath of the Peloponnesian War, to Plato's attempt to unify the demands of social and individual perfection. It is largely familiar, but interest picks up with MacIntyre's distinctive emphasis on the closeness of Aristotle's concerns to Plato's, on the theological dimension in Aristotle's ethical theory, and on the way in which his conception of the relation of ethics to politics is more successful than Plato's:

> There is no standard external to the *polis* by which a *polis* can be rationally evaluated in respect of justice or any other good. To apprehend what a *polis* is, what the good is which it is its function to achieve, and to what extent one's own *polis* has successfully achieved that good, all require membership in a *polis*. Without such membership . . . one is bound to lack essential elements of the education into the virtues and of the experience of the life of the virtues which is necessary for such apprehension.

The *polis* helps us to realize our end in the teleological order of the cosmos: "No practical rationality outside the *polis* is the Aristotelian counterpart of *extra ecclesiam nulla salus.*" And in Aquinas this conception of virtue and practical reason is integrated with Augustine's conception of divine grace. This, MacIntyre indicates in his conclusion, is the tradition he wishes to pursue, though of course he cannot consistently recommend it to everyone.

Whose Justice? Which Rationality? contains a lengthy history of the religious and legal background of moral philosophy in Scotland before Hume and an account of Hume's naturalistic reaction against it. Readers who have not previously encountered the thought of Sir James Dalrymple of Stair will now know why. The material is of some historical interest, but it throws more light on Hume's failure to get a professorship than on his ideas.

Accuracy in reporting what others say has never been MacIntyre's strong point. On the principle that it is easier to shoot a sitting duck, he tends to be most inaccurate when he is on the attack: the representation of Kant's ethical theory in *After Virtue* makes it unwise ever to trust what he says about a philosophical text again, and the treatment of Hume here is not much better. He ignores the theoretical flexibility of Hume's moral psychology because he has decided that Hume is an apologist for the English social order of his day and that the politics drives the moral theory. (Hume's Anglophilia irritates MacIntyre, and he reports with evident satisfaction Walter Bagehot's later judgment that this Scottish turn-coat failed to master idiomatic English style.)

It is true that Hume's examples of objects of pride include importantly wealth, property, and social position, and that his analysis of justice focuses on the rules of property and contract. It is also true that he denied that social or economic equality was an element of justice. And one might add to MacIntyre's indictment that Hume's theory allows him to account for the double standard in sexual morality and the subjection of women. But none of this shows that his psychology presupposes the social and economic arrangements of his day. Conceiving himself as an empirical student of morality, he obviously had to offer a theory that would explain the moral convictions and institutions he was able to observe, but which could also explain how moral beliefs would change under different conditions. The analytic framework he proposes is much more flexible than Locke's theory of natural rights, for example, since it requires us to understand the interaction between external circumstances and individual psychology, and the crucial role of convention, in determining the exact shape of property rights and social hierarchy in a given place and time.

Hume called "artificial" the virtues like justice that are essentially tied to conventions and that achieve their aim only through general and not through individual conformity: he invented the type of moral analysis that led to rule-utilitarianism. MacIntyre's presentation of Hume's theory of the artificial virtues and their psychology owes little to the original; he knows that it must express a particular social allegiance, so he doesn't have to look too carefully at what it says—not an unusual failure among those who urge us to pay more attention to history. He says Hume believes his justification of the rules of property holds for all times and places, ignoring his account of the limiting circumstances—extreme scarcity, extreme abundance, universal benevolence, or universal selfishness—that make the rules inapplicable. And he says, as if it were an objection, that "social instability and disruption might seem to arise in certain circumstances precisely from the enforcement of the rules of property," whereas this is precisely the kind of thing that would on Hume's account result in a change in the rules and conventions defining property. Hume could have provided a very plausible account of the development of the social morality of the welfare state (and also of the liberation of women) along these lines.

I don't defend Hume's ethical theory: it seems to me too flexible and hospitable rather than the reverse—too limited in the sort of criticism it permits of a morality that is psychologically comprehensible or a system of property rights that is not unstable. But MacIntyre's dismissive treatment of it contrasts with the charity he displays in discussing Aristotle's views on the naturalness of slavery and the inferiority of women, about which he says, rightly, "Aristotle's mistake . . . was not to understand how domination of a certain kind is in fact the cause of those characteristics of the dominated which are then invoked to justify unjustified domination," and adds that this mistake can be "excised from Aristotle's thought without denying his central claims about the best kind of *polis*."

MacIntyre's historical examples do not even support, let alone establish, his central thesis. Perhaps he is right that the only path to moral truth is through a historically particular tradition that eschews the search for universal grounds of rational acceptability, but to point out that there have been many such traditions and that the search for universal grounds has not ended moral disagreement provides no reason to believe it. All of MacIntyre's well-taken strictures about the difficulty of translating moral language across cultures and the importance, for any cultural understanding, of looking at the historical background and getting inside the language, are in no way incompatible with a Kantian rationalism about ethics—whether or not such a view is false. My sense is that MacIntyre's religion is driving his philosophy. He wants to produce an argument that does not rely on religious premises to show that only something like a religious morality is possible. This cannot be done. But to him, the conclusion of the argument is evident on other grounds.

We are faced with difficult problems about social justice that MacIntyre's book does not help us to think about, since it contains no substantive moral discussion. At the end, in answer to the question of what we should do if he is right, he replies, "That will depend upon who you are and how you understand yourself." Find your identity, in other words, and if you are lucky, conviction will follow. But this is useless in response to the problems of how to live decently together in a world in which such tradition-bound conceptions as there are lead to conflict as often as they lead to harmony and in which many of us genuinely do not know what we owe to our fellow human beings and believe that others who think they know are mistaken. The continuing search for a more deeply grounded solution to these problems is generated not just by an intellectual but by a moral demand. MacIntyre professes to be freeing us from blindness, but he is really asking for the return of a blindness to the difficulty of moral thought that it has been one of the great achievements of ethical theory to escape.

22

Kolakowski: Modernity and the Devil

This was a review of Leszek Kolakowski's Modernity on Endless Trial *(University of Chicago Press, 1990).*

This book collects twenty-four essays written between 1973 and 1986, expressing Leszek Kolakowski's thoughts on God, man, reason, history, moral truth, and original sin, prompted by observation of the dramatic struggle among Christianity, the Enlightenment, and modern totalitarianism. It is a wonderful collection of topics; unfortunately, most of the pieces in *Modernity on Endless Trial* give the impression of having been tossed off without much expense of time or reflection. They are studded with facile declarations like this, from the title essay:

> [I]n the normal sense of "rationality" there are no more rational grounds for respecting human life and human personal rights than there are, say, for forbidding the consumption of shrimp among Jews, of meat on Friday among Christians, of wine among Muslims. They are all "irrational" taboos. And a totalitarian system which treats people as exchangeable parts in the state machinery, to be used, discarded, or destroyed according to the state's needs, is in a sense a triumph of rationality.

Caricatures of reason to make room for faith contribute nothing to our understanding of Kolakowski's Christian moral position. And he knows better: in an essay called "Why Do We Need Kant?" he acknowledges with respect the attempt to ground universal human rights in moral reasoning

---

Reprinted with permission from *The Times Literary Supplement,* December 14–20, 1990.

rather than in taboos or historical or psychological contingencies. The "reason" that figures in his more reckless remarks is a philosopher's invention, adapted from Hume, and much further from ordinary thought than Kant's concept.

Kolakowski's distinctive point of view would have been worth presenting in greater intellectual depth. He believes the overvaluation of reason is dangerous because its clearest form is merely a method of calculation, useful for discovering means to ends, but quite inapplicable to the assessment of ends themselves. There is admittedly the Kantian hope for a "transcendental" exercise of reason, aimed at discovering a less arbitrary basis for moral requirements than taboos or preferences that are simply given, but while Kolakowski concedes the possibility and admires the ambition, he does not evaluate the attempts to realize it: apparently he believes that a nonrational, religious basis for accepting natural law provides better protection against nihilism.

In "The Illusion of Demythologization" he claims that the faith of the enlightened is still possible, logically as well as psychologically, that there is no inconsistency between our historical knowledge and the belief that Jesus was the son of God, and no inconsistency between our scientific knowledge and the belief in immortality. The Enlightenment's affirmation of the equal value of all human beings was, he contends, a legacy from the Christian tradition against which the Enlightenment rebelled. But the overvaluation of reason and abandonment of taboos that marked that rebellion led finally to the rejection of moral absolutes not defendable by reason, with familiar and terrible results. Blame also attaches to the illusion of human perfectibility that succeeded loss of belief in the inherent evil of humanity, encouraging catastrophic attempts to impose universal brotherhood by political fiat.

"Politics and the Devil" offers a brief history of modern Western culture as a struggle over man's soul. Kolakowski conjectures that the detachment of politics, science, art, philosophy, and technology from the authority of the Church, which is the beginning of modernity, was not just the work of the Devil, but can be seen as a new *felix culpa*, which released our creativity as well as our wickedness. The Enlightenment also contributed to the purification of Christianity by reducing the Church's engagement in politics, war, and the acquisition of wealth. But the Devil made use of it as an antireligious force, leading first to humanism and ultimately to the abandonment of truth in politics in favor of power. In a final twist, he invented a new idea of truth expressed in the absolute claims of ideological States that are caricatures of theocracy, unbridled by religious inhibitions.

I sympathize with two aspects of Kolakowski's worldview. First, he insists on the importance of noncontingent morality, one that assigns an irreducible and unexchangeable value to human beings in the form of natural law or human rights. This rejects both the Marxist position that rights are either a sham (in bourgeois society) or superfluous (under the universal brotherhood of communism) and the nervous relativism that hesitates to apply Western values (even to call them "Western" is a mistake) in judging how other societies treat their members. Second, he recognizes the evil inherent in human nature, and resists utopianism; he admits that the doctrine of original sin has been used as an excuse for doing nothing about serious and avoidable social ills, but thinks the idea of human perfectibility has had even worse consequences. He calls himself a Conservative-Liberal-Socialist, but the political substance of his position is that of a conservative social democrat: attached to individual liberty but eschewing happiness as a political goal, valuing social as well as personal security for everyone, and regarding the market as useful but not sacrosanct. Such values are not unusual, but Kolakowski fears that they are under threat from what he sees as the modernist tendency either to regard all values as arbitrary or to give up when faced with conflicts among them.

It seems to me that he underrates the resources of modern moral reflection. I agree that the question of whether universal moral standards have any basis is of fundamental importance, both theoretical and political, but a religious answer stands as much in need of defense and explanation as does a secular one. It is quite unclear how faith could warrant confidence in a morality without any independent reason to accept its content. Perhaps faith can justify abstinence from shrimp or wine, but it is not enough to justify stoning for adultery, and if that is true, it is not enough by itself to justify a social minimum for the poor or the moral and political equality of the sexes—unless of course faith is sensitive to the content of what it requires us to accept.

Reason, or rather reasoning as a method, tries to find maximally general principles to explain particular cases and to eliminate arbitrary, unexplained distinctions, but it can be applied only in connection with substantive judgments about whatever is being investigated. Its authority in the assessment of moral systems poses deep questions: it depends both on the existence of a specifically practical form of reason—reasoning about what to do—and on the claim of reason not to be merely another socially conditioned practice.

A defender of the Kantian method must claim that it is legitimate to ask for justifying reasons for a contingent social practice in a way in which it is not legitimate to turn the tables and call reason itself into question by appealing to such a practice. The asymmetry arises because any claim to the rightness of what one is doing is automatically an appeal to its justifiability, and therefore subject to rational criticism. All roads lead to the same court of appeal, a court to which all of us are assumed to have access. Reason is universal because no attempted challenge to its results can avoid appealing to reason in the end—by claiming, for example, that what was presented as an argument is really a rationalization. This can undermine our confidence in the original method or practice only by giving us reasons to believe something else, so that finally we have to think about the arguments to make up our minds.

It is hard to understand how faith could occupy a similar position as the final court of appeal for moral belief. It is not a method of inquiry at all and does not seem like the kind of thing to which appeal cannot be avoided in responding to all challenges to its claims. That is why it seems, from the outside, insufficient by itself to support moral principles that can be challenged and that must be compared with alternatives, good or bad.

What is most striking in Kolakowski's cast of mind is an obsession with the moral and philosophical meaning of history, something that is natural to him in virtue of his roots in both the Christian tradition and the Marxist tradition that he long ago rejected. It is a serious lack that this important subject is foreign to the ahistorical analytic temperament; the history of science plays a significant role in thinking about epistemology and metaphysics, but the history of humanity is rarely, in this tradition, made the focus for inquiries into the nature of moral truth and moral knowledge.

The relation between moral theory and the interpretation of historical events is complex, but there certainly is one, since morality purports to reveal possibilities for human development in the direction of greater harmony and decency that people can be induced by that very discovery to pursue. Any moral theory that presents us with such hope must face its own version of the problem of evil: how is the complex history of our species compatible with the hypothesis that most persons are capable of moral decency—a presupposition of any morality that purports to address itself to everyone? How can the supposed authority of morality be reconciled with its frequent impotence?

Perhaps the doctrine of original sin and a belief in the Devil would help in understanding the strange mixture of opposed tendencies that characterizes the modern era: growth of democracy and socioeconomic equality, increased toleration and diminished cruelty in some societies, as against modern totalitarianism with its industrial scale of murder and torture, and the development of mass incineration as a military option. But Freudian pessimism and recognition of the immaturity of the race and the power of poorly understood infantile passions might serve just as well.

It is sometimes suggested that the horrors of the twentieth century and the contemporary power of nationalism refute the values of the Enlightenment. That is not true. Still, a believer in universal, humanistic morality,

whether Kantian or utilitarian, has to say *something* about these events—
something explanatory as well as condemnatory. He needs a conception of
human beings that accommodates both their capacity for morality and
their capacity for monstrosity. Kolakowski rightly insists that the view that
men are naturally good but are corrupted by society is not credible. Kant
attacks the problem directly in *Religion within the Limits of Reason Alone*
and attempts to reconcile the position that morality is the fullest expression of human freedom with the fact that true evil requires free will also.
There is a need for secular theories of evil consistent with universal claims
of positive morality, and exposure to concerns like Kolakowski's might
induce philosophers not accustomed to it to think about the question.
Kolakowski himself, however, seems content to take it easy.

Index

Abortion, 6, 172, 179, 194, 199

Acquisition: of language (*see* Language: acquisition of); of property, 141

Action, 93; commitments of future self to, 189; comparing possible outcomes of, 144; constraints on liberty of, 145; deliberation for, 176–77; individual freedom of, 138; intentional, 69–70; and justification, 42, 169–70; motivation for, 160, 161–62, 163, 166; physiological substructure of, 65–66; primitive nature of, 94; reflection and desire, 180; and rights, 145; on short notice, 150

Active representation, 189

Addition, 48

Adjudication, 196, 202

Adultery, stoning for, 212

Aesthetic response, 35–36, 36

After Virtue (MacIntyre), 204

Agreement, 56, 63; ethical versus linguistic, 123*n*.1; on grammatical rules, 62–63; and justice, 126; in moral sentiment, 172; on use of terms, 55. *See also* Disagreements

Air bags, automobile, 184

Air travel, safety in, 184, 185, 187

Albritton, Rogers, 4

Alcohol, 184; abstention from, 186, 191; forbidden to Muslims, 210

Algorithm, 107*n*.9

Allowance, children's, 192

Altruism, 190

Amoralists, 163

Analogies: between judicial and literary interpretation, 202; with other minds, 18*nn*.10–11 (*see also* Empathy)

Anarchism, 139, 140*n*.2

Anarchy, State, and Utopia (Nozick), 137–49

Animals: ethical treatment of, 149; seen in clouds, 28

"Another Time, Another Place, Another Person" (Williams), 172, 173

Anscombe, Elizabeth, 91

Antimeritocracy, 124

Antiperfectionism, human, 124. *See also* Perfectibility

Antireductionism, 3. *See also* Reductionism

"Appeal to Tacit Knowledge in Psychological Explanations" (Fodor), 65–71

Appearance of time, subjective, 88

A priori concepts, 93–94

I am grateful to Nicholas Humez for compiling the index.

215

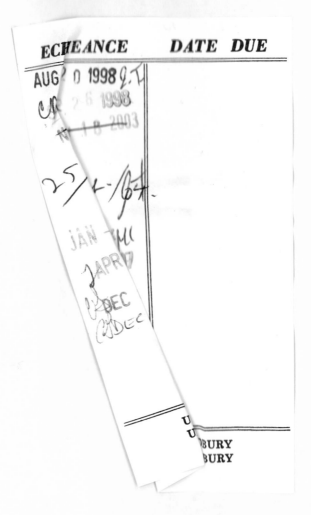